CHOOSE **MEXICO**
FOR RETIREMENT

Help Us Keep This Guide Up to Date

Every effort has been made by the authors and editors to make this guide as accurate and useful as possible. However, many things can change after a guide is published—establishments close, phone numbers change, facilities come under new management, housing costs fluctuate, and so on.

We would love to hear from you concerning your experiences with this guide and how you feel it could be made better and be kept up to date. While we may not be able to respond to all comments and suggestions, we'll take them to heart and we'll make certain to share them with the authors. Please send your comments and suggestions to the following address:

The Globe Pequot Press
Reader Response/Editorial Department
P.O. Box 480
Guilford, CT 06437

Or you may e-mail us at:

editorial@GlobePequot.com

Thanks for your input, and happy travels!

INSIDERS' GUIDE®

CHOOSE RETIREMENT SERIES

NINTH EDITION

CHOOSE **MEXICO**
FOR RETIREMENT

Information for Travel, Retirement, Investment, and Affordable Living

JOHN HOWELLS AND DON MERWIN

INSIDERS' GUIDE®

GUILFORD, CONNECTICUT
AN IMPRINT OF THE GLOBE PEQUOT PRESS

To buy books in quantity for corporate use or incentives, call **(800) 962–0973, ext. 4551,** or e-mail **premiums@GlobePequot.com.**

INSIDERS' GUIDE®

Copyright © 1985, 1988, 1992, 1994, 1997, 1999, 2001, 2003, 2005 by John M. Howells and Don Merwin

Text design: Linda R. Loiewski
Maps by Lisa Reneson © Morris Book Publishing, LLC
Spot photography throughout © Photos.com, Clipart.com, and Pictures Colour Library

ISSN: 1544-2829
ISBN-13: 978-0-7627-3684-3
ISBN-10: 0-7627-3684-4

Manufactured in the United States of America
Ninth Edition/Third Printing

CONTENTS

AUTHORS' PREFACE TO THE NINTH EDITION

When *Choose Mexico* first made its appearance twenty years ago, the idea of retiring in a foreign country was still rather daring. True, small colonies of Americans and Canadians had lived in and around Guadalajara, San Miguel de Allende, and a few other towns for a number of years. But for most people at or near retirement age, places like Florida, California, and Arizona seemed to be more practical options. Two decades later, many things have changed—not least the life experiences of the typical retiree. Persons born in the fifties and sixties are much more likely to have traveled abroad (if only in the military) than those born in the twenties and thirties. They are, as a group, better educated and more willing to try new things. But the changes in Mexico during those years have been even more extensive.

When the authors first lived in Mexico, there was no Internet or satellite television, and there were few American products in the stores. Travel to Mexico and travel within the country was slow and often difficult. A letter mailed in Mexico took weeks to reach the States or Canada. (It still does.) Today, however, e-mail makes communication with friends and relatives an almost instantaneous process. Even if you don't own a computer, Internet cafes where you can use one for as little as a penny a minute are everywhere. Your favorite television programs, sporting events, and up-to-the-minute news are at your fingertips. A vastly improved highway system speeds you comfortably throughout Mexico; and Costco, WalMart, and similar merchants maintain outlets within easy reach of almost anywhere you might live.

Does this mean that Old Mexico is a thing of the past? Certainly not! What it does mean is that you have a far greater range of choices. The new and the old seem able to exist side by side in today's Mexico. It is up to you to decide how much of each you want. A short stroll away from the center of most towns will bring you to neighborhoods largely untouched by American commerce and the lifestyles of the twenty-first century. You can choose to live there, if you wish. Where and how you shop, the kinds of activities you involve yourself in, whom you seek out as friends, and, above all, the time and effort you devote to learning Spanish—all will determine in which of the many Mexicos you will live.

To experience the full richness of Old Mexico, you may want to try one of the retirement sites we have characterized as "For the More Adventurous." There you won't find a K-Mart, a boutique, or an English-language newspaper. You won't hear English spoken, either, so brush up on your Spanish if you are thinking about moving to one of these out-of-the-way places. But you can count on this: The people there, like most Mexicans—and other North Americans who have chosen to live in Mexico—will be welcoming, friendly, and eager to share their beautiful country with you.

Some things in Mexico, as elsewhere in the world, change too rapidly and too often for any book to keep up with, such as the daily fluctuation of the exchange rate (the number of pesos you will get for your dollar), the price of a bottle of beer, or the cost of an airline ticket to Guadalajara. In each revision of this book, we try to keep our readers up to date on those things that change from year to year, such as the laws governing permanent residence in Mexico, the overall trend of inflation, the communities currently most attractive to prospective retirees, and the best sources of up-to-date information on those things that change from day to day.

The task of keeping informed is made easier by the tremendous amount of information available on the World Wide Web and our ability to keep in touch with our sources all over Mexico by e-mail. But nothing can substitute for the feel about life south of the border that we get from our frequent trips there, especially those extended stays when we shop in Mexican markets, get our hair cut by Mexican barbers, and talk directly with native-born and foreign residents.

Because this book is about living in Mexico, we haven't devoted much space to the many new beach communities whose hotels and time-shares are geared to the tourists who spend a few weeks in Mexico. Many of these tourists will, we hope, become residents as they learn to appreciate what the country has to offer.

INTRODUCTION

Are you ready to retire? Your answer may depend on a number of factors such as your chronological age, your family responsibilities, the state of your health, and certainly your financial status. But most of all it will depend on what you mean by "retire." If the word conjures up a picture of days in front of the television set, punctuated by the occasional golf or bridge game, your answer probably would and should be no.

If, however, you would like to enter upon an exciting new life filled with new experiences and new discoveries, retirement in Mexico is one of the options you should be considering. Nothing ages a person like mindless routine, and nowhere is the fountain of youth more likely to be found than in the challenge of building an enriched new life. Of course merely being "different" isn't nearly enough to recommend Mexico as the place where you might want to spend your golden years. There are a number of basic items that most of us would agree on as conditions for considering a place as our future home.

1. It should have a comfortable climate. The extremes of heat and cold and of dryness and humidity that most of us could tolerate when we were younger become much more difficult to deal with as we age.

They can sharply curtail our activities, confining us to a fireside armchair when blizzards howl and to refrigerated interiors when the streets sizzle.

2. It should be sufficiently accessible and attractive to friends and family for them to want to visit you from time to time and close enough to where you now live so that you can get back there when you want to.

3. It should be affordable. What point would there be to consider a place where your income and savings couldn't provide you with a pleasant lifestyle?

4. It should be safe. Urban crime, the threat of terrorism, and environmental conditions have greatly circumscribed our choice of places in the world—our own countries included—where we might choose to live.

5. It should be welcoming. Although the people in most countries make a clear distinction between Americans as people and the U.S. government's foreign policy, there are many places in the world where you might feel a bit uncomfortable admitting your place of origin. Ethnic tensions in some otherwise attractive tropical locations have a similarly chilling effect.

6. It should offer access to good medical care. This, too, is much more important as we grow older.

7. It should offer the companionship of a large number of English-speaking residents. Few of us have sufficient command of a foreign language to enjoy the kind of far-ranging conversation from which friendships are born. It is not enough to be able to order in a restaurant or direct a cab driver to the place you want to go. As important as it is to broaden our language skills, for most of us it is also important to spend time with people who share our native tongue.

In this book we will demonstrate that there are places in Mexico where all of these requirements are met in full measure. Some have springlike temperatures year-round. Most are easily and quickly accessible from the United States. All are economical places in which to live—significantly less expensive than most other North American locations. Mexico isn't crime free, but retirees there uniformly report that they feel at least as safe as in the United States. Good medical care is both accessible and affordable in Mexico. Many doctors are U.S. trained, and the public system is augmented by an extensive private one. You do not have to return to the United States or Canada to get good care.

One of the themes that runs through this book is the warmth, honesty, and decency of the Mexican people. It probably has to be experienced to be believed. If you have never been to Mexico, ask friends who have whether they have ever found another place where they were made to feel as much at home. Most of the places we discuss have sizable expatriate communities with social and philanthropic activities. You should have no difficulty finding like-minded people and making new friends. For the minority who would prefer to avoid the company of compatriots, we do discuss some off-the-beaten track options.

Because Mexico is "next door," just a few days' drive from most places in the United States or Canada, trying it out as a place to live doesn't involve a major commitment. You needn't bother with complicated visa requirements; a simple tourist card allows you a six-month trial visit. Should you decide you like Mexico as a place to live, it's a relatively simple matter to convert your tourist card into a long-term visa. On the other hand, should you discover that Mexico isn't for you, it's a simple matter to pack up and return home for another look at your retirement menu.

The proximity of Mexico is yet another advantage for those who want to experience foreign retirement. Most North Americans tell us they feel a need to renew their contact with home once in a while. They miss friends and relatives; they need a "culture fix." This is easy when living in Mexico, because home is just a few hours away. With your tastefully decorated house in Mexico as an attraction, family and friends will be tempted to visit, and you will have frequent opportunities to play the gracious host. If you lived in Europe, on the other hand, visitors would be few and far between.

The Mexico we describe in this book is not the country experienced by tourists on a two-week vacation. It isn't the Mexico visited by affluent vacationers who move from one luxury hotel to another, seldom coming in contact with the local people. We present you with the Mexico known by residents who live in the *real* Mexico. It is the Mexico enjoyed by North Americans—particularly those of middle age and beyond—who savor the experience and adventure of exploring a Mexican-Spanish culture, making new friends, and beginning a new chapter of their lives. These newcomers want affordable, comfortable places to live, a healthy and enjoyable climate, reliable medical care, and, above all, activities that define the difference between stagnation and vitality.

MEXICO IS NOT **JUST FOR RETIREES**

In many respects the new generation nearing retirement age in this new millennium is very different from previous waves of retirees. For one thing, many people today opt for retirement at a younger age. More people retire in their fifties, some even earlier as they are "downsized" from their professions. It's no surprise that this more youthful group is active and vigorous and demands a lifestyle that doesn't involve sitting on the front porch or passively watching hours of television. "Retirement" isn't precisely what they have in mind. They seek a "new beginning," whether this means starting a business or finding an interesting job in a new field.

Since the advent of NAFTA (the North American Free Trade Agreement), many barriers to going into business in Mexico have been removed. North Americans are experimenting with various enterprises, applying their experience from their business lives, looking for a satisfying niche in an exotic foreign location. Many international corporations have located in Mexico since NAFTA made this practical. The job market for skilled workers has opened windows of opportunity for those who want to work and live in Mexico. The bigger towns and cities have large numbers of North Americans employed in offices, factories, and research labs. Mexico City, Guadalajara, Puebla, and other cities are hosting thousands of expatriate workers. Working papers are required, but the corporations have little trouble acquiring permission for employees to live in Mexico.

LIVING IN MEXICO **PART OF THE YEAR**

More and more people are discovering that Mexico is an ideal place for part-time residence. Uncounted thousands spend pleasant winters there and return to their homes north of the border every spring. When we first started writing about retiring in Mexico, we tended to underestimate this phenomenon. "Wintering" in Mexico, or anywhere else for that matter, seemed like something you read about on the society pages, something that only rich people could do. The more we travel in Mexico in winter, however, the more people we meet who are neither tourists nor full-time residents. Their homes are in Burlington, Vermont, or Duluth, Minnesota. They enjoy a month (or two, or three) in Mexico's sunshine and rejoin their neighbors, children, and grandchildren in the spring.

The opposite side of this coin is the great influx of "summer Mexicans" who flee from the heat and humidity of the southern states, especially Texas, to enjoy the moderate climate of Mexico's central plateau. Some are retirees, some are teachers, and others have jobs that leave their summers free. They, too, develop strong ties to the country, returning to the same places year after year, but their real homes continue to be up north.

Therefore, although this book was written primarily for people who are planning for retirement, we keep hearing from two other groups: (1) people who are already retired but are unhappy with their current situation and are hoping to find something better and (2) younger people, particularly those engaged in seasonal work, who find Mexico a great place to live for part of each year. Why not escape winter by relaxing on a tropical beach or enjoying a sunny mountain village? For those planning to retire "at home," a part-time retirement in Mexico is an excellent idea. Reasonable prices in Mexico make early or partial retirement possible on an income far smaller than you might imagine.

Seasonal retirement is practical for those who don't want to move away from family, friends, bridge partners, golf buddies, their gardens, their hobbies, and so on. Living part of the year in Mexico allows you to choose the best seasons in both your home base and your second home in Mexico. This is possible because of the menu of climates Mexico offers: cool mountain towns to escape Phoenix summers, warm beach towns and sunny desert towns to escape Minnesota winters.

Some part-timers rent the same place every year. They may arrange for a place to store their extra belongings so that they don't have to lug them back and forth every time they visit.

Having a yearly "lease" on the same place permits you to become acquainted with the year-round neighbors. You'll feel at home in your second home, knowing the best places to shop, where to dine, and all the special things your chosen community offers.

Returning to the same town at the same time of the year also puts you into social contact with others who have similar patterns, and you'll make many new friends, who will greet you with joyous homecomings, parties, dinners, etc. Thus you have two sets of friends: those in your home-base town and those in your seasonal home. These second friends have a way of expanding your social connections in the States (or Canada) with visits back and forth while at home.

Obviously retirement in Mexico isn't for everyone. (Thank goodness for that, or the country would soon be overrun with North Americans.) Most retirees decide not to move away for retirement or, if they do move, stay in their own country. Others feel that a total change of scenery is called for. For them, the chance to start a totally new life with new friends and experiences can be an adventure in itself. Still others need to move away from the high-cost areas where they currently live and are looking for someplace more affordable. Fortunately Mexico is an alternative for both full-time and part-time retirement that doesn't involve a total severing of ties.

AN AFFORDABLE **COST OF LIVING**

Over the years Mexico's low cost of living has enabled expatriates to enjoy a fascinating life with a gracious lifestyle far beyond what a similar budget would allow back home. Prices for goods and services, rents, and other living expenses vary from very low to moderate—depending on the particular curve of the currency exchange cycle the country is going through. This is what happens: The value of the peso gradually rises against the dollar, which results in inflation from the standpoint of the person using dollars. Then a sudden drop in the value of the peso brings prices down dramatically, starting a new cycle. The last time the sudden drop occurred was December 1994, when the value of the peso fell from about three to the dollar to about ten to the dollar. Prices remained the same in pesos, but because expatriates received more than twice as many pesos for the dollar, actual prices were more than cut in half. Then the cycle started all over again.

However, the cycle can never zoom high enough to make Mexico as expensive a place to live as the United States. Why? Because of the differences in labor costs, utilities, and locally produced food. When your maid and gardener are happy to work for a couple of dollars an hour, when locally grown foods cost a fraction of what they cost on the other side of the border, and when you needn't spend a fortune to heat your Mexican home in winter or air-condition it in summer, your budget should never stretch to the breaking point. At the time this edition of *Choose Mexico for Retirement* was written, most costs were about two-thirds of those in the United States and the dollar was climbing slowly in value against the peso.

Not everything in Mexico is bargain priced. Some items cost as much as in the United States. Airfare, gasoline, highway tolls, imported foods, and long-distance calls are no bargains. Yet these costs aren't critical in a country where good public transportation abounds, domestically processed foods are varied and delicious, and e-mail substitutes for the lost art of letter writing and for long-distance telephone calls. Room rates in luxury hotels, particularly in resort areas, are pegged to the international, not Mexican, economy. Yet we've found clean, comfortable hotel rooms for less than $50 per night. We ate in good restaurants, paying a maximum of $15 per person for a full-course dinner with beverages.

Living in Mexico can be inexpensive or expensive, depending upon your lifestyle, yet we must emphasize that the biggest attraction here is not cheap living. As we've stated many times in previous editions we do not encourage those with extremely limited funds to move to Mexico. You'll find no "safety net" here— no welfare, no food stamps, no one to take care of you—and the expatriate community resents having indigents descend on them. Furthermore, full-time residency requires a minimum income or else a tedious and expensive return to the border every six months to renew visas. (Even this latter option may not be available forever.) Always make sure you have some money as a backup, because someday you may want to return to your former home. Consider Mexico's affordable cost of living as the icing on the cake, not the only reason to live here.

SINGLES

Although our examples of living in Mexico are framed in terms of couples, there is no community of retirees in Mexico that does not include a large number of singles, both men and women. Single men can and do go anywhere in Mexico that their fancies take them, depending on their

level of adventure. Single women, however, seem to feel more comfortable where there is a concentration of their compatriots.

We interviewed a single woman who moved to Mexico a few years ago about how she felt about her surroundings and whether she felt at ease living Ajijic. She said: "I have no problem living in Mexico as a single woman; in fact, I find my Mexican neighbors keep an eye on me. There is about as much crime here as anywhere else I've lived— about the same as in the California college town I came from. As far as romance goes, there are few available men in Ajijic of my age, in their forties, so ladies, if you're shopping for a man, you could find the pickings slim. Though I keep myself plenty busy with video projects and my newsletter, I do wish I had more English-speaking friends my age."

Judy King, who publishes an online newspaper, *Living at Lake Chapala* (www.mexico-insights.com) had this to say: "I moved here single and feel that is an advantage. I made this choice for me, without trying to coordinate my desires with a mate's wants and needs. I have seen a few marriages split up because one wanted to go back and the other wanted to stay here—so they did! I never am afraid for my personal safety in this country. I have driven from the border alone several times; I walk in the villages at any time of day or night; I live alone. But in Mexico, unlike in the United States, I am always surrounded by families. My homes have been the villages on the North Shore of Lake Chapala, closely surrounded by the homes of my Mexican neighbors. Families are always walking on the sidewalks, people sitting on their stoops, or just inside their doorways, with their families. Even when in downtown Guadalajara, a city of ten to twelve million persons, I feel comfortable walking alone at 10:00 or 11:00 at night, because of the family groups moving about the city."

GAYS IN **MEXICO**

There is a substantial gay/lesbian presence in most resort cities, places such as Puerto Vallarta, Acapulco, and San Miguel de Allende. Certain hotels, bars, and discos are patronized by both tourist and resident gays. The establishments usual operate in a more discreet fashion than do straight bars and night clubs. Away from the tourist centers, however, going to a gay bar or disco can be an adventure; there is always the risk of the police storming in and hassling people just for being gay. That's not likely to happen in the resort areas or centers of expatriate residents, for fear of hurting the tourist trade. This is not to say that there haven't been incidences of antigay violence in Mexico, but our impression is that this has been directed at Mexican gays, not foreigners.

Mexicans seem to accept expatriate gays and lesbians as a fact of life. People here seem to be amused by overt gay manners rather than offended. Cancun is famous for its Gay Festival, held in May, bringing visitors from Europe as well as North America. It's been our experience that the presence of gay couples in a neighborhood doesn't even raise an eyebrow.

> **Note: Unless otherwise stated, all telephone and fax numbers in this book are in Mexico and require that you dial the proper international access, country, and city codes to reach. These numbers are listed under international calling in many U.S. directories; an international operator can help if you have trouble.**

CHAPTER ONE

WHY **CHOOSE MEXICO?**

THE **PEOPLE**

Over the past twenty years of researching *Choose Mexico*, we've routinely asked a series of questions when interviewing North Americans who made the transition to live in Mexico. Our first question is usually, "Why did you choose Mexico?" Answers to this question vary, depending on the respondent's age, social and economic background, personal interests, and other factors. Some say they made the move to Mexico "to escape the rat race." Others wanted to savor the adventure of living in an exotic foreign culture. Many were seeking a more affordable place where they could live better on their fixed incomes. Still others sought an escape from freezing weather, hurricanes, sweltering heat, and other weather-related inconveniences. The second question we ask is: "What do you like most about living in Mexico?" Interestingly, the answer most frequently at the top of the list is "the people."

What is it about friends and neighbors in Mexico that appeals so strongly to North Americans? What qualities transcend the barriers of language, class, ethnicity, and culture to evoke this response so universally? First is Mexicans' friendliness. They routinely treat strangers with warmth and curiosity. The fact that you are a foreigner as well as a

stranger seems to be incidental. Another thing is the innate happiness of the average Mexican. It may be anomalous, but poverty in Mexico is much more common than misery. The people seem to have the ability to enjoy life, no matter how difficult its circumstances.

Related to their friendliness but separate from it, is Mexicans' helpfulness. Mexicans are almost always willing to stop whatever they are doing to be of assistance to a friend, a neighbor, or a stranger. They even seem to welcome the opportunity to be helpful (or perhaps to stop what they are doing). Mexicans appear to possess courtesy and politeness as an ingrained cultural tradition. They preface every request or order with *por favor* (please) and consider it rude to be brusque, loud, or argumentative.

Then there's the love the Mexicans so obviously feel for their children. Much has been said and written about machismo, but it's a rather common sight in Mexico to see a father carrying and caring for his baby or young child. A sensitive observer of the Mexican scene has noted that some North Americans are often distressed by the callousness with which the Mexicans treat animals, yet Mexicans are equally scandalized by the verbal brutality some North American parents visit on their children. Perhaps if Mexican children were not so extremely well behaved, the sight of parents screaming at their offspring would be more common, but we've never seen it.

As you spend more time in Mexico and learn more Spanish, your understanding of Mexicans is likely to undergo many changes. It will become clear, for instance, that casual friendliness seldom evolves into deeper friendships. Mexicans tend to be introverted and family oriented, making close friends mostly among relatives and neighbors. Despite this contradiction of the Mexican character, the appeal of the Mexican people remains an important factor for those choosing Mexico.

Equally important for those moving to a foreign setting is the presence of friendly English-speaking expatriates who can ease your transition into a new lifestyle. Something about foreign ambience tends to draw fellow countrymen together like magnets, creating an intimate and welcoming social scene. Newcomers are routinely searched out and invited to participate in friendship circles. Because the number of expatriates is relatively small compared with native residents, you'll usually not find the usual stratification into social and economic levels that you

expect to see back home. At social occasions such as cocktail parties or other evening gatherings, you are likely to encounter an eclectic collection of guests—artists, college professors, and lawyers chat with computer programmers, carpenters, and waiters. For many expatriates, the Mexican people are the uppermost reason for liking Mexico.

THE **BEAUTY**

Gorgeous beaches flank both sides of the country, some crowded with sun-drenched tourists happy to escape from northern winters, some silently inviting you to explore miles of untracked sand. From the picturesque desert panorama of Baja California to the tropical jungles of the Yucatán, the country abounds in breathtaking scenery. This draws a multitude of Canadians and Americans, who spend billions every year taking in the beauty of Mexico.

Cities with modern buildings and elegant restaurants flowing with excitement thrill many North Americans, whereas others prefer villages with cobblestoned streets and concerts in the town square. Each part of Mexico has its particular character. Each city and village is distinct, its personality differing dramatically from all others. This uniqueness is not found in North America, where so many towns are carbon copies of each other, down to identical restaurants, signs, and mass-produced architecture.

We've heard people state that they think Mexico is ugly because they've visited Tijuana or some other border town and weren't impressed. This judgment is about as fair as one made by a European visitor who, after flying into the middle of Nevada, claimed that the United States was a desert, with almost no one living there! (As you might suspect, we don't particularly recommend border towns as choice places to retire.)

Something that impressed the Spanish conquistadores was the inhabitants' love of flowers. There was something almost religious about blossoms, and they were to be found everywhere: in gardens, along roads, painted on walls. Almost 500 years later the Mexican people's use of flowers continues to impress newcomers to the country. No home is complete without some tenderly cared for potted plants in the windows and perhaps bougainvilleas blooming over the door. In fact Mexicans don't take this floral beauty for granted. So much of it, provided by nature, is all around them, and what requires a pot, some earth, some seeds, or a brush and some paint is considered as much a necessity as food and shelter.

THE **CLIMATE**

Many people whose experience with Mexico is limited to brief visits to towns on the U.S. border, or whose picture of the country was formed from cartoons and Westerns, think of Mexico as a hot, dry place with endless vistas of treeless desert, spotted with cactus and cattle skeletons bleaching in the sun. Of course Mexico has its share of places that are unbearably hot, bone-chillingly cold, too humid, or too dry. However, the good news is that Mexico presents newcomers with a menu of magnificent climates. The country is a checkerboard of valleys and plateaus, often with different climates in neighboring sections. In the tropics, for every 300-foot increase in altitude, the temperature drops one degree Fahrenheit. While Gulf Coast cities like Villahermosa and Veracruz might swelter at ninety-five degrees, Mexico City enjoys temperatures of seventy to seventy-five degrees. There is also a difference in climate between the Pacific and Gulf Coasts. The constant sea breeze blowing across the Pacific keeps summer and winter temperatures pleasant, whereas the Gulf Coast can suffocate in the summer and catch chilly northern winds that whip down from Canada in winter. Not by coincidence, the places where most Americans (and Mexicans) choose to live are either at high enough altitudes to enjoy "eternal spring" or on the Pacific Coast, where the temperatures are higher but tempered by continual ocean breezes.

EXPLORING **FOREIGN LIVING**

When people think about living or retiring in "foreign" countries, Europe probably comes first to mind. However, given the current depressed state of U.S. and Canadian dollars, Europe has become prohibitively expensive for many. Retirement or long-term living in Europe? If you can afford it, be our guest. You'll pay as much for one night in a nice hotel room as you would pay for a month's apartment rent in Mexico. A nice dinner will set you back the equivalent of three weeks' pay for a Mexican gardener. Canada and the United States have too many similarities in language, worldviews, and customs ever to be considered "foreign" by residents of the other country. Therefore, for millions of North Americans, Mexico is one of the few foreign settings where we can afford to travel, where retirement or long-term living is at all practical. The nice part, Mexico is just across the border, an easy drive to many popular retirement areas.

Typically, investigating Mexico as a place to live begins with tourist visits. North American visitors pour billions of dollars into the Mexican economy every year. (The Mexican government refers to tourism as its "green pipeline.") Tourists enjoy beaches, mountains, and fascinating cities. They return home with good memories of a vacation well spent—along with loads of curios, weavings, and pottery knickknacks as presents for unappreciative friends. Yet some tourists bring back something else. They return with a deep appreciation of Mexico's most charming feature: its unique culture. In Mexico you'll find a rich tapestry of customs and beliefs with roots in the Aztec, Maya, and earlier civilizations, blended with European traditions. Add to this a liberal sprinkling of North American expatriates, and you have a culture that is neither American, European, nor Indian. The culture is Mexican. Tourists who grasp this unique situation are likely to be the ones who are reading this book. They want to find out what it's like to live and/or retire in Mexico.

HISTORICAL **BACKGROUND**

At first glance, it doesn't stand to reason that Mexico should be so different from the United States or Canada. After all, the only thing that separates the countries is an artificial line called a "border." Sometimes a high fence or deep ditch—more often just a shallow river or an imaginary boundary that can only be plotted on a surveyor's map. Yet the border is nevertheless real. Once you step across that line, you enter a different world. In some respects you step backward in time half a century or more.

To understand why Mexico is so different from the rest of North America, we need to take a quick glance at history. Beginning in the late 1700s, the United States and Canada experienced heavy waves of immigration, which increased in volume for about a century. For the most part, early immigrants were laborers, farmers, and others who longed for the abundant land in America and sought a new start in life. They knew how to till the land, how to build houses, how to work in factories. They brought the technology of the industrial revolution, which was sweeping Europe at that time.

The immigrants discovered that the choice lands were occupied by native tribes. The newcomers, determined to have the natives' land, either slaughtered the original owners or forcibly moved them ever westward. Small, family-operated farms soon sprang up across the continent. In the towns small mercantile or manufacturing enterprises arose. The United States and Canada thus began as working-class and middle-class societies, and they have more or less retained these traditions.

But Mexico was settled much earlier, in the 1500s, long before the industrial revolution wrought its changes upon the world. The original Spanish settlers in Mexico were hidalgos, the minor nobility and warrior class of Spain, which after several centuries of fighting had just defeated the Moors. Eager for adventure, the hidalgos leaped at the chance of conquering new territories, of becoming lords in a new world.

These soldiers brought with them the ideas of feudalistic Spain with its notions of nobility. The hidalgos' ideas of farming weren't small farms but huge estates operated by serfs, just as was the custom of nobility in Spain.

The conquerors came as an army, without women. But instead of killing off the natives, the early Spanish married Indian women. From the

Spanish point of view, it would have been detrimental to exterminate the natives; they were needed to operate the huge farms, or haciendas. Indian tenant farmers simply shifted from serving Aztec overlords to the new Spanish ones. The Indians thus went on tilling the same lands their ancestors had for centuries.

As Indians intermarried with the Spanish, a new race, called mestizo, was created. The mestizos, with their darker skins and slightly Indian features, became the racial cornerstone of Mexico. As the races blended, so did the customs, traditions, and folklore to create a new, uniquely Mexican culture.

With the conquest of Mexico, Spain quickly divided the country's land among the nobility, and within a few decades the entire country was solidly under the control of the new owners. So unlike the British colonies of North America, Mexico was colonized rather swiftly. Then immigration slowed to a trickle. Modern European traditions were slow in reaching Mexico. While the United States and Europe were undergoing industrialization and modernization, Mexico remained an agricultural country with worldviews formed by feudal Spaniards of the 1500s.

CHAPTER TWO

MONEY **MATTERS**

PRICES **IN MEXICO**

The first edition of *Choose Mexico*, published in 1985, bore the subtitle, "Retire on $400 a Month." Even in those days, two decades ago, that wasn't a lot of money, although the dollar went further in the United States and Canada than it does today. Our assertion that it was possible for a couple, living somewhat frugally, to be comfortable in Mexico on a $400 budget was based on personal observations, numerous interviews, and responses to a questionnaire from retired North Americans all over Mexico. It was realistic at that time. But even then we knew that things could change and cautioned readers to check the book's copyright date and get a newer edition if it was more than a couple of years old.

Things did change. Within three years we had to up that minimum figure by 50 percent, and a couple of years later it had doubled. It has been a long time since we stated our estimate of what it costs to live comfortably in Mexico, partly because change was so rapid and partly because we realized that someone who spends $10,000 a month to enjoy a comfortable lifestyle in the United States (and lots of folks do, if not me or you) may have great difficulty in imagining how anyone could possibly live well on much less.

Finally, we think we have arrived at a way of stating the situation in terms understandable to people at all income levels: If you can afford to live well in the United States or Canada, you can afford to live better in Mexico. And if you cannot quite make it on your income, you might well be able to in Mexico. This is true because your expenses in Mexico will be at least a quarter and perhaps a third less than at home. (You will need to show a minimum income to qualify for residency, which is explained later in the book.)

How much income is needed to maintain a particular lifestyle varies widely between individuals. We've had retirees claim that they do okay on $800-a-month budgets (one man reported living on $400, but he said he admitted he could not recommend it for everyone). Other expats claim a $1,000 minimum is needed, while still others do not believe it can be done on less than $2,000. From our interviews with expatriates living in Mexico, the consensus seems to be that $1,200 to $1,600 is a viable range for a couple with a lifestyle at least as high-quality as they led before they made the move to Mexico. One thing we recommend against is relocating to Mexico if you have little or no funds for those emergencies that are sure to occur. You'll not find any "safety net" in Mexico, no welfare, no food stamps, and you cannot expect much assistance from the North American community. That's one reason the government insists on your proving a minimum income before granting permission to immigrate.

MANAGING **YOUR FINANCES**

Managing your finances in Mexico has become much easier than even a decade ago, but it still requires more work than it did in your hometown. Certainly the Internet has been a tremendous help in keeping in touch with your stockbroker and managing your online banking accounts. If you keep the bulk of your savings and investments in the United States or Canada, as we have always urged our reader to do, you can send instructions to buy or sell securities by Internet or telephone just as quickly as you could back home. If you have residency papers, you can open a Mexican bank account and move funds into your local account from various banks in the United States that maintain relationships with Mexican banks. For example, Banamex in Mexico and Citibank in the United States have announced a new real-time transfer service called Citibank Global Transfers. For a fixed fee of $5.00, funds can be sent from any Citibank account in the United States to any Banamex account in Mexico. The daily limit is $3,500, and the weekly limit $10,500 for most individual accounts. And of course you can get cash immediately at ATMs throughout the country. In fact, ATMs have just about displaced travelers checks as the preferred way of obtaining cash, for tourists and residents alike. Be aware that some ATM transactions will entail higher fees, depending on the bank's policy.

INFLATION **AND DEVALUATION**

Readers of *Choose Mexico* have always been urged to leave most of their assets at home and in Mexico keep a minimum of pesos in a checking account, just enough to pay current bills. The balance of funds in Mexico should be deposited in a dollar savings account. When the peso checking account runs low, simply transfer dollars as needed. Mexican pesos are continually in a state of flux, gaining or losing value against the dollar on a daily basis. For the past decade the change has been almost miniscule, with the exchange rate varying a few cents one way or another. But there have been times when the peso's value dropped dramatically. When a peso devaluation happens, those people holding dollars find that their money buys more, and those with pesos lose out.

It's been more than twenty years since the last disastrous peso devaluation. A decade ago—after another, less serious devaluation—the Mexican government decided to stabilize the currency by allowing it to float daily to reflect the true value of the peso against world currencies. The authors of this book believe the government is on the right track and that future peso burnouts are highly unlikely. But we recommend keeping most of your Mexico funds in dollars, just in case. We do not want to leave you with the impression that Mexican banks are unsafe. The government insures that a bank cannot go out of business, and we haven't heard of anyone losing a single peso in many years.

Inflation in Mexico has been remarkably low over the past ten years, not too much higher than in the United States or Canada. The good news is that when inflation gets out of balance, the government adjusts the value of the peso against the dollar, so there isn't much effect for those holding dollars. As peso prices rise, so does the number of pesos you get for your dollar. For the past several years, the peso-dollar exchange rate has been fairly steady, with the dollar valued around 11 pesos at time of publication.

COST **OF LIVING**

In this section we present current (as of the date of writing) prices for many goods and services throughout Mexico. They are based on the reports of residents; our visits to supermarkets, big-box stores, and corner tiendas; and the extremely detailed data gathered by a Mexican government bureau on food prices in cities all across the country. We are hopeful that this information will be helpful to anyone who is considering moving to Mexico and needs to know whether it is within his or her means. The next step in making a decision continues to be those all-important exploratory trips to see whether you like what you can afford.

HOUSING The biggest item in your budget, wherever you live, is likely to be housing. As in the United States, no other cost varies as widely. Our advice, and we know of no informed writer on Mexico who disagrees, is to rent for some time before even starting to look for a place to buy. It's impossible to give a ballpark figure for rentals in Mexico any more than for the United States. As real estate people are prone to say, "The rent you pay depends on three factors: location, location, location." We've seen advertisements for houses for rent as low as $250 a month, and we are confident that for most Mexicans and some expatriates, $150 a month would be the limit. We also know of homeowners in popular places such as San Miguel de Allende who can get $250 a day for their places! Remember, you get what you pay for. A $150-a-month house is likely to be a place few readers would choose; many would consider even a $300 rental rather basic. Our take is that in a nice area of Ajijic, for example, $600 to $800 are common rents. In more ordinary neighborhoods, half that amount would not be unusual.

Eventually, most people decide to buy, not only for the pleasure of having their own place for gracious living in Mexico, but also to benefit from the steady appreciation of real estate in most parts of the country.

When you own property, you don't hesitate to make changes or remodel to suit your tastes. Also, you have the security of knowing the house isn't going to be sold to a newcomer, and you will be pounding the pavement looking for another rental. (See The Real Estate Game for some typical homes for sale in various parts of Mexico and their prices.)

FOOD PRICES One of the principal reasons for Mexico's low cost of living is the exceptionally low food prices. The traditional Mexican diet of tortillas, rice, and beans is incredibly inexpensive, with the government subsidizing many costs. But foods typically on expatriates' diets, such as fresh vegetables, fruit, meats, and non-imported staples are also bargains, priced at a fraction of what they would cost in the United States. Newcomers soon learn to avoid expensive imported goods and use their Mexican counterparts.

The following table, compiled from a variety of sources, including a government bureau that tracks food prices all over the country, should give you an idea of what impact eating well is going to have on your budget. All prices are in U.S. dollars and are current as of the date of publication. Unless otherwise specified, quantities are in pounds.

Item	Price	Item	Price
Almonds	$4.49	Canned jalapeño chiles	$0.38
Apples—Rome Beauty	$0.79	Canned peaches in syrup	$1.55
Avocados—Hass	$0.96	Canned peas	$0.29
Baby food—		Capers	$1.67
Gerber, fruit flavor	$0.62	Carrots	$0.25
Bananas	$0.45	Celery	$0.26
Beef liver	$0.65	Chard, bunch	$0.44
Beer, Negra Modelo		Cheese	$3.04
—sixpack	$3.75	Chicken breasts	$1.30
Beets	$0.38	Chicken legs	$1.09
Bottled water—1.5 liters	$0.67	Chicken, whole	$0.81
Bread—fresh baked	$1.00	Coca-Cola—2.5 liters	$1.25
Broccoli	$0.51	Coffee—Mexican	$2.48
Canned cherries	$1.21	Cucumbers	$0.27

Dried Pasilla chiles	$0.45	Pears, Bartlett—canned	$1.47
Filet mignon	$4.34	Pinto beans	$0.32
Fresh peas	$0.79	Pork chops	$2.43
Fruit juice, various flavors		Pork cutlet	$1.97
—1 liter	$1.02	Pork loin	$1.31
Grapes	$1.04	Potatoes	$0.40
Ground beef	$1.61	Raisins	$1.50
Ground pork	$1.76	Rolls—fresh baked	$0.12
Head of lettuce	$0.49	Shoulder steak	$2.23
Jicama	$0.26	Skirt steak	$2.21
Lemons	$0.21	Stick butter—quarter pound	$0.40
Mango	$0.32	Strawberries	$1.69
Milk—quart container	$0.67	Sugar	$0.80
Nescafé, decaffeinated—jar	$3.47	Tomato puree—canned	$0.72
Olives	$2.45	Veal cutlet	$2.71
Olives stuffed with pimiento	$2.58	Watermelon	$0.20
Onions	$0.34	Yogurt, flavored—Dannon	$0.36
Oranges	$0.19	Yogurt, flavored—local	
Papayas	$0.39	brand	$0.31
Pears—fresh	$0.67	Zucchini	$0.26

RESTAURANT MEALS Although a smaller budgetary item for the resident than for the tourist, the ability to eat out affordably is one of the things that make living in Mexico enjoyable. The prices listed below include neither the humblest roadside stands (where the authors have had some delicious meals) nor the trendiest resort eateries where the sky is the limit (and the authors have never dined).

Breakfast, full American, for one	$3.50
Lunch, for one	$4.00 to $6.00
Dinner with wine for two	$25.00

CLOTHING Clothing prices—excluding the bargains available at outdoor markets throughout much of Mexico and prices at luxury shops or boutiques, which abound in places popular with tourists—are fairly similar to those in the United States. On a recent visit we found a man's zipper-front sweater for less than $10 and a woman's cashmere sweater for less than $20, the former in a clothing store patronized almost exclusively by locals and the latter in an outdoor market. We also saw (but did not purchase) a very nice looking man's knitted jacket in a Mexico City haberdashery for only $500.

PERSONAL CARE ITEMS Prices for personal care items are similar to those in the United States and Canada. Here are a few examples:

Toothpaste	$1.84
Soap	$0.61
Shampoo	$2.65
Mouthwash	$3.50
Shaving cream	$4.80

HEALTH CARE Particularly for older Americans, the cost of health care is a matter of constant concern. In the United States, even with Medicare, supplemental insurance and prescription drugs take a large and growing bite out of our income. Canadians have excellent government medical coverage, but as far as we can tell, their government insurance coverage doesn't apply in Mexico. U.S. citizens are out of luck also, because Medicare will not pay for treatment they receive in Mexico. In order to take advantage of Medicare benefits, U.S. citizens need to go home. Some U.S. insurance policies are said to cover policyholders in Mexico, but our observation is that most people opt for Mexican private insurance policies when they do not use the Mexican government insurance.

Because medical costs in Mexico are relatively inexpensive, with doctors' and dentists' services and hospital stays costing a small fraction of what they do back home, the lack of your home country's coverage doesn't seem so important. Prescription drugs, too, are cheap by U.S. standards, even costing less than those available in Canada. Your medical insurance choices are discussed in the Staying Healthy chapter.

Here are some of the dollar figures for health care reported by people living in Mexico:

Private doctor's office visit	$20
Specialist's consultation	$30
Dentist's visit with X-rays and cleaning	$35
Hospital, overnight stay	$72
Prescription eyeglasses	$61
Annual premium for coverage by Mexican social security system	Less than $300
Annual premium for Mexican private health insurance	$1,000 to $6,000

ENTERTAINMENT Following are prices you might expect to pay for various entertainments in Mexico:

English-language movie—after 6:00 P.M.	$4.00
English-language movie—before 6:00 P.M.	$1.50
Community theater, opera, symphony, musical	$5.00 to $12.00
Museum admission	$3.50
DVD rental	$1.20
Cable service—basic	$18.00/month
Satellite TV service	$52.00/month

HOUSEHOLD HELP The ability to afford daily or weekly household help is an enjoyable feature of Mexican life for North Americans. A particular delight is to be able to throw a party and spend your time talking with your friends, not waiting on them. Following are some average costs for household help:

Maid—per hour	$1.25 to $2.50
Gardener—per hour	$1.25 to $2.50
Bartender—per hour (for party)	$3.00 to $4.00

PUBLIC TRANSPORTATION Public transportation in Mexico is a cost-effective alternative to driving your own vehicle. Here are some average prices:

Local bus	$0.30 to $0.40
Luxury intercity bus—three-hour trip	$35.00
Taxis – ten- to fifteen-minute trip	$2.00 to $4.00

UTILITIES The cost of electricity varies greatly by location and by the amount consumed. The former may be principally because of differences in climate. The latter is due to a stiff premium for going over the basic consumption level. Some expats seem to do just fine. A couple from Florida reports paying about an eighth of what they were used to. On the other hand, a retiree from the state of Washington (where electricity costs are very low due to extensive hydroelectric power generation) says he pays much more in Mexico. The consensus appears to be that if you come from a location in the United States with cold winters and/or hot summers, you will save money on utilities in Mexico. Following are some basic utility rates:

Water	$140.00/year
Electricity	$50.00 to
	$100.00/month
Per kilowatt (substantially higher	
rate for larger quantities)	$0.05 to $0.14
Natural gas (delivered to roof tank)	$1.40/gallon
Telephone (basic)	$20.00/month

Telephone calls to the United States, once ridiculously expensive, have become entirely reasonable with the right program. Internet-based telephone service is now priced as low as 1,000 minutes per month for $9.95. Programs with fewer minutes can cost even less. Free PC-to-PC service is available, and some users claim that its quality is now equal to or better than traditional service.

MAJOR APPLIANCES Whether to buy major appliances in Mexico or to bring them with you is a topic of endless debate among expat residents.

There is little doubt that appliances are at least as expensive south of the border. The question, then, is whether it's worth the trouble and expense of transporting your old ones from home. One consideration is warranty service. There seems to be general agreement that it is easier to get an item repaired by the shop from which you bought it. Although appliance purchases are not one of the costs of day-to-day living, you should figure them in while computing your cost of building and furnishing your dream home in Mexico. In our comparison shopping, we found that one can choose between low-capacity, low-cost Mexican (and other foreign) brands and top-of-the-line models from major American manufacturers. In the listings below, the low end of each range represents Mexican/foreign brands; the high end represents U.S. goods.

Refrigerator	$350 to $800
Dishwasher—portable	$400
Washing machine	$200 to $500
Dryer	$225 to $500
Washer-dryer combination	$1,400
Freezer—8 cubic feet	$400
Stove	$350 to $1,100

AUTOMOBILE EXPENSE As in the United States, the high price of gasoline is a major factor in the overall cost of operating an automobile. The average cost per gallon in both countries has recently topped $2.00. Although Mexican gasoline prices do not fluctuate as rapidly in the United States, prices here will likely remain fairly close to the U.S. price in the foreseeable future.

Automobile repairs tend to be less expensive in Mexico, as might be expected with the lower labor costs. Mexican mechanics are famous for their ability to find a solution to almost any problem, perhaps because they have had so much experience with keeping ancient autos running. Sometimes repair parts for less popular vehicles can be difficult to obtain in Mexico, and you may have to wait for parts to be shipped in, one reason for driving a model that's commonly sold in the country.

Those who choose to apply for residency in Mexico are permitted to bring in their U.S. automobiles and are not required to change their registration or state license plates. This can be done for a period of five years, even longer under certain circumstances. This is the most economical way to own an automobile in Mexico, because you avoid several taxes and fees. However, some people prefer to buy a new automobile in Mexico, where the warranty is likely to be honored. The table below lists prices for a representative selection of American and foreign cars available in Mexico. It is important to note that U.S. and Mexican models of the same name can vary significantly in equipment and overall specifications.

Make	Model	Dollar price
Chevrolet	Malibu LS	$18,946
Dodge	Neon R/T	$16,029
Ford	Econoline van	$21,435
Lincoln	Town Car	$45,900
Honda	Accord EX	$22,447
Honda	Civic 210400	$18,456
Toyota	Camry XLE	$23,772
Volkswagen	Beetle GLS	$17,269

CHAPTER THREE

MANY **DIFFERENT MEXICOS**

As you travel about the United States and Canada, you'll find remarkable similarities between one section and another. To be sure, the scenery in Maine is different from Alabama or Nevada, but many, many things are the same. Meals served in Denny's or IHOP are indistinguishable from one region to another. People read the same books, watch the same TV shows, discuss the same current events, and generally speak the same dialects of English, using common slang words and sharing common humor, likes, and dislikes.

Mexico is not so homogeneous; its diversity is part of its charm. The country is divided into many physical segments, each separated by geography and history. Each section has its own traditions, cuisine, climate, and, often, even its own indigenous language.

If you take a look at a map of Mexico, you'll begin to see why these differences exist. You'll notice a long, narrow country, with several mountain chains that run north and south, splitting the country and forming barriers against east-west communication. In pre-Columbian times, trails across these sierras were few in number and difficult to travel. Tribes living in the valleys developed unique languages and different civilizations. You'll also notice that today most highways and rail-

roads run north and south. This is not only because of the mountain barriers, but also because most highways and railroads were built years ago by U.S. manufacturing and mining interests that wanted to ship raw materials out of Mexico to feed Northern factories, then ship finished goods back to Mexico.

Furthermore, the country is laterally sliced by rivers and canyons, sometimes thousands of feet deep, that made north-south communication difficult in olden days. It's still not easy today. Each of these sections, over thousands of years of settlement, developed its own variants of culture, food, housing, and style. Today, even though TV and radio have bridged many of the gaps, these differences persist and are a source of local pride. Almost any Mexican you meet will inform you that his or her particular section of the republic is universally recognized as the very best place in the whole world!

CULTURAL **DIVERSITY**

The resident or retiree can choose from an amazing variety of individual cultures as well as climates, each one distinct and a delight to discover. Each is a microcosm with its own cooking techniques, styles of dress, and accents. When you get away from the big towns, you often hear people conversing in Nahuatl or Quechua, the languages of the ancient Aztecs and Mayas. The Mexicans themselves often look physically different from region to region. Because geographical barriers kept them apart for thousands of years, individuals tended to marry within tribes, keeping bloodlines relatively pure. At least forty distinct racial and language groups are represented in Mexico.

On the eastern coast around Veracruz, home of the Huastecan tribes, typical clothing is tropical white, with the men wearing shallow straw hats. The women love bright embroidered trim on their dresses. On the west coast around Tehuantepec, where the temperature is equally tropical, women tend to wear ankle-length skirts. A bit farther north around the Costa Chica area, the Indian women wear long woven skirts of cochineal-dyed yarn and used to go topless. The early missionaries weren't able to completely wipe out the custom, although they did convince most women to wear a white, flouncy overblouse. This outfit is often worn today. Understand, we're talking about traditional dress. Except for traditional

fiestas and national holidays—
when everyone tries to be historically correct—blue jeans and
designer blouses have become
fashion staples, especially among
the younger set.

In the Yucatán women prefer
to wear a loose dress of light cot-
ton (a *huipil*), and the men often
work bare chested, wearing light-
weight, white muslin trousers.
Because temperatures and
humidity can be oppressive, this kind of dress is very practical. On the
other hand, the northern part of Mexico is influenced by the "western"
clothing of Texas and Arizona. There the climate is similar to Texas,
Arizona, and New Mexico, so it isn't surprising that clothing styles should
be influenced by fashion in those states.

In the southern part of Mexico, nearby Guatemalan tribes affect
styles with bright, colorfully woven garments. Depending on the particular tribe, men may wear woolen skirts or knee-length trousers. The pat
terns of the weavings denote which village the wearer is from, and the
colors of the ribbons in the hair indicate whether the person is married or
single.

Although each section of the country has its own clothing styles,
styles from New York, London, Paris, and Mexico City invade the fashions
of young Mexicans, particularly in the larger, more cosmopolitan cities.
The smaller the town or village, the more likely you might find older, more
traditional dress.

REGIONAL **DIETS**

Mexican food varieties are another joy to the authors of this book. Each
section of the country is proud of its own kind of dishes and its own style
of cooking. Part of the fun of traveling in Mexico is sampling dishes from
different parts of the country.

Most tourists think of Mexican food in terms of tacos, burritos, and
chili con carne. This is understandable, because these dishes are just

about all that's served in most Mexican restaurants in the United States. Similarly many foreigners believe that typical American cuisine consists of hamburgers and hot dogs. Just as you can find hamburgers anywhere in the United States, you can find your fill of tacos in Mexico, if that's your dish. Most restaurants that cater to Americans include tacos on the menu, but a really good Mexican restaurant would no more offer tacos and burritos than would a gourmet restaurant in the United States offer hamburgers and hot dogs. There is so much more to Mexican cooking!

In the Yucatán you'll discover such treats as venison cooked with a vinegar-cream sauce, or smoked *jabalí* (wild peccary) or *cochinito pibil* (roast suckling pig, cooked in a pit with a delicious sauce). In the mountains you'll find succulent quail, delicately flavored with herbs and grilled over a charcoal fire, or eggs cooked with a dry cheese that transforms them into a delightfully textured breakfast. Mexican seafood is fabulous. Some of our favorite dishes are *huachinango al mojo de ajo* (grilled red snapper with garlic-butter sauce), langostinos (charbroiled freshwater lobsters), and a bewildering number of shellfish dishes. As an example of menu variety, one favorite Mazatlán restaurant offers almost twenty shrimp dishes. One of the authors even tried iguana stew on a recent trip to Mexico. It tasted a little like chicken but was very bony and had little meat. It's not recommended unless you're truly hungry.

One of the delights of living in Mexico is being able to cook some of these regional dishes at home, to experiment and learn. A trip through a typical market, with its variety of fresh fruits, vegetables, and meats, makes shopping and menu planning a pleasant adventure rather than a chore. With its tropical climate many parts of Mexico have year-round growing seasons for produce that is seasonally unavailable in the North. Just about any time of the year is good for incredibly sweet strawberries and luscious melons. Tropical fruits such as mangoes, pineapples, avocados, and bananas are picked for the Mexican market when they are ripe, not days or weeks ahead to allow for ripening en route, as they must be when destined for the United States and Canada.

Shopping is also fun, because foods are not only fresh but also available in a profusion and quality that most of us barely remember. In time Mexican agriculture may become sufficiently mechanized and chemical fertilizers may become cheap enough to mass produce the tasteless fruits and vegetables that we have learned to settle for in the United States.

But for now Mexican fruits, vegetables, eggs, chicken, and pork burst with flavor and enliven any dish in which they are used.

RETIREMENT **CHOICES**

The difficulty of choosing the right retirement or long-term living spot is finding the section of Mexico that is just right for you. This is where this book should be of help. You can choose a tropical climate to escape winter, or you might want a dry, pleasant summer season. Like cool evenings and warm days? Balmy to warm evenings? Many people select the best of all worlds by living near the beaches in winter and then, when humidity and temperatures begin to rise, moving to their favorite village high in the mountains.

The nice thing about making a search for the right place is that it's fun to do, and you can do it simply by using your tourist card privileges. You can travel about, live a few weeks here or there, and make comparisons. You can see what kind of North American neighbors you would have and get their opinions on living there. One thing you'll find out: There is no one place that can suit everyone. Your needs and desires are unique, so only you can decide.

TWO MEXICOS Many people find it hard to believe that living in Mexico can be economical. "Why, we paid $300 a day for our condominium in Cancun," said one indignant couple, "so how could you possibly live there on a small budget?" Admittedly this was an extra-luxurious, three-bedroom condo with a balcony overlooking the beach. Yet numerous tourists report paying $100 a day or more for rooms.

For tourists Mexico is a real mecca. On a two-week vacation, they can escape the snow and ice of New York or Chicago and do it in real style. In Mexico the beaches are marvelous, and restaurants offer great service, with white-jacketed waiters and menus that are as good as any at a Sheraton or Hilton in the United States. For only two weeks, what difference does it make if you pay $100, maybe $150, a day for a room? One Acapulco hotel charges $300 a day, but this includes your own private swimming pool and a car. If it's minus twenty degrees back home, you may decide you've earned a little luxury in your life. Besides, a $100-a-day room in Mexico is a marvel compared with a $100 room in New York. But with prices like this, how can you possibly expect to live or travel in Mexico on a modest income?

The answer is that Mexico is divided into two realities: one for tourists and one for residents. Tourists make their reservations with travel agents, who earn their living from commissions. They aren't likely to even have inexpensive rooms among their listings. But most North Americans who live in Mexico would think it absurd to lay out that kind of money, not when a $30 room is more than adequate. They can't afford to pay $200 a day for a condo, not when $300 a month can rent a small apartment. People who *live* in Mexico consider it ludicrous to go to a high-priced hotel restaurant and dine on Holiday Inn cuisine, especially when so many marvelous local restaurants offer tasty specialties at a fraction of the cost.

One of the most important changes we've observed in the twenty years since the first edition of *Choose Mexico* was published is the increased difference between the tourist and resident economies. It seems that Mexican entrepreneurs (and the international ones who run the fancy hotels and restaurants) have learned that tourists are willing to pay much higher prices than are common in Mexico.

AVOID LUXURY RESORTS? Is the secret of inexpensive living to stay away from luxury resorts like Acapulco, Cancun, or Puerto Vallarta? Not necessarily. Acapulco, for example, can be one of the cheapest places to live in Mexico. From its initial marketing as a beautiful place for beautiful people, Acapulco has consistently overbuilt hotels and apartments. As soon as one high-rise is completed and half full, another is started. There are plenty of $40-a-day hotel rooms and occasionally $300-a-month apartments. The bargains are to be found away from the beach, sometimes on hillsides with gorgeous views of the Pacific. Twenty-five years ago, these were top-of-the-line accommodations, but in order to compete, the owners of these properties had to continually lower their rents. When you save $100 a day, so what if you have to walk 5 blocks to the beach? If you're going to be a resident, this type of bargain is what you look for.

One thing to keep in mind about living expenses in Mexico is that foreign tourists make up but a tiny part of the population. The vast majority of tourists are Mexican wage earners who can't possibly afford to spend like the foreigners. A $40 hotel room represents about a week's

wages for many Mexican workers. Ninety percent of the people in a resort town work there.
Well-paid workers average only
$250 a month in wages, so they
can't afford to pay much for
rent or groceries. Most of the
housing market is aimed at
them, so rents and prices are
scaled accordingly. You're
either a rich tourist or a resident.

As a potential resident or retiree, you must make this a do-it-yourself
project. Might as well start out traveling like a resident from the beginning! At your bookstore or library, pick up one of the low-cost travel
guides to Mexico—the "Mexico on a Budget" type. They tend to be
accurate about inexpensive hotels and travel tips. Except for the
Christmas holidays and Easter week, you will seldom have problems
booking the hotel of your choice.

Don't bother with a travel agent, because the kind of hotels that
budget books recommend usually don't pay travel agents' commissions
and therefore aren't on their computers. In forty years of traveling in
Mexico, we've never had problems finding an inexpensive hotel. Cab
drivers are helpful, but often they get a tip from the hotels for bringing
guests, so naturally they want to take you to their special hotel. Take with
a grain of salt anything a cab driver tells you. Don't be persuaded to devi-
ate from your original choice, even if the cabby tells you the hotel is
closed or that he knows one that is cheaper. See it for yourself first. The
guidebooks are pretty accurate; cab drivers are not.

HOUSING SEARCH Once you arrive and are safely entrenched in an
economical hotel, you can start searching for an apartment or a house to
rent. If you're in a place where there are a lot of North Americans, you'll
usually find listings and announcements posted on a bulletin board in the
favorite gringo supermarket. Sometimes you'll see FOR RENT signs in windows or advertised in the local English-language newspaper. But the best
way to find rentals is to ask other foreign residents. They always seem to

know what is vacant or what is about to be vacated.

Often your hotel will have an apartment or suite for rent. This is a great way to test the town for its potential without getting involved in long-term rental agreements. (Few landlords are willing to rent for less than two or three months.) A hotel rents by the day, week, or month, and often charges only a little more for an apartment than for an ordinary room. We've rented some nice apartments for between $30 and $50 a day. Particularly common are hotel "efficiencies" in resort places like Acapulco and Puerto Vallarta.

Like most furnished apartments, hotel kitchens come equipped with dishes, silverware, pots and pans, five-gallon jugs of purified water, and even dish towels. The bonus is that every day a brace of efficient maids scours the tile floors, changes the linen, and brings in fresh water, exactly as in a hotel. They do your breakfast dishes and put them away in the cupboard. We usually leave a small tip every day, and it's greatly appreciated.

Our recommendation to nontourists is to take a hotel-apartment that rents by the day or week, even if it costs a little more than an ordinary hotel room and even if you have no intention of cooking many meals. There is nothing like starting off the day by having breakfast on your patio or balcony. Planning the day's adventures while you relax in pajamas is infinitely more fun than spending half the morning getting dressed, then waiting for someone to bring you a second cup of coffee.

For the finicky or those worried about the dreaded "tourist disease," you have the satisfaction of preparing your own meals, using purified water, and taking other hygienic precautions. Your food is as safe as if it were cooked in Omaha.

A few tips about apartment-hopping in Mexico:

- You won't find a can opener in the kitchen. Don't ask why; just bring or buy one.
- Be sure you have matches for lighting the stove and candles for candlelight dining on the balcony (and for frequent power outages in some areas).
- When freezing ice cubes for drinks, use bottled water, not tap water, which probably will not be potable. (We note that many tourists religiously avoid drinking tap water, then brush their teeth with it. And they

wonder why they get sick!) Bottled or boiled water in any form is the only kind that should enter your mouth.

- It isn't necessary to avoid fresh fruits and salads. Just wash everything in a solution of bottled water and iodine drops—five drops per liter of water. Iodine is cheap, readily available, and effective; it is less invasive to health than chlorine and this solution won't spoil the taste of your food.

THE "TOURIST **DISEASE**"

Why do they call it the "tourist disease"? Many people believe that only tourists are affected, that natives "build up an immunity." In fact no one, including local residents, builds up an immunity to the most serious of these disorders, amoebic dysentery. By observing some simple rules of hygiene, residents avoid getting sick. When they don't follow these rules, they get sick just as the tourists do. We know of many people who have been scared off by an unhappy experience with *turista* or have heard of others who suffered through their whole two-week vacation in Mexico. It doesn't have to be that way. Ask anyone who lives there.

We all have bacteria in our digestive systems; they are necessary for good health. But a phenomenon common to anyone who travels from one place to another is encountering a new strain of bacteria. The resident bacteria fight the intruders, and the intestines finally get tired of all the fuss and decide to produce a little diarrhea. This is a mild form of the "tourist disease" and is nothing to worry about. It's the bad-guy amoebas you must worry about. But common sense can avert problems. Most expatriates who live in Mexico report that they seldom if ever have "tourist problems."

As a potential resident, you must relearn a few basic habits. These will distinguish you from the two-week tourist and keep you from a lot of misery. Before long these rules become automatic, and you won't even have to think about them.

Of course don't drink water in any form other than boiled or bottled. By the way, you don't have to boil water for hours and hours. Because no organism can survive at temperatures higher than 150 degrees Fahrenheit, just bringing water to a boil is sufficient. Some water systems are all right, but we recommend boiled or purified water anyway; make it one of your automatic habits. Always soak salad vegetables (lettuce, tomatoes—anything that isn't going to be cooked or peeled) in a solution of water and iodine drops for twenty minutes.

Finally, one of the most valuable pieces of advice this book can give you about avoiding dysentery: When selecting a restaurant, don't be impressed by the nicely dressed waiters, immaculate linen, and sparkling silverware; check out the clientele. Notice if local people eat there. If local people don't patronize a place, there's one of three explanations: The food is overpriced, poorly prepared, or not fit to eat.

Too often a "tourist" restaurant is owned by absentee owners and operated by low-paid employees who really don't care if you get sick or not. They know you won't be back again anyway, and you eat in so many places you won't know where you got the "bug." But a family-operated restaurant, one that caters to local people, can't afford to have anyone get sick. When word gets around, the place is out of business. One of this book's authors as a youth lived in Mexico for many years and has traveled extensively throughout the country for more than forty years. Only twice has he caught the curse. Both times he ignored his own advice and patronized a spiffy, tourist-only restaurant where no Mexicans ate!

Why all this fuss about boiled or bottled water? Isn't any Mexican water fit to drink? If not, why not? The answer is that some water is probably okay, particularly that either coming from desert areas, where the water is pumped from deep wells, or flowing from the high mountains, where few people are around to pollute it. The problem is that Mexico has many priorities well ahead of the construction of modern sewage disposal plants. The costs would be astronomical, and the money is simply not there. Even where there are facilities for modern disposal, expanding home and hotel construction means that sewage production exceeds the capacity of these plants. So most of the sewage goes into septic tanks and eventually seeps into the groundwater. Where there is a high water table, such as you find at the coastal resorts, some sewage, with its amoebas and bacteria, inevitably finds its way into the water system. Wherever water is drawn from shallow wells, you can have problems. A further complication in Mexico City is that the water and sewage pipes are often damaged by earthquake activity, and they leak—not much, but enough to sometimes make you sick. One trend, at least in the expatriate neighborhoods, is the installation of state-of-the-art water purification systems in homes, complete with filters and ultraviolet light treatment. One resident of Mazatlán says, "We and our guests have been drinking directly from the tap for more than six years without incident. Some friends took a water sample back to the United States and had it compared with their tap water. Our water was much cleaner!"

To become a healthy nontourist in Mexico, you have to continually follow commonsense rules. Before long you will become so used to the drill that when you return to the United States, you will hesitate before using tap water to brush your teeth.

TWO PRICE **SYSTEMS IN MEXICO?**

You often hear people claim, "There are two prices in Mexico, one for the Mexicans and one for the gringos." Some believe, for example, that different menus are handed to gringos and Mexicans. This simply isn't true. Most prices are fixed by government decree, and the government is serious about enforcement. When you rent a room, for example, the ceiling price is supposed to be clearly displayed at the desk and in your room.

But, as we have observed earlier, there are two price systems—not for Mexicans and foreigners, but for residents and tourists. You won't find different prices being charged to the two groups in the same restaurants and hotels, because menus and room rates are prominently displayed. You will, however, find higher prices at the hotels into which tourists are booked by travel agents and the restaurants in those hotels. Ironically, the government often turns its head at violations by tourist hotels. Residents, whether Mexican or foreign, know of equally nice places that charge a fraction of the price.

Restaurants and stores, particularly the nontourist places, are anxious to have residents' repeat business; if they overcharge you, you'll never return. However, that old game of bargaining does go on in Mexico. Some merchants feel obligated to quote an unrealistic price, and they often feel cheated out of the fun if you go ahead and pay without a little arguing.

How do you know if you're paying the resident price or the tourist price? Don't all Mexicans expect you to bargain? Should you offer one-third the asking price? These questions are relative to the product being offered and the price asked. For example, if you're in a market and the vendor wants the equivalent of a dime for a handful of onions, ask your-self: "What do I gain by arguing him down 20 percent?" A few pennies or a nickel may mean nothing to you but plenty to the vendor. Actually individual entrepreneurs face a lot of competition in the native markets, so they try to keep their prices attractive. They want to see you become a regular customer, and they usually go out of their way to make you happy.

On the other hand, if you're buying something that costs a lot of money, then a 20 percent discount would be significant. If it's big money, sometimes it's worth bargaining hard, just as you would when buying an automobile or house back home.

NEGOTIATING A PRICE Bargaining is an art form that you might enjoy, but accept the fact that you will never win. Just as you never really beat an automobile salesperson at the car game, you'll never quite get the final value in Mexico. Bargaining is fun to do, and no one gets hurt feel-ings. Yet serious hassling over pennies doesn't mark an American as an astute bargainer; it marks him or her as a cheapskate.

It's interesting to watch the tourists bargain. As soon as they settle down on the beach, a swarm of eager vendors begins landing like flies on a lollipop. They'll offer jewelry, blankets, sweaters, you name it, and the bargaining begins in Spanish, English, and sign language. Everyone has a glorious time, and in the end the poor merchant reluc-tantly agrees to drop the price of the $40 necklace to only $10. The tourist is delighted at his prowess in saving $30, and the vendor is dis-couraged that he allowed such a fine $1.00 necklace to go for only $10. Like the car dealers back home, the beach vendors are experts. But don't get the idea that everyone you meet is trying to scalp you. Most merchants you deal with in everyday living situations are anxious to do business with you and take pride in having a good relationship with *norteamericanos*.

If you visit a store with price tags on all items, it's pretty sure that the owners mean business, unless you're talking big money. If you're thinking about a $100 purchase or a $1,000 deal, then maybe it's worth your while to bargain against the posted price. You may not be successful, but it's worth the try to shave off 10 or 20 percent. But if the price is only $2.00, you're wasting your time haggling.

BEING GENEROUS One complaint occasionally heard about *Choose Mexico* is that it is drawing more and more North Americans into the country. "They come down here, throw money around, pay big wages, leave big tips, and ruin things for the rest of us!" is the way one woman put it.

It's true that when more foreigners move into a town or village, the demand for domestic help creates a boost in wages. It's also true that foreigners tend to pay more than the going rate for lots of things. This means more money circulating in the community and slightly higher prices all around. The final result is that Americans pay a few cents more for goods and services, and Mexicans have more money in their pockets. Because Americans are known to pay higher wages, the local people are eager to work for them. Working for an American family is prestigious, and workers try very hard to be good employees and keep their jobs.

Our stock answer to complainers: Mexico is not your private discovery. Mexico is not for the sole benefit of a few stingy gringos who want to keep the local economy depressed so that they can save a few pennies. We are guests in that country, and as guests we should rejoice in any improvement in the living standard of our hosts. If you have to pay $1.50 an hour for help instead of $1.00 an hour, just remember how much you would pay back home and think of what that extra money will buy for a Mexican family.

Yes, there are two Mexicos. One is for tourists; the other is for residents. The happiest residents are those who consider themselves part of the community, and by the same token, they are the best liked by their Mexican neighbors. The unhappiest residents are those who try to change things and make Mexico into a bargain-basement copy of the United States.

FORMAL **INTRODUCTIONS**

When in a formal social or business situation, using the proper form of address is important. When do you call someone by his or her first name? When do you use a title? A person is addressed by first name only when speaking with close or casual friends, or when the person is your social inferior. But when speaking with new acquaintances of your own social standing or with business associates, you use a title (when appropriate) and their father's last name. Thus when addressing someone with a professional title, such as a doctor or a lawyer *(licenciado)*, it is important that you say, *"Buenas noches, liciendiado Sanchez."* Or if you aren't sure about the last name, simply, *"Buenas noches, liciendiado."* When talking to a friend you'd say, *"Buenas noches, Roberto."* And to the maid, *"Buenas noches, María."* Should an acquaintance begin calling you by your first name, then you can respond in kind. If the new acquaintance has no title that you know of, then by all means use the *Mr.* or *Mrs.* equivalent: *Señor, Señora,* or *Señorita,* as in *"Buenas tardes, Señora Córdova."*

You probably already know that Latin-Americans have two last names. Example: If a woman's name is Matilda Sanchez Alvarado, you know her father's name is Sanchez and her mother's name is Alvarado. When married, she adds her husband's name onto the end: Matilda Sanchez Alvarado de Córdova, showing that she is married to Señor Córdova. Usually she shortens it to simply Matilda Córdova, but when signing legal documents, she signs with the full complement of names.

Some of the aforementioned customs and etiquette may seem trivial to North Americans new to Mexican social and business circles, but they will make a favorable impression on those with whom you interact.

DIFFERENT WAYS OF **VIEWING TIME**

Throughout this book you'll see references to cultural differences in the way time is viewed. *Norteamericanos* are continually surprised, dismayed, and sometimes angered at the casual way many Mexicans view time as unimportant, putting things off until *mañana* and being late for appointments. You ask your gardener to be at the house before noon, yet he arrives three hours late, with no explanation. The electrician promises to be there tomorrow morning to install a new ceiling fan—but doesn't show up until day after tomorrow. You invite guests for dinner at 7:00 P.M., the expatriates are there on time but your Mexican guests don't arrive until almost 8:00. What is going on? Have they no regard for your schedule?

The secret is to understand that you are not going to change the culture and make Mexicans behave like time-driven robots. It isn't going to happen, so live with it. I've learned to accept that when the plumber promises to fix the toilet this afternoon, maybe he will and maybe he won't. By assuming that he won't be there, I'm pleasantly surprised if he actually shows up this afternoon. When a merchant assures me that the ceramic tile I ordered will arrive *mañana,* I fully realize there's a chance that line has been discontinued and my tile will never arrive. He could be avoiding giving me bad news. By assuming the worst-case scenario, I get to enjoy many pleasant surprises, yet not be angry or overly disappointed when things don't happen.

None of this is to say that you can't make some change in people's behavior, especially your employees. If they realize that it is important to you that they arrive at a certain time, they may not understand why it is important, but they will usually be there. Not to do as you wish would hurt your feelings, and that's not the way things should be.

CHAPTER FOUR

THE REAL **ESTATE GAME**

Part of the fun of considering a move south of the border is planning a new lifestyle, a new way of living in an exotic ambience, your own home in Mexico. The mental image could be a colonial-style home with stone walls and an interior garden patio. Others might picture a quaint adobe home, partially covered with flowering bougainvilleas, fronting a cobblestone street where the sound of burros' hooves can be heard early in the morning. Perhaps the dream is a modern home on a hill overlooking a beautiful lake, with a kidney-shaped swimming pool and a large barbeque pit. One of this author's favorite fantasies is to purchase an eighteenth-century home near the central plaza of a colonial town such as Guanajuato or Taxco—an old mansion complete with a roof garden overlooking the ancient city, with a view of the cathedral in the distance.

We all harbor our special dreams. Therefore it's no surprise that one of the first things newcomers are eager to do is locate their dream property and get settled into their new lifestyle. Most realize it's best to rent as they try out a potential location while making a thorough search for that dream home. Should property be too expensive or not high enough quality in one locality, simply move on to another place rec-

ommended in this book. Eventually you will zero in on your future home. Looking is a large part of the fun.

CAN FOREIGNERS **OWN PROPERTY?**

A common misconception is that Americans can't own property in Mexico. For years the government tried to restrict foreign ownership of land, with diminishing success. The fear was that Mexican citizens would have little chance to compete with affluent foreigners and that property ownership for Mexicans would be a thing of the past. In fact this was one of the fears most often expressed by Mexicans when discussing the NAFTA treaty.

Despite the Mexican government's efforts, foreigners seem to have won. For the first time in several generations, all restrictions are off in most parts of Mexico. In most of the country you can buy and sell property just as you might in Omaha or Ottawa. Because of this change in federal law, foreigners can hold an *escritura,* or fee-simple title deed, for the property in their own names.

Foreigners are still restricted within specified distances of the seacoast or international borders—you can't own the property outright; the deed must be placed in a trust.

The way it works is that you purchase the property through a bank. You establish a trust, of which you are the beneficiary, and order the bank to buy the land in the name of the trust. The bank then leases the property back to you for a period of up to fifty years, renewable in perpetuity. This is a government-approved maneuver, which, as one man put it, "is a way for the Mexican government to save face. They can sell beach property to foreigners while claiming that they aren't." Formerly the leases were for thirty years, but the thirty-year leases already in effect will be extended to fifty years.

This bank trust is known as a *fideicomiso,* and because it's renewable, the time limit doesn't really mean much except that you have to set up a new trust when it expires. In the meantime you can do anything you want with your property—live there, rent it out, whatever. The bank charges an administration fee, which varies from $250 to $1,000 a year. When you're ready to sell, the buyer pays you the money and you assign the lease to the new owner. Of course a legal immigrant with FM-2 papers can buy the property in his or her own name, without bothering with trusts.

A welcome change in the *fideicomiso* rules is the elimination of an onerous part of bank trusts. Previously a lease was valid for just thirty years and not renewable; the property had to be sold to a Mexican citizen after that thirty years. If you bought a house with a thirty-year lease and decided to sell after ten years, a new buyer would have only the remaining twenty years of the lease. This meant that the longer you owned property, the less valuable it was for a new owner. But today leases are indefinite and can be renewed without restrictions.

When considering property in the new millennium, our continuing best advice is to consult with local expatriates, real estate experts, and a recommended lawyer to make sure of what you are getting into. Under no circumstances let any money change hands before you have assurances that everything is in order; people have been hurt by real estate salespeople who say, "We'll take care of the details *mañana.*"

A major caution still is that many desirable properties, often choice oceanfront parcels, once belonged to *ejidos* (community-owned farms) that could not be sold without government permission. When those rules were in effect, many North Americans lost money by buying from someone who really didn't own the property. It wasn't always that the seller was cheating intentionally. He may have sincerely believed land that his family had farmed for generations was his to sell.

SHOPPING FOR **REAL ESTATE**

One thing we need to make clear: Real estate agencies do not operate under the same rules in Mexico as where you came from. The United

States and Canada have very strict regulations, and every broker and salesperson is held to certain ethical standards. They must undergo training and pass tests to obtain their licenses. Not so in Mexico. This is not to say that real estate people in Mexico are all crooked. Most are very ethical, but many are amateurs. It turns out that selling real estate to other gringos is the easiest way to get work that pays anything. And just about all that's required to deal in properties is the desire to sell something and make money. It's worth your while to make inquiries among residents as to whom they recommend for agents. The better ones gain their reputations just as the bums gain theirs.

The first thing you'll discover is that the term *multiple listing* doesn't necessarily mean the same as back home. Many real estate agencies will show you only the properties they have under contract and give you the impression that this is all there is available through all other companies. The result is that you're going to waste your time looking at a small range of properties, probably in the upper level of your price range.

The solution is to visit several real estate offices and ask to see a complete list of what they have. This is the only way you can be sure you have access to most available properties. In some of the larger areas, you'll find flyers with pictures of homes for sale and sometimes multiple-listing catalogues showing several brokers' housing inventories. But not all.

SHOPPING BY INTERNET Browsing the World Wide Web in search of your dream house sounds like a great idea, but unless you are looking for something in the upper price ranges, $200,000 and up, you could be disappointed. The kind of housing most expatriates would like to live in, and can afford to live in, seldom makes it to Internet real estate pages. When you research by clicking a mouse, you receive only a partial picture of the housing market in your dream location, a limited view of selected properties. The most popularly priced homes, those in the $35,000 to $100,000 range are almost always sold by private parties via word of mouth, classified ads in the local newspaper, or by listing with a local real estate agent. Therefore the vast majority of privately offered bargain properties will never appear on the Net.

Having said that, browsing the Internet can give you an excellent idea of what kind of housing you can get for your money. For example, at the end of this chapter you'll find a randomly selected list of real estate offerings found on the Web. Compare what is being offered in Mexico for the price with what similar money might buy in your hometown, and you'll get an idea of how far your money can go in Mexico.

MAKING **A DEAL**

When you've found your dream home, be sure you have a reputable attorney who is also a *notario publico,* one who comes highly recommended by your fellow expatriates. Unlike the United States, where a notary public is often a clerk you find working in a bank or real estate office, a Mexican notary has a higher ranking than an ordinary attorney who is not a notary. (In Mexico all notaries are attorneys, but not all attorneys are notaries.) A notary doesn't exclusively represent either party, even though he or she is paid by the buyer. Instead the notary is responsible to the government to ensure that property is transferred free and clear, with a good registered deed.

LOCATING YOUR **DREAM HOME**

If you are willing to locate away from the heart of the expatriate colony, you can find some great bargains in Mexico today. Home prices will inevitably be more expensive in a gringo enclave; however, contrary to popular belief, not necessarily because sellers think *norteamericanos* will pay more. It's more about the things we demand in a house. We want homes with 2,500 square feet or more, several bathrooms, kitchens with marble and granite countertops, top-quality cupboards, brass hinges and top-of-the-line appliances. The garden has to be landscaped, with masonry walls and wrought-iron gates. A price of $160,000 and much higher doesn't seem to scare away buyers.

The $35,000 home in a neighborhood that is partly Mexican will have only one bath, no garage, limited pantry and storage, and only a couple of small closets. The kitchen counters will be of brick and Mexican tile rather than polished granite. Instead of a tastefully carved front door, the house will have a simple metal door leading directly into the living room, with a passageway to the back garden. No phone, no pressure pump, no purification system, no satellite dish.

In a really Mexican home, the plumbing will be sluggish and electric wires will cling haphazardly to walls and ceilings, as though the electrician wasn't serious about his work. The home may be begging to be rebuilt. Depending on your point of view, this wonderful bargain could be either a nightmare or a delightful challenge to remodel with creative artistry. Shopping for just the right tile, looking for tropical woods for the doors and closets, and working with the contractor to rebuild a bargain property is recreation for some people.

In favorite gringo-populated locations, prices will vary for similar homes. To give just one example of local price ranges, in the Lake Chapala/Ajijic area, where most buyers and sellers are gringos, a pleasant home of new construction, suitable for a couple, can be found starting at $100,000, with the top limit depending on whether you need a swimming pool, an adjacent golf course, or a gated community (or all three). Closing costs would run about $2,500, which includes drawing up a trust deed (fideicomiso) or a direct, fee-simple title (escritura). By the way, many choose to go the fideicomiso route rather than buying outright, because it's slightly easier.

WHY NOT **RENT?**

If cost is your primary consideration, you can't beat renting. Do yourself a favor and rent for a period of time to be sure you want to live in Mexico. As we stress repeatedly, Mexico isn't for everyone, and you might be unhappy to have your life savings stuck in a house that isn't selling because of a slow market.

Fortunately for the renter, rentals are abundant in most areas. Prices for a small apartment or plain house can run as little as $350 a month, depending on the neighborhood. Many people we interviewed seem to think $650 to $850 is an ordinary rent, but of course you can pay much more, depending on the level of luxury to which you aspire. Many prefer the ambience of a genuine old adobe home in a rustic village setting rather than one of those modern reproductions of old Mexico in a gated community. These people maintain that the charm of their homes more than make up for the inconveniences of slow plumbing and weak electrical connections. Lower rents are a bonus. We once received a complaint from a reader of Choose Mexico that our book didn't adequately reflect Mexico's "high cost of living." It turned out that he rented a four-

bedroom, luxury home with a view of the ocean, complete with a swimming pool and servants' quarters.

FINDING A **PLACE TO LIVE**

Looking for rentals or homes to buy can be a pleasant adventure. Simply walking around town may give you some leads; a *se renta* or *se aquila* sign might be showing in a window here and there. Don't be put off by the outside appearance of a building. A rough adobe facade with cracked plaster could conceal a beautiful patio with delightful apartments clustered about a flower-perfumed garden. Colonial buildings tend to look inward rather than show themselves to the passerby.

You can usually find a bulletin board in the local *supermercado* (supermarket), where ads for short-term apartment and house rentals are placed, along with ads by domestic servants looking for work. If there's an English-language newspaper or newsletter, it will also contain such information. English paperback exchanges and English-language libraries usually have bulletin boards. However, most news of rentals or homes for sale is spread by word of mouth. This is particularly true of Mexican landlords; they seldom advertise in newspapers and depend on friends and neighbors to let the word out that their house is for rent. It's okay to stop fellow *norteamericanos* on the street or in a restaurant and ask them for leads. Eventually you'll find something.

We know of at least one retiree who returned from Mexico quite disgruntled because he couldn't find suitable housing the first week he was in Guadalajara. Just as in the United States or Canada, you can't expect a dream house to suddenly appear the moment you step off the airplane. You have to look, search, and bargain to find your ideal place. Temporarily rent a hotel apartment, and you won't feel pressured to take the first thing that comes along. You'll have time to explore and compare housing, and you might even have fun making decisions. Our advice is to take your time—and don't expect miracles.

Some of the best housing bargains can be in house-sitting arrangements. Many foreigners who own or lease property in Mexico like to return to the United States for three or so months every year and want other Americans to watch their homes while they're gone. They're also happy to derive a small income to help with the upkeep of the house. Keep your eyes and ears open. You might try placing your own ad in the local English-language paper or posting your availability on a bulletin board. These homes are furnished, of course, and usually come with a maid and/or gardener. (The homeowners don't want to risk losing good help while they're gone, so they pay the wages while they're away.) To be a house sitter, be prepared to furnish good references.

LEASES AND **RENTAL AGREEMENTS**

If you enter into a rental or lease agreement, you may find yourself signing an official-looking document complete with colorful government stamps. If it's a long-term lease, there will probably be an escalation clause that pegs the rent to the value of the dollar versus the peso. More than likely, if the property owner is a gringo, the rental terms will be in dollars rather than pesos. An item to insist upon is a clause on subleasing rights. Many landlords, particularly Mexicans, don't like the idea. Nevertheless, in case you decide to take a long vacation to visit friends and family in the United States, or you feel you've had enough of Mexico and need to get out from under the lease, you should protect yourself against liability. Furthermore, should you obtain a very long-term lease and you plan on putting money into the house to fix it up to your specifications, you'll need a way to recoup this money if you decide to move on. Be sure you have a complete understanding of the rental terms, and insist on a receipt each month as proof that you are living up to your end of the rental agreement or lease.

Most rentals are furnished. For long-term rentals you'll need to be careful about the lease you sign, and make sure it is in English (more likely English and Spanish) so that you clearly understand your rights and responsibilities. Some Mexican owners expect the renter to pay for all upkeep and repairs, which sounds reasonable—but what if you have to repair the roof or some other structural problem? A rental agent can usually provide a lease agreeing that repairs under $50 are the responsibility of the tenant and those over $50 the responsibility of the landlord. Make sure you have a comprehensive inventory, to be sure that the light fixtures, ceiling fans, hot water heater, and so on, are included in your lease.

An important consideration in renting or buying a house or apartment is the presence or absence of a telephone. Depending on the location, it sometimes takes an inordinate amount of time to have a telephone installed in Mexico. With a phone in place, you are assured of communications, and when you decide to sell, rent, or sublease, you'll have an easier time finding clients.

A final caution about rental agreements. Should you decide to rent your Mexican home while you are back in the United States or Canada, you need to be aware of your lease agreement. As in many other Latin American countries, the laws are definitely stacked on the side of the renter and against the landlord.

You must be very sure of the person to whom you rent, and you must have an iron-clad rental agreement. Once someone is living on your property and decides he or she doesn't want to leave, it can be difficult to get the person out as long as he or she pays rent. We've even heard horror stories about tenants refusing to pay rent and staying for long periods of time before they could be evicted.

You could have a similar problem if you sell your property and allow someone to move in before you receive your cash. One reader reported that he believed a buyer when he said he wanted to move in and make improvements on the house so that he could receive a higher mortgage.

The unfortunate seller said he had already spent $8,500 in legal fees to get the swindler out of the home, and the problem still hadn't been resolved.

REAL ESTATE **EXAMPLES FROM THE WEB**

The biggest item in your budget, wherever you live, is likely to be housing. As in the United States, no other cost varies as widely. Our advice, and we know of no informed writer on Mexico who disagrees, is to rent for some time before even starting to look for a place to buy. Where we do present figures on sales prices, it is definitely not an invitation to grab your checkbook and start negotiating. Real estate taxes are extremely low in Mexico, with many retirees reporting annual bills of $100 or less.

Below are listed a few Internet real estate advertisements from some of the communities discussed in this book. We have tried to offer a varied selection with regard to price. The prices are not necessarily typical for any given community; they've been selected to demonstrate the amenities and quality of properties that may be available in your price range. In each location mentioned, you can be sure there are dozens, if not hundreds, of homes listed for sale in classified ads and by real estate agents. If you are seriously exploring a location, we suggest that you use computer searches to look at more listings there (remembering that bargains seldom make it to the Internet). This will prepare you when you visit the place, consult with locals, see real estate agencies there, and view the properties for yourselves.

Lake Chapala Area—This beautiful home is located in La Floresta, about a 10-minute walk from the center of Ajijic. It is almost 1800 sq. ft., 2 bedroom, 2 bath, one-story home. It boasts a magnificent living area complete with a stone fireplace. Because the lifestyle here lends itself to outdoor living, both doors in the center of the house and the master bedroom open to a beautiful patio and garden. This home is listed for $154,900 and, the property taxes run $100 per year!

La Paz—Five-block walk to beach, beautiful area, parking, tropical landscaping. Turnkey. Remodeled and redecorated. 3 bedrooms and small office (or 4 bedrooms), 2 baths. Great condition: $190,000.

Pátzcuaro—Charming 2-story country house 3 bed/2 bath, outdoor terrace and grill. 28,622-square-foot lot with private access to Patzcuaro Lake; $95,000.

San Felipe—Built new in 1998, 2-bedroom, 1-bath home, 1,200 sq. ft. plus storage room. Overhead sundeck, view of ocean. $49,900.

Cuernavaca—Lovely 4-bedroom, 4-bath home with pool and 11,000 sq. ft. tropical garden; $485,000.

San Miguel de Allende—New artist-designed 3- bedroom house in el centro. Property is 1,679 sq. ft., has large patio and terrace, boveda, 3 bathrooms, many charming details; $319,000.

TOWARD **THE HIGH END**

Ajijic—Spectacular hacienda-style estate in the heart of Ajijic. Old-world feel with every modern convenience. Beautifully maintained, with mountain view. Single story, 5 bedrooms, 8 baths, set amidst lush gardens around a large heated kidney-shaped pool. Construction size 8,930 on a 24,200 sq. ft. lot. Separate fully furnished casita with kitchen, bedroom, bath & living area with its own street entrance, and private car park. Separate laundry. Commercially equipped kitchen, separate bbq. area, magnificent terraces, exterior sound system and formal dining room. 3-car garage, potting shed, pantry, wine cellar, 2 gas fireplaces, satellite TV, automatic sprinkler system, & waterfall are just some of the features of this exceptional estate. A must-see for the discriminating buyer. Unfurnished, $695,000.

APARTMENT AND **HOUSE RENTALS**

San Miguel de Allende—Cozy, one-bdrm apartment in San Miguel, all-wood paneling, secure parking, 10-minute walk to Centro, off-street but near shops, bus. Monthly only; $300/month.

Puerto Vallarta—Furnished, penthouse rent to one single adult; patio and terrace overlooking Rio Cuale, in Puerto Vallarta. Tranquil, cool, close to town and transportations; tropical vegetation and mountains all around; $250 per month.

Playa Del Carmen—2 ocean-view efficiency apartments for rent in North on 5th Ave. $350 per month each apartment.

Guadalajara—2-bedroom apartment available immediately. Close to downtown. All furniture and utilities included in price (water, electricity, and gas); $357/month.

Ajijic—2BR furnished house in the east end of the village with off-street parking and a large backyard with avocado trees, a lemon tree, and ornamental garden for $450/month.

CHAPTER FIVE

AT HOME **IN MEXICO**

Most Americans of ordinary means have had little experience with servants, other than having a cleaning woman come in once or twice a week. During the past forty years, even in homes affluent enough to afford hired help, the trend has been to substitute "labor-saving" devices for human assistance. The middle-class homemaker spends more time in the kitchen and laundry or behind a vacuum cleaner than his or her counterpart of a generation ago. Not only has help become expensive, but in the United States it is a rare employer or employee who is fully comfortable with the employer-servant relationship.

When Americans hear that domestic help is readily affordable in Mexico, they often wonder whether they would like to hire someone to cook, clean, and do laundry. They visualize someone who is a servant because he or she is unable to find other employment, although domestic service in Mexico is considered an entirely acceptable occupation. Domestic servants often prefer working for foreign residents because we usually treat them better than local employers, being more egalitarian, paying higher wages, and being generous in ways that sometimes aren't apparent. When American residents speak of the loyalty and good nature of their servants, they are being neither naive nor

condescending. Servants can truly help increase your involvement with the country, as well as make life easier and more comfortable.

When we first lived in Mexico, we initially resisted the idea of employing a maid. We value our privacy and hate the idea of a person living with us twenty-four hours a day, constantly scurrying around the house trying to look busy. However, we discovered that servants often work for more than one employer and are happy to work for us two or three hours a day. We were able to find someone who would come in mornings after breakfast and after doing the breakfast dishes, scrubbing the tile floors, and doing laundry, would sometimes prepare our noon meal. She spoke no English, but even if we had spoken no Spanish, it would not have been a problem for these chores.

The workers' energy and efficiency will amaze you. They evidently feel that because they are being paid by the hour, they must fill up each hour and thus will look for things to do. With one maid we had to be careful not to lay clean clothes on the bed so that we could wear them after showering—when we were ready to put them on, they would be hanging on the line, already washed. Anything that wasn't hanging up or in a dresser was fair game for the washtub.

If you wish your employees to do anything complicated, they must be taught procedures that will be strange to them unless they have had experience working for Americans. If you want a roast chicken for lunch, you must make clear how long you want it cooked, what kinds of seasoning you want, and what, if anything, to put inside. Even something as simple as making picnic sandwiches can be a mystery to someone for whom bread is a luxury, seldom if ever used in her house. If, on the other hand, you want to try chile con queso or chiles rellenos, the maid will need no instruction. Unless you're willing to take time teaching and explaining, you're better off doing the complicated American cooking yourself and letting the maid help you with shopping and cleaning up the kitchen afterward.

Often you can hire someone who will take care of your garden and also serve as a repairman, a bartender, and a watchman. He helps the maid, runs errands, and negotiates with local businesspeople for you. If you're going away to Acapulco for a week, often the gardener will stay in your house to watch things. Many gardeners have several clients, so it's easy to find someone who only wants to come in for an hour or two a day to water plants and make sure everything is working properly. Above all, treat your servants with respect, and don't talk down to them. Being a domestic servant in Mexico isn't a low-status job, and you want your employees to be proud of working for you.

One reason you may not wish to hire a maid and gardener is the legal obligations you have toward them as employees. They have certain rights under the law: annual vacations, severance pay, notice of dismissal, and things of that nature. People who do employ full-time servants recommend that you have your lawyer draw up a one-year contract. As one expatriate from Acapulco says, "You can't argue with the intent of the laws. These people have been taken advantage of for years, so maybe it's a good thing some laws are slanted in their favor."

OPEN-AIR MARKETS **AND THE KITCHEN**

Long before the Spanish arrived, the *tianguis* (open-air market) was a prominent feature of Mexican life. A few tables shaded by awnings, farmers with something to sell, and townspeople with money or items to trade were all that were needed. From Mexico City to the smallest villages, that tradition is still alive today and continues to be much more than just a commercial institution.

Outdoor markets are common throughout the world. Even in the United States they are staging a comeback in the form of farmers' markets (in big cities), garage sales, and flea markets (just about everywhere).

In few places, however, are open-air markets as prominent or as important to the life of the community as they are in Mexico, where on one or more days of the week, a whole neighborhood may be transformed into a sprawling marketplace with most of the residents drawn into its transactions.

For the North American resident or visitor, these markets are an opportunity not only to buy everything from produce to machine parts at substantial savings but also to observe closely the inner workings of Mexico. One thing that fascinates us is the juxtaposition of items as traditional as tethered chickens and trussed-up (live) pigs with other articles as contemporary as radios and DVD players.

In addition to these informal, weekly outdoor markets, every city and town has one or more permanent *mercados*, usually under public auspices. Usually these markets are housed in great tin-roofed sheds but spill out into the surrounding streets. They, too, are operated by a collection of entrepreneurs, each offering his or her own specialty—fruits or vegetables, meat, even clothing and hardware. At first you might feel intimidated by this seemingly disorderly hive of vendors vigorously hawking their wares, but remember they cluster according to the products being offered. Thus, for vegetables, you wander about the section where stand after stand of produce—tomatoes, onions, avocados, and potatoes—is displayed in attractive arrangements. Wander a few steps away and you might find yourself in a profusion of clothes, or birds in cages, or perhaps stands where cassettes and CDs are sold, with boom boxes blaring at top volume. If you live near the ocean, look for the area where fish is wholesaled. Fishermen bring their catch to sell to the wholesalers, who in turn sell it to the stores. By going directly to the fishermen, you not only save money but also buy the freshest possible catch.

MANY **OTHER SHOPS**

Not everything in the *mercado* will appeal to you, at least not until you are used to the system. Those stalls where sides of beef, dotted with flies, hang in the open can be passed by in favor of meat markets with sanitation and refrigeration. Modern meat markets can usually be found inside the *mercados* or at least nearby.

Melons and other displayed fruits are often cut and sliced. These are best enjoyed for their aesthetics. Be sure the melon you buy is whole; when you get home you can slice it with the assurance that it hasn't been a parade ground for flies. Any fruit that can be peeled is perfectly safe to eat on the spot. With fruits and vegetables that need washing, better wait until you can purify them in your kitchen.

Before you begin to worry that you're going to have to do all your buying from street vendors, rest assured that the *supermercado* has arrived in Mexico. Even smaller towns have miniature versions of the U.S. supermarket. Although you could do all your shopping there, you would not only miss one of the delights of Mexican living but also severely limit your choices. Like its counterpart in the United States, the *supermercado* is a convenient, usually economical place to buy packaged foods, domestic paper goods, laundry soap, beer, and liquor. For fresh fruit and vegetables, meats and poultry, and baked goods, go to the *mercado*, or community market.

SHOPPING FOR FOOD

Because most fruits and vegetables sold locally are grown in small family plots, without the aid of U.S. mass-production techniques and not force-fed with chemical fertilizers, they taste great. The variety of oranges (which have seeds) is amazing. Their juice is sweet and refreshing. Avocados are an adventure. There are

at least a hundred different kinds, each with a slightly different flavor and texture. The bland U.S. varieties pale in comparison. Carrots are often small, but they are so sweet and tasty that you could make a meal on them alone. Asparagus, broccoli, and Swiss chard are so flavorful that you wonder if they're the same varieties as we get up north. Indeed they may not be. This is not the produce that Mexican agribusiness ships to the north. Like its U.S. counterpart, it concentrates on a few varieties of produce—generally those that will survive the long journey. In the *mercado*, however, you are buying from small farmers who raise the same crops their fathers planted. The emphasis is on flavor, not convenience or uniformity.

Cattle are seldom grain-fed in Mexico, which means it takes longer—six months to a year longer—to raise them for market. This extra maturity accounts for the rich flavor of Mexican beef. Of course range-fed beef is tough and stringy, which for some folks counterbalances the tasty flavor. Beef can be aged in your refrigerator, and it can be cooked in ways to compensate for toughness. At better meat markets you can purchase grain-fed beef if you prefer an extra-tender steak. Most good restaurants serve tender beef—well, tender for Mexico.

Pork is another story. Most pork sold in the markets does not come from pig farms, where animals are penned so tightly they can't move and fed until they pack on enough weight to go to market. In Mexico, pigs wander loose around farmhouses and in small villages, almost as if they were family pets. They exercise and run free until they are ready for market. The result is a lean, red-meat pork, sometimes with the consistency of steak. The flavor can be incredible. If you cook this pork until it's well done, it's perfectly safe.

Outside the *mercado* you'll find many other food shops, bakeries, and small markets. Those that cater to foreign residents have higher prices. Yet food prices are so low in Mexico that it's difficult to be concerned that the dozen eggs that cost the equivalent of $1.00 in the *mercado* are selling for 25 cents more in the shop where the proprietor speaks English.

FOOD PRICES One difference between food shopping in the United States and in Mexico is the frequency with which one needs to shop. You can buy food so fresh in Mexico that it seems a shame to let it sit for several days in the refrigerator. In addition, going to the *mercado* is fun. People who normally shop once a week at U.S. supermarkets quickly fall into the Mexican habit of shopping daily. They discover the fun of planning a menu around what looks enticing in the market, rather than what's available in the freezer. Shopping is an engaging form of social interaction and a fine way to practice Spanish. The standkeepers quickly recognize you and often, as a token of goodwill, put something extra in your bag after you've paid. Once, when we bought a cut-up chicken at our favorite poultry stand, the owner placed an extra neck and two gizzards into our basket. When we indicated that we really had no use for the extras, he nodded his head in understanding and replaced the neck and gizzards with three large, yellow chicken feet.

You can bargain in most markets, but it's hardly worthwhile because of the low prices. You will quickly learn to identify those who take advantage of your relative wealth by jacking up their prices. In this case, rather than waste time bargaining, simply avoid those stands and deal with friendly merchants who give you the right price and who show you they appreciate your patronage.

Outside of a few convenience foods, most items that Americans are used to are available in Mexico. Food packaging of local products, however, tends to be several years behind. Maybe this is because people prefer fresh foods to prepackaged mixes or frozen TV dinners. Bacon, for instance, is usually sliced to order rather than prepackaged in transparent material. Sometimes seemingly arbitrary little shortages can be annoying if you allow them to be. Once, for several weeks we searched for oatmeal that was not presweetened, although it had been available a month earlier and was available again later. Some things are sold in different base quantities. For example, eggs can be bought by the dozen but are cheaper by the kilo. Oranges, though available by the kilo, are cheaper when bought by number. Go figure. When you shop every day, getting your purchases home is not a serious problem, even if you don't have a car. All over Mexico, Americans and Mexicans can be seen carrying groceries in locally produced straw bags. In some parts of the country, the bags have straps that go over your shoulders; in others, straps that you hold in your hand. (If you get tired of walking, taxis are affordable.)

Wherever you are, the straw bag filled with groceries proclaims that you are not a tourist but someone really living in Mexico. Lately, however, plastic shopping bags have been pushing aside the woven ones. Although they're cheaper and can be thrown away, they will never be quite the same as the straw bags.

MEXICAN COOKING Once you get those delicious meats, fruits, and vegetables home, what you make them into will be up to you. There are Americans in Mexico whose menus seldom stray from those of their former neighbors still living in Dubuque or Toronto. (We think they're missing something.) On the other hand, if you want to experiment with the varied cuisines of Mexico, your kitchen is an excellent place to do so. You are in control and can adapt seasoning to suit your taste.

Diana Kennedy's *My Mexico: A Culinary Odyssey* (Clarkson/Potter Publishers, 1998) is an excellent English-language cookbook for Americans who want to share what Mexico's many peoples have to offer. You can use this book as a source of recipes, as a guide to ordering in restaurants where menus aren't in English, or as a source of answers to your maid's questions about what you'd like for dinner. Don't expect your maid to be able to prepare all the dishes in the book; however, if you speak Spanish well enough, or are skillful at teaching by example, you may have your maid cooking Mexican food of which the neighbors have never heard.

A pleasant though not essential part of your preparation for retirement in Mexico might be studying Mexican cookbooks and trying some dishes. Even if the ingredients are not all readily available, you will find some recipes you can make with what is at hand.

As we've asserted several times in this book, Mexican cuisine is rich and varied and by no means limited to chiles, beans, and tortillas. Nevertheless, were it not for the creative use of maize (corn) tortillas, beans, chiles, and cheese, there would be many more people suffering from hunger and malnutrition in Mexico. These inexpensive ingredients formed the foundation of the pre-Cortez diet and are staples of Mexican cooking today. Meat, poultry, and fish are used sparingly, almost as one would use a seasoning. The result is comparable to much Asian cooking: delicious, inexpensive food that is actually more healthful than the standard American diet, which emphasizes red meat.

Years ago nutritionists wondered why Mexicans seem to thrive on a combination of foods that violate many of the basic nutritional values held by most Americans. They discovered that the nutrients, particularly the proteins, in the daily Mexican fare fit together in an almost perfect balance. Also the Mexican custom is to eat the principal meal, *la comida*, in the middle of the day. Traditionally this is a leisurely meal that is eaten during the long siesta hours and that might include a nap afterward. Mexicans tend to limit *la cena*, or the evening meal, to a light snack. Elaborate evening meals, if eaten at all, are eaten very late. In Mexico City, for example, many restaurants don't even open their doors until 9:00 P.M. and are still serving meals at midnight. Enjoying the main meal during the siesta is ideal for the retiree. The maid will be there to prepare it, and you can make your own supper from the leftovers or enjoy *la cena* in a restaurant with your friends. In addition it is healthier and more comfortable, particularly as you grow older, to avoid heavy meals late in the day.

MAKING FRIENDS IN MEXICO Moving to a community in Mexico where there are substantial numbers of fellow expatriates, who are likely to be there for the same reasons you are, presents an outstanding opportunity to meet kindred souls. Jennifer Rose, who lives in Morelia, says: "For North Americans it's fairly easy to make friends when joining most established gringo communities. You'll be treated by the local community much differently once you've laid down roots here than being a tourist. As a new resident, you will be treated as a novelty, a breath of fresh air, welcomed as someone new joining the community. As far as the expatriate community is concerned, most are unwilling to make an emotional investment in developing friendships with transients. However, every community is different. Some factions bring out the Welcome Wagon, while others can be as chary of newcomers as fifth-generation Mainers.

"As for Mexican friends, don't expect to make a great number of them at once. Understand that Mexico is a very stratified society No matter how democratic you may consider yourself, inviting the bricklayer and the bank president to a dinner party is going to make both feel very uncomfortable. Expect different levels of friendship. There's the 'drinks but not dinner,' the 'let's meet at a restaurant,' and the 'inner circle' where you socialize in the homes of friends."

DO YOU NEED **TO KNOW SPANISH?**

If you're going to fully enjoy Mexico, of course, you will need to learn to speak Spanish. However, you won't starve if you don't know Spanish, and you won't lack for social connections just because you are too lazy to learn more than a few phrases of the language. You'll survive. Many North Americans have lived in Mexico for years and learned just enough Spanish to ask where the restroom is or order another round of drinks. Occasionally they enter the wrong restroom, that's true, but rarely does a waiter misunderstand an order for more drinks. If you plan on hanging around with Americans for your entire stay in Mexico, or if you insist on living in expensive hotels and condos, then it really doesn't matter whether you learn Spanish or not.

Once you learn to communicate in Spanish, though, you suddenly find new doors open to you. Mexico becomes a totally different place. Instead of being limited to a small circle of English-speaking friends, you can venture out into the exciting world of Mexico. You can participate in everything that is going on around you instead of being puzzled and mystified by it. You will find yourself being invited to visit homes and join in festivities that before were inaccessible. You will have fun dealing with merchants, servants, and neighbors, entering into much closer relationships with them. You will no longer fear hassling with bureaucrats or arguing with the police and taxi drivers. When traveling like a resident in posh resort towns, you will be in a much better position to locate those inexpensive hotel rooms. In short, when you learn Spanish, you truly become a resident of Mexico who is ready to enjoy the country to the fullest.

But isn't it difficult to learn a foreign language? Yes, it is; language learning is not easy. You often hear someone say: "Oh, I won't bother studying the language now. I'll pick it up when I get there." Unless you're younger than ten years old, the chances that simply by being around Spanish speakers you will be able to "pick up" the language are less than zero.

The only way adults learn a foreign language is the old-fashioned way: through study, practice, and more practice. Studying Spanish can not only be enjoyable, it can be a rewarding activity, part of getting settled in your new home.

Even if you already speak some Spanish, we highly recommend that one of the first things you do upon arriving in Mexico is to enroll in a language class. Besides polishing your command of the language, you'll find classrooms excellent places to meet people and enlarge your circle of friends. Your fellow students will form their own social groups, which hold parties and get-togethers—any excuse they can find to practice Spanish.

CHAPTER SIX

LIVING WITH **MEXICAN LAWS**

YOUR **LEGAL STATUS**

We are often asked, "Do I have to give up my citizenship if I retire permanently in Mexico?" Of course not. Very few North Americans would consider Mexican retirement if this were the case. Fortunately there are a number of ways to become a legal resident of Mexico, and none of them affects your citizenship in any way. The options open to you range all the way from using tourist cards (readily available to anyone wishing to visit Mexico) to *inmigrado* status, which gives you all the rights of a Mexican citizen, except the right to vote.

It seems as if the rules for becoming a resident of Mexico are continually undergoing changes. Following are the latest regulations for the four basic types of resident visas, but realize that more changes are always possible. One pleasant change in the recent past is that it is no longer necessary to be older than fifty-five to become a resident. As long as you meet the financial requirements, any age will do. Another welcome change is that it is easier to meet the financial requirements (more about this later).

TOURIST VISA (FM-T) As its name suggests, the tourist visa is essentially for people vacationing in Mexico. All that is required is proof of citizenship. However, we strongly recommend a passport, because you'll find you will need one to cash travelers checks, rent an automobile, and all other cases that require identification. When you cross the border in a car, be sure to request a 180-day visa; otherwise you might end up with a 30-day visa. This allows you to stay a total of 180 days in any one-year period. If you travel by air, you might be told there's a 90-day maximum when traveling by air. However, a 180-day visa will often be granted at the airport if you give them a good reason for needing more time.

If you do not get the full 180 days, you can request an extension up to the 180-day limit. We recommended that you request this extension at least fifteen days prior to the expiration of the visa. You go to the nearest *Instituto Nacional de Migración* (National Immigration Institute) office to request the extension. You'll find an office located in most areas where expatriates live. You will need the following documents to request an extension: a valid passport (original plus one copy of every passport page, whether annotated or not), your original FM-T, and a letter in Spanish requesting the extension of time in Mexico.

When a minor travels alone, when accompanied by only one parent, or when traveling with someone other than parents, the nonaccompanying parents must provide notarized consent letters. If divorced, parents can sign a notarized Parental Custody document.

Advantages of a tourist visa (FM-T): No income requirement. No charge. No need for legal help to obtain a visa. Once your FM-T has been stamped by Mexican Immigration, you are free to travel back and forth across the border as often as you like during the time the FM-T is valid.

Disadvantages: Only good for six months. For years people would simply return to the border and apply for another six-month visa. But with today's computers, this has become a thing of the past. We have been told that immigration officials at the border will often refuse to grant a visa for more than one or two months to those who have used up their 180 days for that year. If you decide that you want to stay longer than six months at a time, or if you decide to move to Mexico permanently, you must apply for the next level of visa, FM-3 status.

VISITANTE RENTISTA (FM-3) A *visitante rentista* is a one-year visa designed for those who want to live up to a year in Mexico but may not want to make the move permanent. This document can be renewed each year for a total of five years, after which you can either upgrade to an FM-2 or simply apply for a new FM-3 visa. To ensure that applicants have enough income to live in Mexico without working, you must show bank statements for the previous three months (sometimes six months, depending on the consulate). The statements must show that at least $1,500 for a couple or $1,000 for a single person has been deposited to the bank account each month. These figures are approximate; they vary with the peso-dollar exchange rate, and the amount is tied to a multiplier of the minimum wage. If you own property, your income requirements are reduced by 50 percent. You are entitled to a one-time tax-free import of a reasonable amount of household goods within three months of securing the FM-3 status. (This is called a *Menaje de Casa* and is discussed later in this chapter.)

You can apply for your FM-3 visa before you leave your home country by applying in person at the nearest Mexican consulate. You then have ninety days to activate the visa by entering Mexico and having it stamped by Mexican immigration. Alternatively, you can apply at any Mexican office of the *Instituto Nacional de Migración* (INM). You simply enter Mexico on a regular tourist visa and apply for a change later, before your tourist visa expires.

Something Important to bear in mind: Mexican consulates in the United States and Canada do not necessarily operate under the same set of rules. Each has its own requirements and procedures. For example, some consulates require a criminal background check; others may not. Some require three months of bank statements; others want to see six months worth of deposits. Some consulates grant FM-3 status only to those who are fifty-five or older, while others have no age limit. We've been told that some consulates insist on higher income requirements. Unfortunately, "shopping" for a more relaxed consulate in the United States or Canada is not permitted. You must apply at the one nearest your home. Okay, so the consulate rules seem harsh? Simply wait to apply when you get to Mexico with a tourist visa.

Approval of your visa can take from a month to six weeks after your paperwork has been filed. You will be wise to hire a "facilitator" to help you with the procedures and guide you through the process. You should be prepared to have the following items:

- Your original FM-T tourist visa.
- A valid passport.
- Last three bank statements proving minimum income of $1,000 USD per month for the head of household and $500 USD for each dependent. (It wouldn't hurt to bring six statements, just in case.) The bank statements must be originals, not copies or printouts of your Internet online banking program.
- Your marriage license, which may be notarized at your nearest consulate before leaving or notarized and translated into Spanish by an official translator in Mexico. It wouldn't hurt to do this before you leave.
- Birth certificates for your dependents.
- Four front and four right-profile pictures measuring 4 cm by 4 cm. Pictures must be taken without jewelry or eyeglasses; hair must be off the forehead and ears.
- Proof of your an address in Mexico, such as your phone or electric bill or your house lease or deed.
- Three copies of the SAT-5 form showing that you have paid the immigration taxes at a bank in Mexico. Current taxes for an FM-3 are 1,038 pesos.
- A letter of application, written in Spanish, requesting conversion of your FM-T status to FM-3 status.

Every year you must renew your FM-3 visa, and you'll need the same type of documentation you used for the original visa, except for the photos. This must be done thirty days before the expiration date. The FM-3 visa can be renewed four times, for a total of five years, at which time you must either apply for a new FM-3 visa or upgrade to an FM-2 *immigrante rentista* status.

Advantages of a visitante rentista (FM-3): Applications processed routinely. The easiest way to reside legally in Mexico. May bring in household goods tax-free. Your automobile is legal as long as your FM-3 is valid. You can work if you can get a work permit. You can own a business, although you cannot work in the business without a work permit.

Disadvantages: Not too many; this is the route most people take when retiring in Mexico. Requires some red tape and dealing with

Mexican consulates. It's possible to do it yourself, without the assistance of a facilitator or lawyer.

INMIGRANTE RENTISTA
(FM-2) *Inmigrante rentista* status is for those who are serious about living and making their homes in Mexico. The income requirements are higher— again based on a multiple of the minimum wage, which comes to about $l,500 for the retiree and $750 each for dependents. Again, this amount is cut in half if the applicant owns a Mexican home. This status requires renewing an FM-2 visa yearly for five consecutive years, then applying for permanent immigrant status. Once you have *inmigrante* status, you can work at almost any job or endeavor you please, including a business. You will have all rights of citizenship except for voting.

Advantages of **inmigrante rentista** *(FM-2):* After renewal for five years, leads to *inmigrado* status if you so desire, but you also have the option of remaining on FM-3 status.

Disadvantages: Need to show higher monthly income. Longer, more difficult process to obtain. Restricted from leaving the country for long periods of time.

INMIGRADO Once you've been in the country for five years as an *inmigrante rentista* (FM-2), you can apply for permanent residency as an *inmigrado*. This is for those who have decided to make their homes permanently in Mexico. Those with *inmigrado* status have all the rights of a Mexican citizen except for the right to vote. They can work or operate a business without restrictions such as permits. They no longer have to prove financial capability. It isn't necessary to give up U.S. or Canadian citizenship. The only restriction is that more than thirty-six consecutive months' absence from Mexico, or accumulated absences of five years over a ten-year period, will result in cancellation of the visa.

Disadvantages: Granted only after five years as *inmigrante rentista.* Requires an attorney who is aware of the rules. Restrictions on amount of time allowed out of the country. An *Inmigrado* is not allowed to own a vehicle with foreign license plates.

MENAJE DE CASA Once you have your FM-3 status, you can begin packing the things you want to bring with you to your new home in Mexico. *Menaje* translates as "household goods." You should coordinate this with your FM-3 visa, because from the time the FM-3 is activated, either by crossing the border or when receiving the visa in Mexico, you have six months to obtain approval of your *Menaje de Casa* list of household goods you want to import. After that, you have ninety days to move everything into Mexico. Since the rules can change without notice, it's good to ask to be sure these time periods are correct.

IMPORTING YOUR AUTO An automobile is not considered part of the *Menaje de Casa.* That makes it easy to import. The car permit you receive at the border is valid for as long as your visa is good. That means 180 days for an ordinary tourist visa and up to a year with FM-3 status. Should you decide to upgrade your visa to a one-year FM-3, the good news is that the car permit will be valid for as long as your FM-3 visa is good. However, you do need to notify Mexican customs that you have a new status within ten days after you get your FM-3. This can be done at any *aduana* office in the larger towns for no fee.

WHICH STATUS **IS RIGHT FOR YOU?**

The process of obtaining the longer-term residential statuses is, like any dealings with the Mexican bureaucracy, complicated and exasperating. If you are blessed with the patience of a saint, you can probably do it all yourself. If not, it may be worth the additional expense to retain a Mexican lawyer or facilitator who has been recommended by fellow expats. If you are going to Mexico for relaxation, you may not want to spend your time in lines in government offices. Besides, in Mexico, even lawyers' fees are moderate.

Which status is right for you? You'll probably want to start with a 180-day tourist card before making any binding decisions. While in Mexico you will undoubtedly receive advice from longtime residents, and you'll hear more arguments than we could possibly make for or against each option. You can always upgrade to FM-3 status while you are in Mexico.

DIFFERENCES BETWEEN **U.S. AND MEXICAN LAWS**

Many Americans are concerned about the differences between the legal systems of Mexico and the United States. Some dread the possibility that they might, because of some misunderstanding, end up in a dreary Mexican jail. This fear evaporates in the Mexican sun, however. We have found no American resident there who expressed concern about the law. Of course if your retirement plans include dealing illegal drugs, this reassurance does not apply. On the other hand, we've encountered a few gringos who, for one reason or other, spent some time in a Mexican jail. From their experiences we can safely say that you don't want to do time there! Mexican law, like most European systems, is one of codified statutes. This is often referred to as Roman law or the Napoleonic Code. North American law, on the other hand, is based on English common law, in which each case may be considered unique and each decision may be based on prior decisions in other courts. Under Mexican law almost every possible violation or transgression is thoroughly codified or listed in law books, and extenuating circumstances play little role. Instead of long jury trials to determine punishment or damages, the magistrate simply looks up the law code that applies—and that's it. Awards in damage suits are usually limited to the actual proven losses.

Sentences for criminal acts are longer, and parole is not as easily available as in the United States. On the second conviction (even for relatively minor offenses), a person is judged to be a "habitual" criminal, and on a third conviction is sentenced to twenty years away from society. That doesn't mean nine months in the slammer and then parole. It means twenty years. Perhaps as a result, serious crime, particularly in smaller towns and cities, is much less frequent than in most places in the United States.

BRINGING YOUR **CAR INTO MEXICO**

In an effort to control illegal importing of automobiles, the government devised a system of bonding your car as you enter the country. This is done when you enter Mexico with a tourist visa. To enter with your vehicle, the customs authorities at the border will require the following:

1. Valid proof of citizenship (passport or birth certificate)
2. A valid, original vehicle registration or original certificate of title, which must be in the vehicle driver's name
3. If the car is being financed, an affidavit from the lienholder authorizing you to take the car out of the United States
4. A valid driver's license,
5. A U.S.- or Canadian-issued credit card—VISA, MasterCard, or American Express (not a bank debit card)—in the driver's name, which will be used to pay a $18 to $19 fee (depending on the peso exchange rate) for a multiple-entry permit valid for a total of 180 days in a one-year period. Your credit card also backs up your promise to remove your car at the end of the 180-day permit period. (If you don't have a credit card, you'll have to post a cash bond equal to your vehicle's value.)

An entry permit copy is given to the driver and a hologram applied to your windshield. It's important to remember that the permit and hologram must be returned at the border (look for a HACIENDA office sign) when leaving Mexico. Otherwise, the vehicle could be refused entry into Mexico on your next trip. Obtain a return receipt from the *aduana* officials.

You should either have a Mexican insurance policy in hand or be prepared to buy one immediately after crossing the border. Technically, Mexican insurance isn't required, but if you don't have it, you're taking a real chance. Your U.S. or Canadian policy won't help you, because Mexico does not recognize any insurance not issued by a Mexican company. Here's the main reason you should never drive in Mexico without Mexican insurance: The law says that the person who caused the accident must demonstrate that he or she is capable of paying damages. There's nothing unreasonable about that. An insurance policy is perfect proof of ability to pay. But if you do not have Mexican-issued insurance and you have an accident, even though you may think it was not your fault, you will have to post a cash bond until the guilt is decided by law. The police officer who investigates the accident cannot make the determination of who is at fault; only a judge can do that. So unless you can come up with the cash, your car will be impounded until a decision is made. If it is a serious accident, perhaps with injuries, the consequences can be serious. Be aware that should it be determined that the consumption of alcohol or drugs contributed to your accident, your Mexican insurance may not be valid. Bottom line: Do not drive while even slightly "under the influence."

Nowadays, with the ability to buy insurance online over the Internet, there is no excuse not to have your car insured the moment you cross the border. If you are only going to be in Mexico a couple of weeks, you can buy insurance by the day. But if you are going to be in the country for several months, you'll save big money with a six-month policy. Daily coverage can run $10 to $25 a day, depending on the value of your vehicle. If your daily rate is $15 a day, then a thirty-day policy would cost $450. By shopping Internet, you might find a six-month policy for only $300 or a one-year policy for $450.

If someone other than the owner or owners will be driving (such as your spouse if not an owner of the car), be sure to have this noted on the car permit by the Mexican official. That will make the person an authorized driver. Any licensed person can drive the car as long as the owner is in the vehicle, but unless that person is noted on the car permit, he or she is not considered an authorized driver. Do not under any circumstances permit an unauthorized person to drive the car when the registered owner is not in the vehicle! The fine can be truly substantial. If a Mexican national is driving the car, the police are more likely to impound the vehicle, possibly never to be returned. And make sure every legal driver is mentioned in the insurance policy. And save all the paperwork; you'll need it when you return. Caution: If your car is found in Mexico beyond the six-month term or without the proper documents, it can be confiscated. For more information contact your nearest Mexican consulate.

If you plan to stay in Mexico on a *visitante rentista* visa (FM-3), you will probably want to legalize the vehicle for a year at a time to match your visa. You first enter on a regular six-month car permit, and then within thirty days of receiving your FM-3 status, you apply for a one-year car permit. This permit, along with your FM-3 visa, must be renewed each sub-

sequent year. You will have to keep up your U.S. state license in the meantime. (Some people feel it's simpler to buy a Mexican car and be done with it!)

After five years you can apply for your *inmigrante rentista* (FM-2) status, and if you elect to do so, you'll have to pay taxes and nationalize the car. FM-2 residents aren't permitted to own a foreign-registered car. Of course you can simply renew your FM-3 status should you so choose.

At one time, those entering on tourist papers could obtain an automobile permit good for 180 days, return to the border for a short visit in the United States, then obtain another 180-day permit. Not so today. The Mexican government has begun enforcing the 180-day limitation rule on both tourists and automobiles. Thanks to new computer technology, they can track the number of days your car is in the country as well as the number of times the vehicle crosses the border. The computer records your car's vehicle identification number, and when you exceed the 180-day limit with that particular vehicle, you could be in trouble. The recommended procedure, if you are traveling back and forth, is to request a permit for only a few days longer than you expect to be there, and then keep close track as to how many days you've spent in Mexico during a year's period.

A car with foreign plates remains legal as long as its owner maintains the immigration status that he or she had when the car entered the country. Obviously this means 180 days for tourists. For those who apply for a one-year FM-3 visa, the automobile is legal in Mexico—as long as your visa is renewed every year, up to a period of five years.

As noted previously, Mexican police are not empowered to assign fault for an accident, so whether or not it was your fault, you'd better have the appropriate proof of insurance with you; always keep the policy with you when you drive. The good news is that Mexican insurance companies are very good about helping you and making sure your auto is fixed. We've heard of them finding hotel accommodations for clients whose autos are being repaired. So drive as carefully as you do in the United States, and stop worrying.

MEXICAN **LABOR LAWS**

In many aspects Mexican labor laws are similar to those in the United States as they apply to the maximum workday and workweek and the employment of minors. There are, however, some special rules regarding vacations, bonuses, and termination of employment that have particular relevance to those of you who plan on hiring a maid or a gardener.

Workers with more than one year's service are entitled to an annual vacation of at least six workdays. This increases at the rate of two workdays a year for the next three years (to a total of twelve days' vacation a year). In subsequent years, two workdays of vacation are added for each five years of employment. Thus, if someone worked for you for nineteen years, he or she would be entitled to a vacation of eighteen workdays, or three six-day weeks.

After one year of employment, workers are also entitled to an annual bonus equal to fifteen days of wages (paid before December 20). Those who have not been employed for a full year get a bonus prorated for the time they have worked.

There are a number of grounds for which an employee can be dismissed for cause (including more than three unauthorized absences from work within a twenty-eight-day period). The rules and their enforcement vary from one locality to another. Check with your neighbors as to the guidelines in effect for hiring help. In general the labor laws do a good job of protecting workers without unduly burdening employers. To avoid having a terminated employee bring a case to the State Labor Board, an employer should insist that the employee sign a form in front of witnesses, then file it with the authorities. Again, check with neighbors or acquaintances as to what form this document should take in your area.

EMPLOYEE BENEFITS If you have employees, you are liable for more than just their wages. The national labor code stipulates a number of benefits that you must pay by law, not just out of the goodness of your heart. In addition to holiday and vacation pay, you must provide Social Security, a Christmas or New Year's bonus (called an *aguinaldo*), and severance pay. Check with your neighbors to find out where to sign up and pay.

Some people think that by paying much more than minimum wage, their generosity negates their obligations. Not so. The benefits are due and payable no matter how much extra you pay. Some feel it's better to pay minimum wage and the benefits based on that salary, then give the employee a monthly bonus or regular gifts.

POLICE **IN MEXICO**

Police officers in the United States and Canada are generally thought of as highly trained and professional. Taking bribes is considered sleazy in the extreme; we are horrified when a cop is "on the take." Although not exactly highly paid, most U.S. police officers earn from $30,000 to $50,000 a year, more with overtime and bonuses. American taxpayers consider this a good investment; they feel they get what they pay for.

But Mexico is reluctant to pay public employees decent wages, sometimes even living wages. Therefore, many government employees, including police, feel they should be compensated by the public for any services they perform. North Americans have difficulty accepting this practice; they harshly refer to it as bribery and corruption. However, Mexicans choose a softer term, *la mordida* (the bite), and take a more tolerant attitude. They consider these payments tips, just as one might tip a waiter for his services.

In contrast with the adequately paid and professional U.S. police officer, police in Mexico come from the lower socioeconomic classes, have little or no training, and are pitifully underpaid. Many Mexican police earn the minimum wage. From this meager amount they must pay a *mordida* to their superiors for the "privilege" of holding this low-paying job.

Nobody could possibly expect a police officer to feed and clothe a family on such low wages, not even in Mexico. Therefore, he is expected to supplement his salary by "collecting fines" or taking *mordidas*. Officially, this is frowned on, but the officials who frown disapprovingly over the practice fully expect the collection of *mordidas* to continue, and they encourage it by refusing to pay a living wage. Furthermore, higher officials routinely hold their hands out for their share of the *mordidas* collected by the cops. Again, a police officer feels that he's doing nothing wrong by collecting the fine from you. He considers it a favor to you by not issuing a traffic ticket and making you go to police headquarters to stand in line to pay your fine (while, outside, another cop is removing your license plates because you've parked in a no-parking zone).

If you ask Mexican taxpayers why they don't pay police a living wage, you'll hear: "What? Spend my taxes to pay a cop to chase speeders? Let the foolish speeder pay the cop's wages, not me. If and when I get caught speeding, I'll pay. Not before!"

This is not to say that all Mexican police lack professionalism and pride or that they cannot be honest, competent, and conscientious. (Again, they don't consider taking *mordidas* to be dishonest.) They can be very tough on real criminals. As a matter of government policy, when it comes to minor indiscretions, police are far more tolerant with foreigners than with Mexican citizens. We've seen North Americans get away with offenses (such as public drunkenness) that would land an ordinary citizen in jail for three days. Treating tourists or foreign residents roughly or unfairly is a serious matter, which can cause repercussions throughout a department. Should you have an unpleasant experience, you are obligated to report it by calling the Ministry of Tourism's twenty-four-hour hot line (in Mexico City) at 5–250–0123.

In Mexico City you'll encounter "tourist police" who speak English and whose job is to see that the tourists are assisted. They have a tendency for overkill, however, and will attack you with friendliness, practically insisting that you visit the places they think you should. They'll flag down a cab, push you inside, and send you off to the tourist market before you know what's happening. (While this may seem very friendly, you must realize that the cab driver is probably the cop's brother-in-law, and they split the commission for delivering you to the tourist market.)

MEXICANS ARE **SERIOUS** **ABOUT THEIR LAWS**

Many laws in Mexico seem to be honored in their violation, which sometimes gives an American the wrong impression. For example, the largest piles of trash and garbage are invariably found stacked around signs that proclaim, DO NOT THROW GARBAGE HERE! Speed limit signs have no relation to the speed of the traffic. Stop signs seem to be invisible to most drivers, and stern prohibitions are simply a challenge. The foreigner residing in Mexico, however, would be wise to consider himself or herself a guest. Obeying laws should be no more an imposition than it would be in the United States. If you park in a no-parking zone, you might find your license plates impounded. To get them back, you must first go to a bank where you get a receipt for the fine you must pay, then to the central office where confiscated plates are held.

Some legal matters are taken more seriously in Mexico than back home, especially business relationships. If you break a lease, for example, you may discover that the landlord has impounded your belongings, and the judge agrees with him. The law might come down very heavily on you if you cheat someone out of money or refuse to pay a legitimate bill. As we've noted above, there are special rules for hiring employees, such as your maid or a gardener. Trying to get away with something on a real estate deal can be expensive, as many an American who tried to circumvent the laws against buying *ejido* property and lost all his or her investment can attest. (New laws have all but eliminated the *ejido* problem; some of these properties can now be legally sold.)

One way to ensure an extremely unpleasant stay in a Mexican jail is to be illegally in possession of firearms in Mexico. As attached as you may be to your trusty rifle, shotgun, or handgun at home, don't try to sneak it past the customs officers at the border. Even if you succeed, chances are very good that the police at your destination will find out about it and will not treat it as a minor matter. There are several North Americans in jail at this moment because they brought a gun across the border.

According to the U.S. Department of State, some of the arrested U.S. citizens were simply driving across the border on a day trip to shop or to eat in a restaurant. They inadvertently carried a firearm which was licensed in the United States, without realizing they were violating Mexican laws. If a visitor is caught bringing in a firearm, ammunition, or other weapons, Mexican authorities may confiscate the person's vehicle or other personal property and place the individual under arrest. Detainees may spend months in pretrial detention while their case is being investigated.

A North American who normally obeys the laws in his own country can expect no more trouble in Mexico than he would at home—probably less, because he usually behaves as a guest in a foreign country. But those who think that the law applies only to others, those with contempt for the customs of their host country, or those who feel that the law shouldn't apply to Americans as it does to Mexicans are likely to be quickly disabused of these attitudes.

CHAPTER SEVEN

STAYING HEALTHY
SOUTH **OF THE BORDER**

Far too much of the discussion of whether Mexico is good for your health boils down to the question "Can you drink the water?" The short answer to that question is "Yes, but not water from the tap." We'll cover that in detail a little further on, and we hope that we can persuade you that it is a relatively trivial concern. Far more important is the fact that the vigor and happiness of the typical U.S. retiree in Mexico points to the ways in which the country is indeed a very healthy place for older people.

There are both physical and emotional reasons for their well-being. The climate in most places where retirees have chosen to live is healthier in several ways than in the communities they have come from. For one thing, it is drier. For generations the attractions of a low-humidity climate have been bringing people who suffer from respiratory and rheumatic diseases to the American Southwest. With the exception of its coastal areas, Mexico is blessed with a climate that is at least as dry. In addition Mexico possesses something the southwestern states do not: It has (again, in the communities favored by retirees) temperatures that are moderate year-round.

Some people avoid Mexico because they fear for their health. They have heard that no one escapes *turista*, or "Montezuma's revenge," and imagine a stay made miserable, if not dangerous, by gastrointestinal woes. Some Mexican water supplies are indeed contaminated, but clean, safe water is available almost everywhere. Furthermore, the contaminated water can be purified easily, as can vegetables and fruits that have come into contact with that water. As we've noted, every prudent Mexican and foreigner recognizes the importance of guarding against the hazards of impure water and untreated raw fruit and vegetables. The necessary steps are incorporated into his or her life so that these precautions become as natural as washing one's hands before meals. (This practice is a very good idea in Mexico as elsewhere. Some studies report that a person's hands are likely to be a major source of the bacteria that get into his or her mouth.)

Water is safe after being boiled for a few minutes. Treating it with iodine drops or a reliable filtration device also takes care of bacteria or amoebic problems. If you have a maid, she will make sure you always have an ample supply of purified water both in the kitchen and in the bathroom so that you will not be tempted to brush your teeth or swallow a pill with tap water. Fruit and vegetables fresh from the market are stored separately from those that have been made safe by a brief soaking in purified water to which some iodine drops have been added (available inexpensively at any drugstore or market).

Ice must be made with purified water and, like fruit and vegetables, should be consumed only in places where you can be confident that the necessary precautions have been taken. The law in Mexico is that ice cubes must be made from purified water. That requirement, however, does not extend to bulk ice. Almost always restaurants and stores will use purified water for ice cubes; because it is so inexpensive, there is no reason not to. If a restaurant doesn't follow the law, cheating by using tainted water, its customers will soon know about it and will no longer patronize the place. Bad restaurants don't remain in business for long. In the beginning you'll have to rely on the knowledge of the local Americans about which restaurants to avoid. In time you'll develop your own sound instincts.

Some travelers, worried about gastrointestinal illness, dose themselves with antibiotics, which are readily available in Mexican pharmacies.

However, this is a bad practice; these medications can have dangerous side effects. Recently the fad has been to take hefty dosages of Pepto Bismol as a preventative. Carl Franz (in *The People's Guide to Mexico*) swears by the efficacy of Pepto Bismol and confirms that it works. This is fine for travelers, but if you're going to be living in Mexico, you don't want to spend the rest of your days pouring that pink stuff into your stomach. Once you've settled into your new life, you'll find this kind of self-medication unnecessary.

Good health, however, is more than avoiding unfriendly bugs. It involves your total physical and mental well-being and your whole outlook. If Mexico is the right place for you, you can be healthier there than you could be anywhere else. Almost everything that can make you happy—the climate, the good food, the constant activity—will also help keep you healthy. These elements, in addition to the commonsense principles of sanitation discussed above, are the essential prescriptions for good health. If you have a chronic illness, your doctor will have some additional rules and perhaps some medications for you, but you should find them no more onerous in Mexico than in your hometown.

HEALTH **CARE**

Americans living in most parts of Mexico report good availability of competent English-speaking doctors and dentists in most cities of any size. Quality hospitals are within easy traveling distance, and most commonly prescribed medications are stocked by Mexican pharmacies. One problem is that U.S. Medicare coverage is not valid in Mexico. Several respondents stated that they might go to the United States for an unusual or extremely serious illness, but most indicated that they thought they could find sophisticated facilities and medical staffs here in Mexico.

Mexico has both private and public health care systems. The government insurance, known as IMSS—usually referred to as "Social Security"—is the government's public health care system. The government maintains large hospitals in the principal cities and uses local public hospitals and clinics in smaller ones. For an annual fee of approximately $300, those enrolled in the Mexican health insurance program receive total coverage. Government medical facilities are described by expatriates as "no frill," but adequate. As with public systems everywhere, there are complaints of impersonality and long waits. Many expatriates purchase this inexpensive coverage as a hedge against catastrophic illnesses but also use private doctors, paying for office visits and minor surgery out of their pockets. One person pointed out that the premiums paid to a private insurance plan cost much more than the cost of any medical treatment she would be likely to need. "One plan has a $1,500 deductible. That would pay for a lot of doctor visits and medications." Should anything serious arise, she plans either to fall back on the government plan or to return home and take advantage of her Medicare coverage. Many Canadians do the same, returning home for serious medical problems.

Private health insurance is available from both U.S. and Mexican companies, with premiums reported to be from $1,500 to $2,000 and up to $6,000 per year. Some policies include the option of air evacuation to a hospital in the United States. The private system includes many excellent facilities, and their charges are surprisingly low. Since many Mexican doctors have served as interns or residents in American hospitals, finding one who speaks English is seldom difficult. Some retirees who are in good health prefer to "pay as they go" and do not enroll in IMSS or private plans, feeling that they can afford to handle routine medical bills out of pocket. Considering that a four-day stay in a private room can come to less than $300, they may have the right idea.

Nursing home care is available in some locations and, according to those who have experienced it, is of excellent quality. Certainly it is possible to employ caretakers for the elderly or disabled who can remain at home for a tiny fraction of what this kind of help would cost in the United States.

DOCTORS Many doctors in the United States are Mexican trained. As the number of qualified students seeking entrance to U.S. medical schools exceeded their capacity, many young Americans went abroad for their medical educations. Mexico was one of the countries in which they found top-quality training facilities. In short there is no more reason to be concerned about the qualification of a reputable Mexican doctor than there is to be about an American one. Two nice things about Mexican doctors: They still make house calls, and office visits are usually not much more than $20. Specialists, of course, are more expensive.

Although not every town is blessed with a first-rate hospital, few towns are far from one. Few drugs require prescriptions in Mexico, and those that do can be filled at any pharmacy. If, however, you need some special or unusual medication, it would be wise to bring a supply with you on your initial visit to Mexico and, if you find it is unavailable there, to confer with your physician when you return to the United States. Your doctor can tell you what may be substituted. If there is no substitute available in Mexico, receiving a regular supply from the United States,

though a nuisance, should pose no problem. Incidentally, in Mexico many prescription and over-the-counter drugs cost less than 40 percent of their U.S. price.

DENTISTS For years Americans living in the Southwest have been visiting border-town dental and medical clinics. Some border towns have become low-cost medical centers, attracting patients in search of affordable care. Border towns such as Las Palomas (across from Columbus, New Mexico) and Los Algodones (near Yuma, Arizona) attract thousands of patients daily, with dentistry and medical treatment the major business in the town center.

Throughout Mexico, some excellent dental facilities provide quality care at truly affordable prices. Many tourists pay for vacation expenses with money saved by having needed dental work performed in Mexico. For those who live in Mexico, the low cost of dentistry is part of the low cost of living. Prices can be as low as one-third to one-fifth what you would expect to pay in the United States. Residents report paying $20 to $25 for teeth cleaning, $85 for a porcelain bridge, and $20 for a filling.

Of course, not all Mexican dentists are equal, so recommendations from local residents are essential to make a proper choice. Dental offices and skills vary widely, depending on the type of clientele and the location. Some are low-budget, basic-care dentists taking care of working-class clientele, using minimal equipment, and charging next to nothing for treatments. Don't expect these dentists to speak fluent English. Other offices will be high-tech and modern, specializing in treating expatriates living in affluent enclaves. English will be spoken here, and prices can be almost as expensive as back home. As one reader pointed out, "Dentists who advertise in English-language publications that they speak English and are 'U.S. board certified' will double their prices!" The trick is to choose one of the numerous offices between these two extremes—with personal recommendations, of course.

PRESCRIPTION MEDICATIONS Most medications, with the exceptions of "controlled substances"—e.g., tranquilizers and pain killers—are available at Mexican pharmacies without a prescription, often at prices less than half those in the United States and also significantly lower than in Canada. The wise patient does not, however, self-prescribe. Just because a medicine is easily available "over the counter" does not mean that it is harmless. It is also advisable to seek a physician's advice on whether a Mexican generic or equivalent can be substituted for a prescribed medication.

Returning to the United States with medications purchased in Mexico is usually not a problem, providing they do not fall into the controlled category. When crossing the border, be sure to carry a prescription for the medications you are bringing with you, and do not fail to declare them if questioned.

MEDICARE

As we've said, routine and emergency medical care of high quality is available in many places in Mexico. Nevertheless, those retirees who are eligible for Medicare (which does not pay for care or treatment received in Mexico) or who have a trusted physician in the United States will wish to return there if they become seriously ill. If they're not well enough to travel by routine means, there is a commercial "air evacuation" service that provides emergency air transport to destinations north of the border.

For a monthly fee you can arrange to have this service available when needed. Air transport of casualties, which was first employed in Korea and came into its own in Vietnam, has been adopted in civilian medicine and without question has saved many lives. How appropriate this air service is (except to enjoy the financial benefits of Medicare) may be a moot point. If nothing else, it gives Americans in Mexico the emotional security of knowing that in the event of serious illness, within a few hours they can be under the care of American doctors in an American hospital.

On the other hand, we've interviewed retirees living in Mexico who are convinced that medical care there is as good as back home. One man claimed that hospitals in Mexico don't have a "factory" mentality, where doctors worry more about malpractice lawyers than they do about patients. Also physicians in Mexico are willing to prescribe medication for pain, which some doctors in the United States will only do "if you are screaming and threatening bodily harm." To this add the practice of doctors making house calls instead of requiring you to travel back to the hospital for postoperative follow-ups.

Of course you must recognize that not every town in Mexico will offer top-quality care; some clinics—especially rural ones—are quite rustic at best. You'll need to check out facilities and make your own decisions.

HEALTH **INSURANCE**

Of course many Americans retiring in Mexico are too young to qualify for Medicare and have to rely on other health insurance to pay major medical expenses. Some U.S. insurance companies cover you wherever you travel or live. Certain carriers pay a slightly smaller percentage of the total when you are out of your home area, but because health care in Mexico is so inexpensive relative to U.S. costs, that won't be a problem. Most Blue Cross plans will pay for your hospital stays while in Mexico but usually require that you pay for your hospitalization at the time of service and wait for reimbursement. We advise that you check with your insurance broker to determine the extent of your coverage while in Mexico and to discuss any adjustments necessary to maximize your protection at minimum expense. In Guadalajara the American Society offers low-cost health insurance to its members.

As noted earlier, another option available to North Americans in

Mexico is low-cost medical coverage by the national health system. Twice a year there are open enrollment periods when you can join. For the $300 annual fee, this plan covers medical, hospital, prescription drugs, even dental care and eye examinations. We believe this is something to investigate after you have been here awhile and have had the opportunity to check out the quality of the hospitals and physicians in the community in which you decide to live. Our understanding is that there is no age limit; we know of a woman who joined the plan when she turned eighty-six years old.

Several folks we interviewed stated that although they had insurance coverage back home, they rarely used it. One man said, "I have a major medical plan that covers everything over $15,000. But when I went to the local hospital here for emergency treatment, the bill came to less than $2,500! This covered several doctors for separate opinions, surgeons, an anesthesiologist, hospital stay, laboratory work, X-rays, electrocardiograms, sonograms, prescription drugs, and follow-up care for three months following surgery." He added, "A friend of mine paid more than $2,500 for just one night in a Las Vegas hospital!"

OTHER HEALTH **CONSIDERATIONS**

Many of our readers have inquired about the provisions Mexico makes for people with physical handicaps. From what we have observed and been told by people who face the problem, Mexico is still far behind the United States in dealing with accessibility. On the positive side the gentle climate does make getting around somewhat easier, and the low pay scale enables people who need help to afford it more readily. On recent visits we noted more curb cuts, particularly in the larger cities. Most airports and many bus terminals have wheelchair access. Each airline, domestic or foreign, can give you information on the arrangements it can make for wheelchairs or other assistance.

For the tourist traveling in Mexico and eating in restaurants, adhering to a special diet—perhaps one low in sodium, carbohydrates, or fats—could be difficult, though clearly not impossible. For someone who lives in Mexico and prepares his or her own food (or has it prepared by a servant), there is no real problem. One of the delights of living in Mexico is the abundance of fresh fruits, vegetables, and poultry year-round. In many places fresh fish is always available. Most diet convenience foods are now available in Mexico, and with reasonable inventiveness almost any dietary prescription can be followed.

Mexican cuisine is discussed in greater detail elsewhere in this book. But we add a brief reassurance here for those potential retirees who may feel intimidated by the food's notorious spiciness: You could live in Mexico for years without ever being forced to eat anything the least bit *picante,* even if all your dining were in restaurants. Any town is likely to have several restaurants where the food is continental rather than Mexican, and not all dishes in thoroughly Mexican restaurants are highly spiced. In the more elegant restaurants, the dishes are not spicy at all, but with an emphasis on French sauces, they are not guaranteed to be low calorie.

Volumes have been written about the role of lethargy and stress as aggravating factors in chronic conditions that are common in people past middle age. Lethargy comes from inactivity, from boredom and fatigue. Perhaps because of the stimulation of the unfamiliar or because of the vibrancy of Mexican culture—its sights, sounds, and smells—one encounters few bored and unhappy retirees there. Visitors to Mexico, almost without exception, comment on the lack of stress and the relaxed atmosphere. So maybe it is the absence of many negative and unnecessary forms of stress that makes so many expatriates consider Mexico a healthful place to live.

CHAPTER EIGHT

GETTING **AROUND MEXICO**

One big advantage to living in Mexico is the opportunity for travel. You have the entire country to choose from, with many interesting locations just a few miles from anywhere you decide to live. At your leisure you can afford to visit little-known or out-of-the-way places that ordinary tourists seldom see. You can lope on down to Acapulco for a weekend as casually as you might visit the local lake or seashore back home. All of those exotic beach towns you've read about are just a bus ride away: dream places like Mazatlán, Puerto Vallarta, Cancún, plus dozens of hidden beaches and fascinating villages no one outside Mexico has ever heard of. You'll probably discover your own personal hideaway.

Mountain gems such as Zacatecas, San Cristóbal de las Casas, and Taxco beckon to you, and for a welcome change of pace, the cosmopolitan atmosphere of Mexico City invites shopping and elegant dining. Fortunately travel in Mexico costs far less than it does in the United States. Most people find they can take regular excursions and still stay within the boundaries of their basic budget. With abundant hotel rooms for less than $50 a night, how can you miss?

Because Mexican culture—cuisine, handicrafts, music, and architecture—is, like the climate and scenery, intensely regional, travel

within the country offers the stimulation that people living in the United States and Canada often have to go abroad to find. Another advantage of traveling and living in Mexico is that when, in your travels, you come across the unusual piece of pottery or furniture you just can't resist, getting it home is easy—there are no shipping and customs problems caused by crossing an international border. Many North American retirees' homes in Mexico look like miniature museums, because their owners are so carried away by the beauty, variety, and inexpensiveness of the handicrafts they encounter on their trips around the country.

BUS **TRAVEL**

The mainstay of the Mexican travel system is the nation's vast network of buses. Bus travel in the United States, where one company has a virtual monopoly on interstate service, is neither particularly inexpensive nor enjoyable. In Mexico it's a different story. Many companies, each one eager to take you anywhere you can possibly wish to go, compete for your business. You get the feeling that your patronage is important to them. The government is building new terminals—central depots where all bus lines meet—as quickly as possible in each town. There's little waiting time because buses for most destinations depart every few minutes. Yet the cost of a ticket is a fraction of the price charged by intercity, monopoly bus lines in the United States. The latest thing in Mexican bus travel is the "executive" bus, which is equipped with an amazing bump-free suspension; a restroom; the latest-release films shown on closed-circuit TV; and a friendly attendant who serves coffee, tea, and soft drinks, hands out pillows, and generally assists the passengers on the trip. By the way, all seats are reserved on first-class service in Mexico.

The best part about the Mexican bus system is that rural areas are not devoid of bus lines as they are in the United States. We've traveled in some of the most remote areas in Mexico—to high mountain villages, through jungle country, and across desert terrain—but no matter how isolated the area might seem, before long a bus comes rumbling and bouncing along, carrying passengers from one village to another.

Mexico offers several levels of bus service, and not all buses operate with the newest equipment. Sometimes the vehicles are ancient, dented, and in need of paint, but often the equipment is the latest in air-conditioned luxury. Officially, there are three types of service—first, second, and executive class—but these terms don't necessarily describe the equipment. The main difference between first and second class is that first-class buses take reservations and can sell only as many tickets as there are seats. Executive class is just a bus company term for a step higher than first class. There could be meals or drinks available or maybe a TV movie shown. Second-class buses are permitted to crowd on as many passengers as possible, allowing people to stand in the aisle. Additionally second-class buses are slower because they make many more stops, sometimes stopping to pick up passengers whenever anyone waves a hand at the driver. Also some second-class buses traveling through truly isolated rural areas permit passengers to carry produce, chickens, and piglets to market. This adds immensely to the adventure of bus riding in Mexico. Your living adventure in Mexico isn't complete without at least one ride on a second-class bus with a squealing pig in the aisle!

Most North Americans choose first-class service. However, if you'd like to see Mexico on a different level than other tourists and you speak some Spanish, second-class travel may be an adventure you'd enjoy. Second-class buses are usually older and always slower. They turn off the pavement at every opportunity and bump their way over unpaved roads to visit any number of picturesque villages. While the bus takes on passengers and disposes of cargo, you often have fifteen or twenty minutes to wander about the square, inspect the inevitable church, or order a bowl of steaming chicken *caldo*. If you were driving, it would never occur to you to detour off the busy highway. The other passengers take pride in pointing out landmarks as you go along; they seldom have the chance to talk with a real *norteamericano*.

MEXICAN **RAILROADS**

For more than a century Mexico's government-subsidized passenger train services linked isolated communities scattered across the country's rugged terrain. The rail network provided a much-needed transport system that allowed farmers, workers, and merchants as well as adventurous tourists an exceedingly cheap way to travel. Train fares were much lower than bus fares. Passenger service provided trains connecting Nogales and Nuevo Laredo on the U.S. border with Merida in the Yucatán and Oaxaca in southern Mexico. Traveling in swaying old coaches right out of the 1920s, sometimes in ornate drawing rooms or tiny sleeping cabins, a special breed of travel buff was drawn to Mexican train travel.

Since the railroads were privatized, profit has become more important than convenience and service. Despite protests from poor families and farmers who cannot afford automobile travel or relatively expensive interstate bus service, the government is withdrawing support for all but a few lines. Eventually only passenger service to the Copper Canyon and the Tarahumara Sierra will be supported. This is because of the extremes of the terrain and the difficulty of building roads there for alternate transport. With much nostalgia we announce the end of an era.

AUTOMOBILE **TRAVEL**

Chances are wherever you live in the United States or Canada, existing without an automobile is next to impossible. Our society has forsaken public transportation to the point that it's almost nonexistent. We depend on our cars just as cowboys depended on their horses back in the Wild West days. Without an auto, even the simplest shopping errands are all but out of the question. Fortunately Mexico hasn't "modernized" itself to the point of phasing out public transportation. Taxis are cheap and plentiful, and buses are everywhere. Just stand still, and before long, one will come along to take you where you want to go. Because public transportation is so convenient, many retirees elect not to have a car in Mexico, particularly if they're trying to live on a budget. Nevertheless, there are times when a car comes in handy. You might want to show visitors the sights or drive to the next town to do some heavy shopping. Car rentals are readily available for these special occasions. By renting a car whenever you need to make a jaunt to Acapulco or Guadalajara, you can enjoy motoring without the expense of maintaining an automobile.

But many North Americans are so automobile dependent they can't visualize life without a car. They either bring one with them or buy one in Mexico.

DRIVING A CAR INTO MEXICO Detailed rules for entering Mexico with your automobile are found in the Bringing Your Car into Mexico section

within the Living with Mexican Laws chapter. Your vehicle's permit is good for a maximum of 180 days as a tourist. You can enter with the vehicle several times, but you need a permit every time you enter Mexico and go very far past the border.

Any current driver's license from the United States or Canada is valid in Mexico. You need no other. However, you must have Mexican automobile insurance, which can be bought at the border and renewed in most places in Mexico. This is just about the most important advice you'll find in this book. The law doesn't mandate that you have insurance, but common sense does. Also bring proof of your U.S. or Canadian insurance. (We've never been asked for it, but everybody seems to think it's necessary.)

We've heard several horror stories about Americans who drove without insurance in Mexico. Even in the case of a noninjury accident, the police must, by law, arrest anyone who doesn't have insurance—at least until they can prove financial responsibility. You can't blame them for this; a gringo would be sorely tempted to abandon his wrecked auto and return home if the damages might be more than his car is worth.

To make another point: It's important not only to have insurance, but also to carry the name and phone number of an insurance agent and lawyer with you at all times. Lately there's been a disturbing trend in the way the police handle accidents. When a traffic accident occurs, the police have the right to impound your vehicle. They don't always do this, but they can. When this happens, you need to have an insurance adjuster or an attorney come to your defense.

An injury accident, however, is considered more serious; police may hold a driver for up to three days to be sure there is no criminal fault. Usually, when it's pretty clear what happened and criminal intent doesn't enter into the picture, they won't hold you—but they can. So be sure your insurance policy provides for the services of a lawyer in the event of an accident. For example, if someone is injured and it's your fault, you could be held financially responsible not only for damages to the car of and medical expenses for the injured party, but also for supporting the victim's dependents until he or she recovers. The insurance company should be liable for these expenses, but it takes an attorney to keep you out of the fray.

We've heard many heartwarming stories of insured motorists who were given excellent treatment by their Mexican insurance companies. Typically, the insurance agent found them a place to stay and had someone watch over the vehicle to supervise repairs and make sure the work was done satisfactorily.

Another tip on insurance: Report accidents as soon as possible. If you wait until you return to the United States to make your report, there's a good chance you've lost your claim. You must report the accident where it happens. And, if you are driving a rental car, you must report an accident within six hours of its occurrence, or the insurance company won't pay. Too often the driver of a rental car simply leaves the car where it was damaged, thinking it is the rental agency's problem and that the insurance will cover it. Days later, by the time the rental agency appears on the scene, the car may have been vandalized or stripped to the frame. Again it's your liability if not reported immediately, and the insurance company could refuse to pay.

BUYING **INSURANCE**

Insurance rates for daily coverage in Mexico are set by the government, so there is very little difference between companies. However, when buying policies for six months or more, you can save a bundle by shopping. Some companies sell only by the day, so a one-year policy would be astronomical, as much as $2,500. But insuring by the year might cost $350 with another company. It used to be that the only way to save money on insurance was to go through an RV travel club or special brokers. However, at least one U.S. company, Sanborn's, also offers Mexican long-term insurance at discounts. One insurance strategy is to purchase enough daily insurance coverage to get you to the region where you want to settle, then ask local residents which insurance agents they recommend. They'll have the up-to-date information on rates and coverages.

A typical policy on a recent model car should cover collision, upset, and glass breakage, with $100 deductible; fire, "total theft," wind, hail, flood, and earthquake, with no deductible. People often decline full coverage on older cars; auto repair in Mexico is cheap, so they're willing to gamble. It would have to be a serious accident to cost more to repair an old car than the cost of an extended, full-coverage policy. While you might gamble on collision, property and bodily injury insurance are essential—no matter what you're driving. Only a fool would drive in Mexico without liability insurance. On the other hand, it's unnecessary to overinsure; because insurance awards in Mexico are usually limited to actual damages, it isn't necessary to insure more than $25,000 for property damage and $30,000 per person bodily injury.

Although these amounts are adequate under Mexican law, there's always the possibility of having an accident involving a U.S. citizen, with subsequent litigation in U.S. courts. Therefore, some people feel better with higher liability insurance.

THE END OF AN ERA, NO MORE BEETLES! At one time, we believed the most practical and economical car in Mexico was the old-style Volkswagen workhorse, the VW Beetle. It's still the most popular car in Mexico, with more than a million old-style models toodling along Mexico's highways and byways, accounting for one of every eight passenger cars in the entire country. Favored by Mexico City cab drivers and painted a distinctive vivid green, some 70,000 Beetle taxis roam the streets of the Mexican capital. In Puebla the taxis are black with yellow roofs; police cars are painted green.

One of the VW Beetle's best features used to be the price. They could be purchased new for around $7,500 at the time of the last edition of *Choose Mexico*. However, 2003 saw the end of an era for the traditional old-style VW Beetle. A new, modern model, the Volkswagen GLS, with a slicker body style and larger engine is now in production at the Puebla plant. The base price is about $17,000, not much different from the cost of the same model car in the United States.

For years, automobiles not produced in Mexico could not be marketed in Mexico, making the Beetle the only rational choice for an economy automobile. The implementation of the NAFTA treaty changed this. Today most makes and models are available, and parts are readily obtainable. This changes our opinion about VW being the best buy in Mexico. Also, since with an FM-3 visa you can drive your imported automobile in Mexico for five years, there seems to be little reason for purchasing an automobile in Mexico. Drive your car for five years, then bring in another vehicle.

GAS STATION **SMARTS**

Gasoline comes in three flavors in Mexico. *Nova* is the lowest grade of gasoline—and also the most common diet for Volkswagens. For most other vehicles, use *Nova* only if nothing else is available. If you notice your engine knocking or pinging when using this grade of gasoline, upgrade your fuel choice to avoid engine damage. *Nova* is sold from blue dispensing pumps. Contrary to popular belief, *Nova* does not contain tetraethyl lead. These additives were phased out of all Mexican gasoline in the late 1980s.

Mexican midgrade fuel, *Magna Sin,* has an octane of about 86 and can be used in most automobiles without problems. Again, listen for engine ping and have the ignition timing adjusted if necessary to avoid engine damage. *Magna Sin* has an octane rating a little less than no-lead regular in the United States. *Magna Sin* is dispensed from a bright green pump.

Mexico's newest gasoline, *Premium,* is not always found outside larger cities. It is dispensed from silver pumps. Even though it has the top Mexican octane rating, *Premium* isn't much better than ordinary U.S. regular unleaded gasoline. When you can, fill up the tank with *Premium* and give your engine a treat. Mexican diesel is dispensed from red pumps and is called *Diesel Sin*. Truckers and RV drivers consider it to be equal to or better than U.S. diesel.

Beware of kids who come running to start pumping gas into your car before you have a chance to think. Some of them have a scam where they clown around and get your eyes off the pump so that you don't know how much gasoline has been put in. They then quickly set the meter back to zero, quote you an outrageous amount, and pocket the difference. In addition, if a pump isn't brought back to zero before pumping begins, you'll pay for fuel you haven't received. Keeping your gas cap locked until you are ready to stand by and watch will ensure that no one can play games.

Here's a little more advice to prevent you from ever being scammed at a gas station. Before you pull into the station, make a close estimate of how many liters you will need. (There are 3.64 liters to a gallon.) Then multiply the number of liters by the price, which is standard at all stations. Round this figure off to the nearest even amount, and try to have the exact change ready. Next get out of your car and carefully watch the whole proceedings. Check that the pump has been reset to zero; don't let anyone distract you from this mission. Always have a calculator in your hand. This makes the person pumping gas think you know what you're doing (even if you don't). Then ask for the exact amount of pesos you want to spend, rather than the number of liters—for example, *"Cien pesos, por favor."* (Or write it on paper: "100 pesos.") This way, you only have to watch the pesos meter on the pump. If you have exact change or ask for an even amount, you cannot be shortchanged. If you hand the attendant bills larger than the amount on the pump, carefully count it out; a favorite trick is for the attendant to innocently say, "But señor, you handed me a 50 peso bill, not a 100!" (The bills look enough alike that you could feel you've made a mistake.)

When a boy wants to clean your windshield (this service is never provided by gas stations), remember that he's doing it for tips. We usually say yes, even if the windshield doesn't need cleaning, because it's probably the boy's only way to earn a peso. The spare change isn't going to make a difference to us; it will to the boy. If a herd of kids comes around, choose one youngster and wave the rest away, or you'll have a forest of hands seeking tips. Once a little entrepreneur (about five years old) pounded all four of our tires with a chunk of wood, then seriously announced that he had checked the air in the tires and that they seemed to be full. We gave him the customary coin plus an old tennis ball for his services. His look of delight told us that he will be pounding on tourists' tires for some time to come.

RULES OF **THE ROAD**

As in all countries there are special customs and rules for driving in Mexico. When you're on the road, you need to know these rules in order to understand what's going on around you. These customs vary from region to region. For example, in the northern desert, where you might expect lots of high-speed driving, you'll find that some Mexican drivers refuse to drive faster than 30 miles an hour in the belief that slow driving prolongs the life of the car. They're probably right—you'll find a plethora of 1980-vintage cars still creeping along the highways. They aren't driven fast enough to wear out.

Slow driving may be interesting, but it's also dangerous for the American who whips along at 60 miles an hour while others cruise at 30. A good rule is to drive as if there were a 25-mile-an-hour car around every curve, and be prepared to slow down. On the other hand, in Mexico City, where congestion can be appalling, drivers go as fast as they can. Sixty miles an hour seems perfectly reasonable to a cab driver in the capital; after all, he's getting paid by the mile, not by the time.

We try to avoid driving in Mexico City. If possible, we enter the city early Sunday morning, when traffic is lightest, park the car, and take buses or taxis for the rest of our stay. Driving anywhere else in Mexico is a piece of cake, but Mexico City turns many a macho driver into a trembling wimp.

TURN SIGNALS **AND RIGHT-OF-WAY**

In the United States, our system of turn signals seems self-evident. When the left signal is blinking, it means, "Be careful, I'm going to turn left!" However, in Mexico, a blinking signal could mean any number of things, depending on what the driver wishes it to mean. Often a left signal doesn't mean a left turn at all. It means, "It's okay to pass if you want; I don't see anyone coming in the opposite direction, but if I do, I'll pull over to let you get by safely." On the other hand, it could mean the driver is actually planning on turning left. If there's any possible left turn ahead, you'd better wait. A flashing right blinker usually signals a right turn—but not always. Sometimes the driver is saying, "Don't pass," or he may just be blinking for the hell of it. You never know. A flashing of both lights at once seems to say, "Look out, I'm going to do something silly, so stay clear!"

All of this makes sense of some sort when you consider that, under Mexican law, the vehicle in front has the right-of-way. If the guy in front of you decides to make a left turn, make a right turn, swerve into the next lane, or suddenly stop and ask directions, you have to be prepared to avoid him. The people in back of you give you the same courtesy. Well, usually they do.

At first this system of right-of-way can be puzzling for the tourist, especially in heavy city traffic, with cars swerving from lane to lane in front of you. What you must realize is that you have the right-of-way over all those behind you. Therefore, instead of worrying as you must in the United States about all the cars on the road, you can concentrate on trying to outguess the idiot in front of you. Whatever lane changes you make are cool, because those behind you are watching you very carefully. You'll find that when you cut in front of people, they will obligingly drop back and give you room, instead of honking their horns and waving their fists as gringo drivers might. Actually we consider it a fairly good system, and most drivers, once used to it, find it rather easy to get around in Mexico (except in Mexico City). The smaller the town, the lighter the traffic, and the slower people drive. Again, remember that the guy in front is always right. If you're in front, that guy is you. Having said all of this, we urge you not to totally give up worrying about the driver behind you, who could be a gringo who doesn't understand the system!

One exception to this rule is when someone is passing you; then you must concede the right-of-way. Always be prepared to help him get safely around you. Even if the other driver is breaking the law by passing on a hill or curve, you're equally guilty if you don't drop back and let him pass.

HIGHWAYS **AND BYWAYS**

During the oil bonanza of a few years ago, Mexico embarked on an ambitious road-building project. The emphasis was on constructing new highways to reach areas that were previously accessible only by dirt or gravel roads. So you'll find miles of fine highways that lead you to some great places, areas where you can drive all day on new roads and seldom see another vehicle. Because of a lack of funds, though, many other highways—the busy ones—haven't been maintained, and they tend to disintegrate rapidly.

North American drivers aren't used to watching out for road hazards. We take it for granted that manhole covers will be in place and that a sign will give adequate warning when a bridge is out ahead. We assume that shoulders are safe to park on in an emergency and that farmers will keep their livestock off a busy highway. But in Mexico the motto is "Driver beware!"

What does this mean for the novice driver in Mexico? Simply that you must slow down and drive cautiously, just like most of the Mexican drivers. So you take an extra twenty minutes for your trip because you drive 50 miles an hour instead of 70. You'll find that you'll see more of the country and arrive a lot more relaxed.

The most important motoring advice we can give is never attempt to drive the highways at night. There are several good reasons for this. One is that livestock roam freely throughout the country. It can be somewhat disconcerting to be driving along at 70 miles per hour on black asphalt and suddenly come across an almost invisible black bull sleeping on the road. Animals love to bed down on the pavement at night because it holds the daytime heat and makes a cozy place to sleep. A 1,000-pound animal can neatly remove the wheels from your car if you collide with it at high speed. Even worse is clipping a burro. This cute little animal also finds the warm asphalt a great place to stand and snooze. When a driver zooms around a curve and cuffs a burro with his bumper, he finds that the animal is just the right height to flip up in the air and glide across the hood at 50 miles an hour. Burros stop looking cute when 200 pounds of bone, hide, and muscle come crashing through your windshield.

Another hazard of night driving is suddenly finding the lane blocked by a line of large rocks. "What the devil are rocks doing across the road?" you may well ask. I once heard a nervous American speculate that maybe *bandidos* had placed the rocks as a roadblock. No, no. No *bandidos!* The rocks are actually placed there by truck drivers. Here's what happens: Truckers prefer traveling at night because the traffic is much lighter and they make better time. When a truck breaks down (a frequent occurrence), the driver has no choice but to stop in the right-hand lane (there's rarely a roadside shoulder). But he doesn't want to crawl under the truck to make repairs if it means taking a chance that another driver will not see him and will crash into the back of his truck. So he first goes back 50 yards and places rocks—the biggest rocks he can carry—across that lane to warn other truckers and motorists. Oncoming drivers are thus alerted that something is wrong up ahead and will have time to stop or swerve. If the oncoming driver doesn't see the rocks, his vehicle will tangle with a barrier of 20-pound boulders, and the trucker will be safe. Usually, when the repair job is finished, the trucker will roll the rocks off the road. But not always; the driver is anxious to get on his way.

A related problem occurs when a truck has to stop on a hill for any reason. Once he's ready to get started again, the driver finds it a hassle trying to work clutch, brake, and accelerator at the same time. So he puts a heavy rock behind each rear wheel to prevent the truck from rolling backward. With the truck wheels braced against the rocks, it's much easier to get going. The rocks remain on the road, waiting for you as you round a curve. You can imagine the damage they can cause. Rocks are easy to avoid in the daylight, but not at night.

Another hazard about night driving is that some Mexican drivers routinely turn their lights off, to see if anyone is coming, when passing on a curve. Guess what happens when the car coming the other way also has its lights out? Also, some older cars don't have working taillights. Occasionally a car won't even have headlights; its driver is content to drive along simply using the moonlight for illumination.

Do you now understand why you don't want to drive at night? We have to admit that we violate these warnings from time to time, when we have a schedule to maintain and driving after dark is the only way to do it. We've never had an accident, but the tension level involved tells us driving at night just isn't worth it.

The speed limit on good highways is usually 100 kilometers (60 miles) an hour; the posted limit is much lower in towns. Sometimes that limit is ridiculously low, and you'll notice that few people observe the signs unless a cop is in sight (which is rare). Without many police around to enforce the rules, your chances are excellent for getting away with driving 50 kilometers an hour in a 30-kilometer zone. Yet why take the chance? Drive slowly and safely in Mexico, and you'll seldom get into trouble.

HIGH-SPEED TOLL ROADS Built by private enterprise (with much government help), a significant portion of Mexico's high-speed, 75-miles-per-hour divided highways are in the hands of the private sector. Because the tolls are relatively expensive, most local automobiles and slow trucks prefer to use the free roads. This means little traffic other than buses, tourists, and affluent Mexican drivers. These roads are well worth the money, however, for the convenience of getting to your destination in about half the time you'd spend on the free roads. The low traffic flow and absence of cross traffic makes for high safety. These superhighways would be the only place where we break our rule of not traveling after dark. The downside to toll road travel is that all you see is countryside, cattle, and an occasional farmhouse. You miss the interesting (although crowded) towns and cities of Mexico. Below are some of the major toll roads and current charges.

Nogales to Mazatlán: Running south from the U.S. border through the states of Sonora and Sinaloa, the drive takes fourteen hours covering 1,200 kilometers. One-way toll is about 450 pesos.

Mazatlán to Los Mochis: This fast route whisks you across the state of Sinaloa in about four and a half hours, avoiding kilometer after kilometer of crowded and poorly maintained free roads. The toll is about 230 pesos.

Puerto Vallarta to Guadalajara: A scenic 360-kilometer drive over green-clad coastal mountains and past fields of maguey (for making tequila). The drive takes three and a half hours with a toll of about 225 pesos.

Guadalajara to Mexico City: This toll road also cuts the free-road driving time in half, only four hours as opposed to eight. The 500-kilometer trip costs about 440 pesos.

Mexico City to Acapulco: This high-speed, low-traffic route takes you to the beaches of Acapulco and saves at least three hours of slow driving. The 350 kilometers is covered in just three and a half hours and costs about 430 pesos.

Mexico City to Oaxaca: What used to be a tiresome ten-hour drive now takes only four hours to cover 460 kilometers. The toll is about 260 pesos.

Mérida to Cancún: The fastest way to get to Chichén Itzá now takes three hours to cover the 315 kilometers (cutting the time in half). The toll is 240 pesos.

TRAFFIC **TICKETS**

If you are stopped for a violation such as speeding or failing to observe a stop sign, the police officer will probably hint that you can save a lot of time if you pay the fine directly to him. That way he won't have to take your driver's license and license plates to ensure that you'll show up at the station tomorrow to pay the fine.

Don't get upset and accuse the officer of being a crook. In the unofficial system of Mexican traffic rules, a traffic cop can accept a cash donation in lieu of a ticket and keep the money as part of his salary. Most officers are paid minimum wage or less, so they're expected to catch speeders to earn enough money to live on. Technically they aren't supposed to do this, but in practice, almost all of them do take payoffs, or *mordidas* (little bites). For the police officer it's sort of like working on commission. Even with low prices in Mexico, a person can't feed his family very well on a cop's wages, so most Mexican drivers expect the police to take the money.

If you've actually violated the law, you have no cause to complain; just negotiate the fine and pay it. The police officer is actually doing you a favor by not taking your license plates. You either pay the cop, or you waste a day by going to the police station to pay. Haggling over the amount of the fine is usual, and the money is traditionally folded and passed surreptitiously. We keep a couple of dollars worth of pesos folded behind our drivers' licenses and simply hand it over when we're caught doing something wrong. You can expect the cop to lecture you as to how dangerous it is to be going the wrong way on a one-way street, or whatever, then apologize for stopping you, and that's that.

What's the safeguard against a cop's stopping you for something you didn't do? Simple: Insist on taking the ticket. That way he's wasted his time by stopping you, because he gets nothing if you pay at the police station. For that reason a cop seldom hassles motorists unless he can convince them they've broken a law. If you're innocent say so, and don't even discuss paying a fine. It will be an inconvenience for you, but it will make it easier on the next driver. If you're guilty, just pay up. Until Mexican taxpayers agree to pay police decent salaries, as we do in the United States, the system of *mordidas* will continue. You don't have to like the system, but don't try to change it single-handedly, or you may make an enemy of the police. We've often been criticized by people who point out that the practice is morally wrong for suggesting that drivers pay *mordidas* to cops. But we have to tell it like it is—not how we'd like it to be.

HELP ON **THE ROAD**

Don't be discouraged about driving in Mexico. If you take normal precautions and understand what's happening around you, it's perfectly safe. (John Howells has driven many thousands of miles in Mexico, with only two minor accidents. Don Merwin has never had an accident in Mexico but admits to having driven far fewer miles.) What if your car breaks down on the road? Chances are one of the first cars along will stop to help if you are stranded on the highway. You'll quickly find that mechanics are everywhere: men who've spent their lives keeping their old machines running with innovative, creative repairs.

If you sit long enough, you might see a Green Angel (*Angeles Verdes*) coming to the rescue. What's a Green Angel? To promote tourism and to help motorists in general, the Mexican government has a fleet of repair trucks that cruise the highways, looking for cars in trouble. These Green Angel trucks (painted green, of course) patrol the major routes and try to cover each highway at least once a day and occasionally twice a day or more. The trucks are loaded with gasoline, oil, spare parts of all descriptions, plus two trained mechanics. Usually one of them speaks English. If you're in trouble, it's their duty to stop and make the necessary repairs. You pay the cost of parts, gasoline, and oil, but the labor is courtesy of the government. Lately some of the Green Angels' funding has been reduced, but the workers are still trying to cover their routes once every day.

You might want to take note of this phone number—it's the twenty-four-hour hotline for the Green Angels: 01–800–903–9200. You can call from anywhere in the country (assuming you have access to a telephone), and the dispatcher will get in touch with a Green Angel by radio. If you park by the side of the road and raise the hood, someone will surely stop to help. At the next town this good Samaritan will phone the Green Angels for you or notify the police, who can call the hotline.

If you drive a lot in Mexico, you will from time to time come across random customs inspections on the highway. Officials—sometimes military, sometimes civilian—stop traffic and check for contraband. The main items they are looking for are drugs, guns, and ammunition. Please, don't carry any guns or ammo unless you have the proper permits, or you can really get into trouble—big trouble—jail!

Often a tourist misunderstands and feels threatened by these inspections. This misunderstanding, we fear, has given rise to stories of *bandidos* or shakedowns. We've heard of people nervously thrusting money into the inspectors' hands, thinking that's what they want. These stories would be funny if they weren't so damaging to tourism. The inspectors aren't interested in tourists other than to make sure they are really tourists and not loaded down with illegal contraband or .30-caliber ammunition. They want nothing other than your cooperation in letting them look in your trunk or under the hood. But if you are going to force money upon them, most will gratefully accept it.

ONE-WAY **STREETS**

Perhaps a word or two about a few other traffic customs are in order here. The system of one-way streets puzzles some American drivers. Because the streets in most older towns were designed for horse traffic, they are often quite narrow and, by necessity, one-way. The direction is indicated not (as you find back in Buffalo) by a large sign on the street corner, but by small arrows high up on the corners of the buildings. These signs also control traffic in a unique and commonsense manner. The arrows come in three colors: red, green, and black. If the arrow you can see on the building is green, that means you're on a major street and have the right-of-way over any car coming along the cross street. A red arrow means you must yield. Black means it's first come, first served. But remember that the first one there always has the right-of-way. Actually this system works rather well and keeps traffic flowing along the narrow streets with a minimum of congestion or accidents. Of course just because you have a green arrow doesn't necessarily mean you can charge ahead with confidence. Always slow down and look both ways; you might run into a tourist who doesn't know the system.

Please don't let any of these cautions frighten you. Driving is an excellent way of seeing the country. You can amble along at your own pace and stop where you like to explore villages or have a picnic on a country lane. The pace of driving is slow in Mexico, but it matches the pace of living. Above all, don't worry about getting off the road and into remote areas. Just as in the United States and Canada, the more rural the countryside, the more simple and friendly the people. Farmers and other Mexican villagers are every bit as hospitable as farmers in Tennessee or Iowa, maybe more so.

RV TRAVEL **IN MEXICO**

The first thing some people do when they retire is buy a motor home or a travel trailer. They envision themselves living the carefree life of bohemian vagabonds, following the pleasant weather and enjoying the good life. A few actually do this; they become "full-timers," as RV people call folks who live year-round in their rigs. But most end up using their RVs for temporary quarters, driving or dragging their portable homes to winter quarters in Florida or Arizona.

Given Mexico's variety of climates and interesting places to stay, it's only natural that many RV retirees are interested in Mexico as a place for full- or part-time retirement. RV travel in Mexico is quite popular, with untold thousands returning year after year. From our perspective there are severe drawbacks to using RVs for retirement in Mexico, although we admit there are some positive aspects of *seasonal* RV living there.

First let's dispense with the idea of mobile homes in Mexico. With few exceptions dragging one of those monsters into Mexico for retirement living is highly impractical. By the time you purchase a mobile home, struggle to move it to your location, set it up, and make the connections, you could have built a quality home and saved money in the bargain. The exceptions we've found are in Baja California, just a short distance from the U.S. border. Because mobile homes contain wiring and plumbing, all set up and ready to use, they have the advantage of being able to be installed on a lot—ready for immediate occupancy. Getting them to some sites in northern Baja is relatively easy because of an excellent four-lane highway that extends as far south as Ensenada. However, according to Mexican law, anything longer than 40 feet long or more than 8 feet wide requires special permits, which could mean yards of red tape. There's good reason for this law: Mexican highways are simply not designed for 12-foot-wide packages. When you try to haul that clumsy box through towns where the narrow 400-year-old streets were laid out for horses and carriages, you could learn the full meaning of the word *impossible*.

Recreation vehicles—whether motor homes, travel trailers, or pickups with campers—are fine for vacationing and part-time travel in Mexico. However, living full-time in a tin box in Mexico leaves a lot to be desired. First of all, in most charming Mexican towns and villages, RV facilities aren't all that great. In most places RV parks are nonexistent. As a rule trailer parks are located on the outskirts of town, so you end up living where the trailer park is located rather than where you'd like to stay.

This leads to our second objection to long-term RV living in Mexico: It separates you from the everyday life of the community. You'll be staying in an enclave of North American RV travelers and will have few, if any, Mexican neighbors with whom to interact. You'll be insulated from the traditional neighborhoods and the everyday events that make life in Mexico so fascinating. Instead of living near the *zócalo*—where you can stroll around in the evening, socialize with friends, or lounge on a bench while reading the morning papers—you'll be parked out in the boon-docks. You'll have to make a special effort to get into town. You might as well be camped in an RV park in Kansas for all the indigenous Mexican culture you'll be experiencing.

Having said these negative things about RV living in Mexico, let's examine the positive side for a minute. Many RV people regularly travel to Mexico for winter retirement and wouldn't consider any other style of living here. They counter our objections by pointing out that they enjoy living in a closed, gringo-style community. "We don't want to learn a foreign language," one woman emphasized, "and we didn't come here to absorb another culture. We simply want to spend a pleasant winter with our friends and return home when the weather thaws out back home." One couple we know drives to Ensenada every winter, parks their rig in the enclave, and for the entire season rarely set foot outside the protected walls of the trailer park. That behavior is a little extreme, but it makes them happy. For those who are somewhat paranoid about Mexican food, having their own kitchen is very comforting. They can prepare their own meals and feel safe. "Yes, RV people do eat out occasionally," said one woman, "but most of the time we prefer to eat the same kinds of meals as we do back home."

Others disagree that you necessarily have to be isolated from the Mexican community. One woman told of a Halloween party held in San Carlos Bay: "We informed a few taxi drivers that we were having a 'trick or treat' party for kids, and could they find some kids to attend. Come Halloween night, the taxi drivers brought over 250 children to the party! Most were dressed in costumes, and we gave out 150 pounds of candies and treats. What a wonderful night!" Halloween has become an annual event, looked forward to eagerly by the gringo and Mexican adults as well as by the kids of San Carlos Bay.

WHERE DO RVERS GO IN MEXICO? RV people tend to return to the same Mexican RV parks every year for their "winter retirement," just as they do in the United States. They eagerly look forward to meeting their friends of last season. Many long-term friendships have been forged in Mexican RV parks. The seasonal residents organize and plan activities, from potlucks to dances. RV owners probably aren't any more friendly than other travelers in Mexico, but because they are quartered so close together, they have more opportunities to be friendly. Before long, everyone knows everybody else.

The most popular places for winter retirement are in Baja California and along the mainland side of the Sea of Cortez. At last count more than a hundred RV parks in Baja catered exclusively to North American snowbirds. From the border down to Ensenada, throughout the zona libre (free zone), where some entry laws are less restrictive than elsewhere in Mexico, many thousands of "winter Mexicans" (temporary retirees) settle in each year. Unlike most other parts of Baja, year-round RV retirement is feasible here because the climate is pleasant: High temperatures range from sixty-six degrees in January to seventy-seven degrees in August.

The accepted way of life in the *zona libre* is to reside in commercial trailer parks, although some retirees purchase lots and set up their trailers on a permanent basis. But farther south, on the shores of the Sea of Cortez—where the population is almost nil—there's a different way of RVing. It's called "boondocking"—parking for free or almost free for months on end. In fact, boondocking is the only way to enjoy some of these beaches. Because of the absence of fresh water, there are no hotels or tourist accommodations of any sort. Unless you camp, no matter how rich you are, you can only glimpse these beautiful sights as you drive past beaches and scenery that money can't buy. For RV residents a weekly trip to the nearest town to replenish drinking water and stock up on groceries is all that's needed for a winter's stay. (Almost nobody stays for summers; it becomes a furnace here!)

The mainland side of the Sea of Cortez—particularly places such Puerto Peñasco, Bahía Kino, and San Carlos Bay also draws large number of winter visitors. The climate is about the same as in most of Baja: pleasant winters and horribly hot summers. Some intrepid travelers go farther down Mexico's west coast, as far as Mazatlán, San Blas, and Puerto Vallarta. When you get this far south, RV facilities aren't as plentiful. Summers are tolerable, but fewer RVs are on the road then, and parks are practically empty.

CHAPTER NINE

WHERE NORTH
AMERICANS LIVE

Our discussion of specific Mexican communities that you might want to make your retirement home is divided into two groupings. The first deals with the most popular locations, those with a substantial North American presence and a long history of welcoming retirees. Without doubt, these places will be the choices of most of our readers. However, because the most popular places are not the most economical, and because we know that some of you crave adventure, we discuss a number of other locations in a second grouping. These places have few year-round foreign residents and are, occasionally, harder to get to than the communities in the first group. When there are few North American residents, some communities are likely to offer a lonely life for those who do not speak enough Spanish for meaningful communication with their Mexican neighbors. At the same time, any town that has electricity is within range of satellite television, and any house with a telephone can be hooked into the Internet (although in some areas is can be expensive due to high phone rates). So maybe isolation is a thing of the past.

Rather than weigh down our discussion of Mexico's off-the-beaten-track retirement possibilities, we will repeat what we feel is the most

important caveat for anyone considering retiring abroad: If you feel a place might be right for you, before you make any important decisions, spend some time there seeing what living there would be like.

THE GUADALAJARA/**LAKE CHAPALA AREA**

No part of Mexico attracts more North American retirees than Guadalajara and neighboring towns around Lake Chapala. Estimates of the U.S. and Canadian expatriate population hereabouts range between 15,000 and 20,000, with about 8,000 living by the lake. An unusually large percentage of the expatriates here in the winter are Canadians, almost equal to the number of U.S. citizens. However, longtime residents say that during summer months, U.S. residents outnumber Canadians by four to one. Part of the explanation for this is that more Canadians began coming here as Florida became more crowded and expensive. Furthermore, Canadians have to be back in Canada for six full months to maintain their national health care benefits. It's understandable that they avoid the cold winter by escaping to Mexico and then return to enjoy the delightful Canadian spring and summer.

When you ask why so many choose to live in the Guadalajara area, the list of reasons typically starts off with "climate." The weather here, North American residents brag, is the finest in the world, and statistics consistently confirm this opinion. The Guadalajara area experiences an average of only one day completely without sunshine per month. The average daily temperatures are in the high sixties in winter and in the high seventies to mid-eighties in summer. Most rain falls on summer evenings (actually, May through September) after a day of basking sunshine. Guadalajara's claim to being the site of "perpetual spring" obviously has some basis in fact. Should you crave the heat of a tropical sun and the crashing of waves on a sandy beach, a three-hour drive takes you to Pacific beach resorts where you can escape those "frigid" spells of sixty-degree weather that occur during January.

One reason we would recommend Guadalajara or Lake Chapala as excellent places to start your quest for a retirement home is the large number of expatriates already there. By acting as a support group, they can ease the tension of your transition into a new lifestyle. Helping one another is an unwritten expatriate rule. This can make for an easy intro-

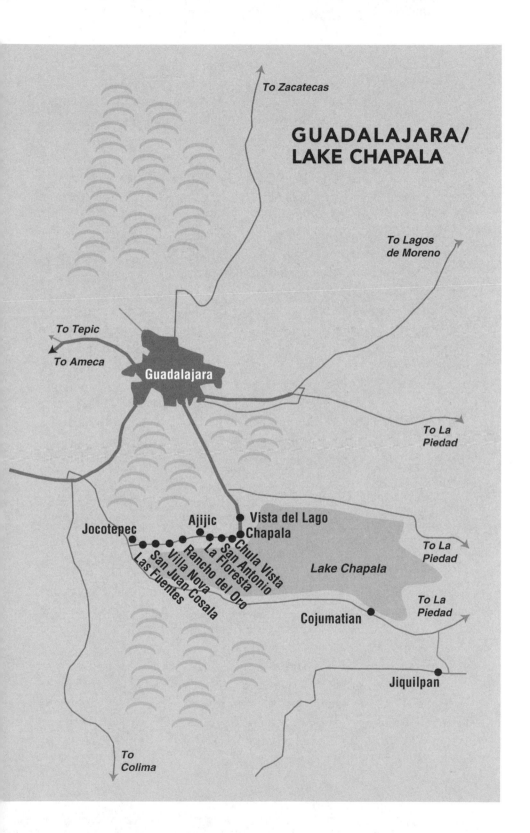

GUADALAJARA/
LAKE CHAPALA

To Zacatecas

To Lagos
de Moreno

To Tepic

To Ameca

Guadalajara

To La
Piedad

Jocotepec

Ajijic

Vista del Lago

Chapala

Chula Vista

San Antonio

La Floresta

Rancho del Oro

Villa Nova

San Juan Cosala

Las Fuentes

Lake Chapala

To La
Piedad

To La
Piedad

Cojumatian

Jiquilpan

To
Colima

duction to living in a foreign country. That's not to say that you will be living in an exclusively gringo compound, isolated from your Mexican neighbors. On the contrary: the vast majority of U.S. and Canadian citizens here live in homes and apartments interspersed throughout several attractive Guadalajara neighborhoods or in villages along the shores of Lake Chapala. If your next-door neighbors turn out to be fellow *norteamericanos,* it's usually a coincidence. Almost all the retired residents with whom we talked reported wonderful relations with their Mexican neighbors.

In Guadalajara a variety of neighborhoods in and around the city are popular with expatriates. These neighborhoods come in all degrees of prices and elegance. According to residents some of the nicer locations are Lomas del Valle, Colonias de San Javier, Rancho Contento, Club de Golf Santa Anita, Providencia, Ciudád Buganbilias, and Barrancas de Oblatos. Housing prices in general, although fairly typical for Mexico as a whole, are somewhat lower here than in Mexico City and in some popular resort areas.

Understand that these are not gringo enclaves; these are the neighborhoods where most middle-class and wealthy Mexicans live. In fact, the general affluence of Guadalajara is one of its hallmarks: The city is one that has truly benefited from NAFTA. With large companies like IBM and Motorola operating factories here, large payrolls stimulate the economy.

Medical care in Guadalajara is tops, with two medical schools, excellent hospitals, twenty-four-hour emergency pharmacies, and other medical care services. A hospital affiliated with a high-tech facility in California brings the latest in medical treatment to the area. Through efforts of the American and Canadian expatriate associations, many U.S. health insurance companies, such as Blue Cross and Blue Shield, are accepted here. A Guadalajara clinic, Sanatorio Americas, advertises that it not only accepts Blue Cross and Blue Shield but also charges no deductible.

Guadalajara is one of Mexico's major transportation hubs, with an international airport and high-speed tollways connecting the city to both the U.S. and Guatemalan borders as well as to other parts of the country. These facilities make it easy for your friends and family to visit you and for you to return home occasionally, whenever you need a cultural "fix."

THERE'S ALWAYS **SOMETHING DOING**

One of the reasons for Guadalajara's appeal is the plethora of recreational and cultural activities available there. Only Mexico City and Cabo San Lucas offer more golf courses than Guadalajara's five. Tennis courts, swimming pools, and health clubs are plentiful. Guadalajara offers a number of movie theaters showing films in English, frequent concerts, operas, and, with the great number of social organizations serving the retiree population, no end to parties, trips, and other organized activities. There are at least two libraries with books in English and many bookstores and newsstands that sell U.S. publications. Cable and satellite television have revolutionized home entertainment, and videotapes and DVDs of American films circulate freely in the retiree community. More than thirty religious, civic, philanthropic, social, and special-interest organizations serve this huge and diverse collection of individuals.

Most American cities the same size or even larger might envy Guadalajara for its cultural richness and diversity. There is hardly a day in the week when there isn't a concert, a new art exhibition, or some other event at the Institute Cultural Cabanas, the Degollado Theater, or one of the city's many other museums and concert halls. A typical weekly issue of the *Guadalajara Reporter* lists twenty or more such activities. The fare is thoroughly international, and, like everything else in Guadalajara, the price is right.

A striking part of Guadalajara's cultural life is the city's numerous museums. Perhaps the best known of these was made from the studio of Clemente Orozco after the artist's death. Guadalajara residents are proud of this famous native son, whose murals embellish many public places. Many other museums display the work of great artists of Mexico and the world. It is not without reason that Guadalajara has been described as "Mexico's Florence."

Shopping isn't the authors' favorite leisure activity, but we can't deny that it seems to be a popular one in Guadalajara. Every time we turn around, there seems to be a new and fancier shopping mall somewhere in the city or its environs. NAFTA opened the flood gates for North American merchandise, and Guadalajara has taken full advantage. The huge WalMart stores here, for example, are open twenty-four hours a day. You'll also find such familiar stores as Costco, Sam's Club, Sears, Radio

Shack, Baskin Robbins, Ace Hardware, and Office Depot. These stores are joined by Mexican shopping jumbos such as Gigante, Sanborn's, and others equally modern but with less recognizable names. All of this commercialization is a far cry from the way it was when we published the first edition of *Choose Mexico*; in those days you had difficulty finding toothpaste and diet soda. Many retirees bemoan this modernization, but they shop anyway.

We doubt that anyone has ever counted the restaurants in Guadalajara, but we have no doubt that you could go to a different one every night for several years. Before you reached the last restaurant on your list, you'd have to start over so that you could try all the new ones that had opened while you were sampling the others.

If all that shopping and restaurant-hopping sounds exhausting, there's no reason you can't do as we do and spend a lot of time sitting in one of the many beautiful parks and plazas scattered around the city, enjoying the sunshine, the sights, the sounds, and, yes, the smells of Mexico. One of our favorite little parks is decorated with the busts of Mexicans whose heroic stature was earned in such unmilitary pursuits as poetry, philanthropy, education, and music.

The center of much retiree life in Guadalajara is the American Society of Jalisco. The American Society, known to its members as AmSoc, is headquartered in the pleasant Chapalita section of Guadalajara. The society's facility is a hive of activity, with bridge games, meetings (to plan the members' frequent and very economical outings), community service projects, and just plain companionship that spills out of the meeting rooms and library into the lobby and dining area. The society offers low-cost medical insurance to its members and in other ways too numerous to count helps them to feel secure and at home in their adopted community.

LAKE CHAPALA **AND AJIJIC**

A fifty-minute drive from Guadalajara brings you to the shores of Lake Chapala, where thousands of *norteamericanos* make their homes. These are folks who prefer smaller towns or village living to big-city Guadalajara, with its eight million inhabitants. When we speak of Lake Chapala as a place to live, we actually refer to twenty or so communities lining the northern shore of the lake, with the charming town of Ajijic as the focal point. Driving along the lakeshore you'll encounter the villages in the following order: Vista del Lago, Chapala, Chula Vista, San Antonio, La Floresta, Ajijic, Rancho del Oro, Villa Nova, San Juan Cosala, Las Fuentes, and Jocotepec. We might also mention La Cristina, Las Palmas, Los Arroyos, and the San Juan Racquet Club. American residents are dispersed throughout these towns and villages. They live in all manner of homes, condos, and apartments, as well as in several exclusive, gated communities and on small farms in outlying areas.

You'll find an interesting dichotomy between those who adore the intimacy of village life and those who prefer the luxurious gated villas on the hillsides. Each group can't quite understand why the other chooses the opposite lifestyle. To be perfectly honest, we can't quite figure out which side we're on. On the one hand, during a gorgeous sunset we love having cocktails while sitting on the elegant terrace of a tasteful hillside estate (our friends', not ours). Yet there's something to be said for the quiet exhilaration of village life: the sound of church bells in the morning, the sight of burros bearing firewood, the interaction with your Mexican neighbors, and the quaint restaurant around the corner. Each lifestyle has compensating pleasures.

The mountains that loom high above the lakeside villages not only create a panoramic backdrop but also protect the lakeshore and the villages from prevailing northerly winds. This effect contributes to the delightful climate here and explains why the southern shore is comparatively undeveloped; the mountain ridge deflects blustery winds in that direction.

The lake does something else for the climate; the large body of water acts as a climate control. Winter days in Ajijic, for example, tend to be five degrees warmer than in nearby Guadalajara, and summer days can be five to ten degrees cooler in Ajijic. People who live around the lake are quick to point this out. This fact is ammunition in the ongoing feud over which place, Guadalajara or Lake Chapala, is the best place to live. It's entertaining to listen to each camp ridicule the other's choice of living arrangements. The feud extends to the individual lakeside villages, with residents of each community maintaining they live in the best place of all. Personally we think they're all correct.

The lake itself serves as more of a scenic treasure than as a source of recreation. Few people swim there, and fishing isn't great—it never has been. From time to time the water level drops drastically; currently the lake is almost full. In *Village in the Sun,* the charming 1945 book that popularized Lake Chapala and started the immigration of North Americans to the area, Dan Chandos described the lake:

> *It is an unusual lake. Its waters, heavy with silt, are never transparent, and reflect colors in curious half-tones that can turn a vulgar Wagnerian sunset into the blue-and-red fuchsia shot silk that Victorian parasols were made of.*

Our observation is that sunrises are just as spectacular as Lake Chapala sunsets. The lake does contain fish—several kinds of small whitefish, carp, and similar species—but not the kind sportsmen go after. Local fishermen harvest them with nets.

The center of the town of Chapala looks more like a small city than a village. A wide boulevard is Chapala's main street, a kind of open mall with a tasteful center island of flowers, shrubs, and tropical trees. The town's centerpiece is a charming plaza, complete with a graceful bandstand where townspeople like to congregate in the evenings. At the other end of the spectrum is the fascinating village of San Antonio Tlayacapan. With cobblestoned streets and weathered adobe buildings centered on an ancient church, San Antonio is the epitome of a Mexican village. This is the place Dan Chandos described in *Village in the Sun.* Curiously, though, the gringo population isn't very dense. This makes San Antonio Tlayacapan a place for total immersion in Mexican village living. Prices are affordable here as well, with some homes being offered, when we were last here, at what seemed like bargain prices to us.

A popular lifestyle on Lake Chapala (for those who can afford it) is the country-club atmosphere of Chula Vista Country Club and the Vista del Lago. Beautifully landscaped homes—many with lake views—overlook the golf courses, with access to lighted tennis courts and swimming pools. Home prices vary from moderately to really expensive. Chula Vista maintains an active neighborhood association, which continually strives to maintain the quality of services in this area. As a result, Chula Vista is one of the few communities on the lake that enjoys pure drinking water (Villa Nova is another). Everywhere else you must use either bottled or boiled water.

The town of Ajijic boasts the largest number of North Americans in residence. Most lakeside expatriates live either in Ajijic or scattered among towns or villages along the lakeshore. Estimates of the expatriate population range between 25,000 and 35,000. Numerous residential developments along the lake cater to North Americans and wealthy Mexicans. Home styles vary from relatively inexpensive homes to luxurious colonial-style mansions in gated communities. Even the newest developments try to present a Mexican village ambience, complete with cobblestone streets and houses designed to look like Old Mexico. Distant Jocotepec attracts a growing number of new residents, partly because homes and land are less expensive.

For many residents the *only* place to live is in the village proper, where housing is typically Old Mexico. They live in houses hidden behind high walls or in buildings with plain exteriors yielding no hint of what lies inside. Streets are typically cobblestoned, and many buildings are of adobe construction, occasionally of stone or antique brick. Real estate in the villages varies from cheap to expensive, and the interiors vary from rustic to fantastic. Again, the exteriors give few clues as to what lies inside.

Ajijic serves as Lake Chapala's cultural and social center. It's where the Lake Chapala Society (an expatriate association with almost 4,000 members) is headquartered. Even if you have no intention of choosing Lake Chapala as your retirement paradise, you owe it to yourself to take a look at the society's library complex. Located in the center of the village, on a large estate with landscaped gardens and surrounded by a wall, the facility is the heartbeat of the expatriate society. This was the estate of Neill James. A fascinating woman who lived in Ajijic for several decades, she was well liked by expatriates and adored by natives of the area. She donated everything except her living quarters to the society and on her death, at the age of ninety-nine, bequeathed these to the people of Ajijic. (By the way, it's pronounced *Aah-hee-HEEK*, with the accent on the last syllable.)

The Lake Chapala Society's centerpiece is an extensive lending library, which includes 30,000 volumes as well as 5,000 videotapes, but that's only a part of it. The association sponsors numerous social events, fund-raising activities, and special cultural offerings such as lectures, concerts, and other top-notch entertainment. The library hosts a computer club and a ham radio club with regular broadcasts and far too many activities to be listed here. The grounds have separate rooms for lectures, classes, and meetings; a snack area with tables; and quiet garden areas for reading and relaxing. Even though North Americans thoroughly enjoy the library complex as a meeting place and learning facility, one of its most important functions is public relations for the expatriate community. While local people take English lessons, their children take art classes. Over the years many successful artists have received their start here, and today they donate their time to teach a new generation of artists. When we last visited during the holiday season, local residents were feverishly working on a Toys for Tots program, raising money to bring Christmas joy to more than 6,000 local children. These activities go a long way toward creating a favorable image of local gringos. You sense a genuine feeling that North Americans are accepted as valued members of the community.

Another tradition here is the American Legion post. Its large membership reflects the presence of retired military personnel near Lake Chapala. Its tree-shaded clubhouse is set behind brick walls on a quiet side street. Its members take an active part in community affairs.

The large number of active civic and social groups in Ajijic makes it easy to meet people and become a part of the community. Take a look at the following list of activities and social groups in the area: Humane Society, Computer Club, Chess Club, several garden clubs, Culinary Arts Society, the Writers' Group, Genealogy Club, Duplicate and Progressive Bridge Clubs, Needle Pushers, Texas Line Dancing, Daughters of the American Revolution, Lakeside Little Theater, and two yacht clubs. This is only a partial list. All in all, more than ninety English-language clubs and charitable organizations keep people busy by the lakeside.

If the foregoing activities aren't enough, you can also take classes in art, handicrafts, music, computers, and Spanish (both conversational and structured). Or you can participate in tennis, golf, walking, jogging, horseback riding, boating, fishing, mountain biking, tai chi, and various exercise groups. A variety of passive pleasures are available, too, such as taking in concerts, art galleries, and museums.

In summary, we feel that unless you are familiar with Mexico or have already picked out another community in which to live, the Guadalajara–Lake Chapala area is probably the place to start your search for the ideal retirement site. It may or may not end up as the place you decide to live. Nevertheless, given its convenient location and good transportation to most parts of Mexico, and given the unequaled support expatriates offer newcomers, going there first can make the choice easier and less intimidating.

SAN MIGUEL **DE ALLENDE**

Every time we return to San Miguel de Allende, we are afraid we will find it so crowded, so Americanized, and so filled with traffic as to destroy its legendary charm. The bad news is that it is more crowded, some parts of it are Americanized, and a few of its major streets—at least at certain times of the day and week—have more traffic than we would like. The good news is that it is still a charming and delightful place for vacationers and retirees. A few blocks from the town's center, in a prosperous commercial and residential area, we could easily believe that we were the only gringos around. True, San Miguel has a high proportion of foreign residents. San Miguel's mayor estimates that it is as high as 7,000 out of a population of 70,000 in the urban area, but that seems to have little impact except in the center of town.

We were also worried that the relentless march of "modernization" might have destroyed San Miguel's colonial flavor. That fear, too, proved to be unfounded. The laws that require all new building to conform to the town's architectural character continue to be enforced.

The existence of a huge, modern shopping mall (including a well-stocked American-style supermarket, Gigante) on the outskirts of San Miguel de Allende may be an affront to those who would like time to stand still, but it is a huge convenience for anyone who would like to purchase such essentials as laundry detergent, vodka, and lawn chairs quickly and painlessly.

San Miguel is served by a well-equipped, modern hospital operated by a private nonprofit association. Its staff includes six specialists and one general practitioner.

There are few places in Mexico where North Americans have been as happy as in San Miguel de Allende. A colonial city just less than four hours' drive or bus ride from Mexico City, it draws both visitors and residents from all over the world. What many of them share is an interest in the arts. These people are attracted both by the handsomeness of the town and its natural setting and by its several excellent art schools.

The 6,300-foot altitude produces a climate that is comfortable year-round, if you don't mind winter evenings that are chilly enough for a wood fire and summer afternoons that are warm enough to make swimming pool owners especially popular. San Miguel owes much of its attractiveness to three events in its history. The first, the depletion of the silver mines in Guanajuato, rendered San Miguel obsolete as a way station en route to Mexico City and left it a backwater. Consequently its fine colonial architecture was not demolished to make way for the progress that afflicted many other Mexican towns.

The second event was the arrival in 1938 of an American, Sterling Dickinson, who founded the art school that became the world-renowned Instituto Allende, which continues to draw outstanding artists and craftspeople from all over Mexico, the United States, Europe, and Asia. A second school, Mexico City's Palace of Fine Arts, affiliated with Bellas Artes, also welcomes foreign students, but it places more emphasis on the education of younger local artists. In addition to these larger institutions, several smaller schools and artist's studios offer training in everything from painting and photography to weaving, stained glass, music, and dance.

The third event contributing to San Miguel's unique flavor was the Mexican government's promulgation of a law designating the entire town as a national monument. Hence, any development or construction that would change San Miguel's character or appearance must now have express permission.

Some grumble about San Miguel's narrow streets, paved with what must be the world's sharpest and most irregular cobblestones. These same people lament the government's stubborn refusal to allow the erection of gleaming aluminum and glass facades on the homes and shops facing onto the streets. But Los Angeles, Houston, and parts of Mexico City are always there to welcome anyone who cannot do without these symbols of progress.

Since one out of every ten residents of San Miguel is a foreigner, that ratio is sufficient to support an active English-speaking social and cultural life, but it's not large enough to make San Miguel a little bit of the United States in Mexico. There is no American enclave where foreigners are concentrated, and when North Americans there say that what they like best about Mexico is the people, they mean their Mexican neighbors (not just servants and shopkeepers) as well as their compatriots.

RECREATION Particularly for a town of its size, San Miguel has remarkably diverse opportunities for recreation, which ranges from golf, tennis, and riding to classes in yoga and dance. You can attend lectures, play in an amateur string quartet, and go bird-watching with the Audubon Society. Organizations you can join include a duplicate bridge club, an amateur theater group, an American Legion post, and a garden club. There is also an annual chamber music festival.

Spanish is taught at the Instituto Allende, the Academia Hispano Americana, and several smaller and more informal schools. Depending on the school, these programs range from a couple of hours a day to more than forty hours a week. There are students of all ages, and, among other benefits, classes, whether in language or the arts, provide excellent opportunities for meeting people.

If the concerts, dance, and theater in San Miguel and nearby Guanajuato do not satisfy your cravings for culture, Mexico City is three and a half hours away by car or bus. Some residents wish that it were a little closer, forgetting that the distance is just about right to save San Miguel from being overrun by day-trippers and other tourists (especially because there is no airport in the town or nearby).

Within a short drive there are several hot spring resorts that are open to the public, where you can swim or just soak contentedly in the naturally heated water. We are not aware of any claims of curative powers, but we can testify to their calming effect on the spirit.

RESTAURANTS Because San Miguel is a magnet for North Americans and other foreigners, it is amply endowed with good restaurants. These range in ambience and cuisine, from spartan vegetarian to elegant continental. Italian, French, Argentinean, and Spanish restaurants have all been around for some time. More recently the choice has been expanded to include two Chinese, a German, and an Irish restaurant. The latter features live Irish music one evening a week. Hamburgers, pizza, and bagels are widely available, but we are happy to report that the golden arches have yet to appear in the central area. Specialty food stores feature items as exotic as Danish cheese, German sausage, Arab pita bread, and the international bagel. Although these delicacies may not be as economical as tortillas and frijoles, they are quite reasonable by U.S. standards.

San Miguel has so many groceries, drugstores, meat markets, and vegetable stands (as well as a large indoor municipal market with surrounding outdoor stalls) that each North American resident you consult is likely to give different advice about which are the most reliable and most economical. Actually quality, selection, and price tend to be similar in all stores. When you have been in San Miguel awhile and acquire Mexican friends, they can tell you the best places to buy such national specialties as *carnitas, chicharones,* and *mole.*

A MOST UNUSUAL LIBRARY San Miguel's unique public library serves a wide variety of functions. Its outstanding collection of English-language books, including many current best-sellers, is supplemented by an ample selection of classical and popular music on tape. After payment of a nominal membership fee, cassettes and books can be borrowed free of charge. (Most small or middle-size towns in the United States do not have these extensive literary and musical resources.)

The library is in a restored colonial mansion, whose handsome inner court serves not only as a pleasant spot to sit and read but also as a place to meet friends. Concerts and lectures are often given there in the evening. Once a week *Conversaciones con Amigos* gathers there to provide English-speaking students of Spanish and Spanish-speaking students of English a chance to practice with one another. (Another weekly meeting of this group is held in the courtyard of one of the town's several language schools.)

On a recent visit to the library, we were pleased to find a well-equipped computer center where, for a modest fee, you can check your e-mail, surf the Web, balance your checkbook, or do anything else a PC can do.

In addition to the solace and stimulation the library provides to North Americans, it is also the base for an ambitious program of reading instruction and academic scholarships for underprivileged local children.

The library and its philanthropic activities are supported financially by weekly house and garden tours that allow both tourists and curious residents to see how the most affluent live. Helping with these tours is one of the many ways that retirees in San Miguel can repay the community's hospitality. Those we questioned described a number of opportunities for public service, such as helping with the school for the handicapped, working with the local humane society, contributing to *Atención* (the weekly English-language newspaper), and participating in the cooperative burial society. In recent years the library has expanded into an adjacent building that once was a church and has added a pleasant cafe. One room in its original space now serves as headquarters for its computer classes. The *Biblioteca* now provides free wi-fi Internet access in its courtyard and cafe. Library members have free use of Internet-connected computers. In addition it provides numerous satellite library facilities to the Spanish-speaking residents of surrounding villages. Work on behalf of the community and the demonstration of genuine concern for the people of San Miguel are two of the reasons for the excellent relationships that most North Americans there enjoy with their Mexican neighbors.

EXPLORING SAN MIGUEL For anyone trying to find his way around San Miguel as a visitor or start enjoying all it has to offer as a resident, Archie Dean's masterful guide, *The Insider's Guide to San Miguel,* is indispensable. This 250-page book will help you find a doctor, get your watch repaired, or relish the best ice cream. It can be found in shops and hotels all around San Miguel or purchased directly from the author, who is frequently on the streets or in the Jardin with a pack full of copies on his back and his distinctive sombrero on his head. Archie's Web site, where the book can also be purchased, is http://insidersma.tripod.com.

Because San Miguel attracts the wealthy as well as the artistic, the town is reputed to be the most expensive location outside the seaside vacation playgrounds. This may well be true of real estate prices in the town's center, but certainly not with regard to restaurant, supermarket, or year-round rental prices. As we've noted elsewhere, get a few blocks away from the Jardin and you are in the world of ordinary Mexicans.

The residents of some other expatriate centers have made the point that if you have little interest in the arts or in community involvement, you could feel a little out of place in San Miguel. They may be right, but this town has so much to offer that you might want to see for yourself.

MORELIA

Ask a Mexican which is his country's most beautiful state and, unless pride in his birthplace triumphs over objectivity, he or she is likely to answer Michoacán. In summer much of Michoacán's green, rolling landscape reminds the traveler alternatively of New England's Berkshire Hills or a painting of peaceful rural China. Michoacán stretches from the Pacific almost to Mexico City.

Morelia is the capital of the state of Michoacán, and the city's colonial flavor has been maintained by ordinances that strictly control the styles of new construction. Several downtown banks, which conform to these rules, are lodged in restored mansions that preserve the elegance of forgotten centuries while providing a place to exchange your traveler's checks for pesos.

At the heart of the city, Morelia's massive cathedral boasts two soaring towers that are said to be the tallest in Mexico. Although construction began in 1640, the towers and dome took an additional hundred years to complete. Flanking the impressive cathedral, the Plaza de Armas serves as the social and commercial center. Tourists and residents gather (in cafes under the plaza's elegant arched portals) to have coffee and chat while waiting for the *Mexico City News* to hit the newsstands. Shopping, restaurants, museums, and other attractions are within easy walking distance of the Plaza de Armas. The plaza is located a block from the city's university. Dating from 1580, it is the second oldest university in the Western Hemisphere.

Morelia supports an active cultural life—music, drama, and dance thrive there, as do the visual arts. Recent additions to the cultural scene are the spectacular Palacio del Arte, which boasts 5,000 seats and features internationally famous artists, and the even larger Pabellón Don Vasco at the fairgrounds. The city also hosts several excellent language schools—one connected with its own bed-and-breakfast and others that can arrange homestays with Mexican families. A homestay is an excellent way to get to know Morelia, meet other people studying Spanish, and make some friends among the Mexican community.

Morelia is indeed a colonial town, but it isn't all monuments, ancient homes, and narrow, cobblestoned streets. Once away from the city center, a startling modern facade contrasts with the colonial style. Such contrasts are more typical on the southern edge of the city, where many expatriates prefer to live. Perhaps because Morelia's population and prosperity have increased so rapidly in the past decade, some sectors are modern and elegant. The Plaza de las Americas shopping mall is among the largest and most luxurious malls that we have ever seen. It's as though Saks Fifth Avenue, Sears, Macy's, and K-Mart were combined with a luxury supermarket and, for good measure, packaged with marble floors and ultramodern fixtures. Costco, Suburbia, HomeMart (a Mexican version of Home Depot), Ace Hardware, WalMart, and Office Depot have graced the mercantile landscape in recent years. Sears has undergone a complete renovation, emerging as the city's "fancy" store, carrying name brands ranging from Maytag to Lancôme. For lovers of the outdoors, another modern convenience in Morelia is a golf course.

Despite the fact that Morelia has been slow to catch on as a retirement site, we feel it could be a viable alternative to Guadalajara. Overall it is much cleaner, and the nicer sections of town are just as attractive and convenient as Guadalajara. Moreover, Morelia is only a fifth of the size of Guadalajara. A major difference between Morelia and other places of similar size is that Morelia doesn't seem to support a well-organized expatriate group. Once a week in the Holiday Inn (formerly the Hotel Calinda), there's an informal gathering (with an unofficial chairperson), but this meeting is more of an excuse to get together and exchange news than an integrated association as you would find in Guadalajara, San Miguel de Allende, or Ajijic. One resident approved of this casual approach, saying, "All that politicking that usually marks political ascendancy in many expatriate organizations is not demanded here."

How many foreigners live in Morelia? Jennifer Rose, a longtime resident of Morelia, says, "How many? That's a good question—kind of like counting the number of angels who can sit on the head of a pin. About six or seven years ago, I sat down with some friends one evening and we wrote down the name of every single expatriate we could think of, just to get a count. We quit at around 600. Some people will claim there are only 150, but they're only counting those with whom they're acquainted." She further points out that although the loose network isn't extensive, it's nevertheless big enough to have among its population "some of those gringos you assiduously avoid!" In short, the foreign colony here is large enough to support an active social life, and settling in Morelia today hardly qualifies you as a pioneer.

Easy outings from Morelia include Pátzcuaro and Uruapan. The latter, justly renowned for its lacquered boxes and trays, also attracts special attention for the nearby volcano, Paricutín. In 1943 the volcano suddenly erupted and spilled molten lava over the surrounding villages and countryside. Pátzcuaro owes its reputation to the loveliness of its colonial buildings and of Lake Pátzcuaro. The lake is dotted with islands, including one covered by the Tarascan Indian village of Janitzio. The island is topped by a gigantic statue of José Morelos, one of Mexico's greatest heroes and a native of the locality. The lake is also the home of the *pescado blanco,* a delicious whitefish caught by the Indians in their delicate "butterfly" nets and featured on the menus of the neighborhood's numerous restaurants. Pátzcuaro is another location that would seem ripe for retirement relocation, but so far only a handful of North Americans have taken up the invitation.

QUERÉTARO

One of Mexico's earliest colonial cities, Querétaro was colonized in 1531 after a bloody battle with tribal defenders. Legend has it that the Spanish were getting the worst of the fighting until Spain's patron saint, *Santiago Apóstal,* miraculously entered the fray. He turned day into darkness with a solar eclipse, spurring the Spanish conquistadores to victory.

From very early times, Querétaro served as a second-home destination for wealthy families who wanted a respite from Mexico City's cool climate. The weather here is ideal, with sunshine and seventy-five-degree temperatures most of the day. Those who didn't have weekend homes in Cuernavaca felt obligated to own a place in Querétaro. Today, away from the bustle of Mexico City yet only a couple of hours distant from the city via toll road, Querétaro is the "in" place for weekend homes and retirement. The fact that Querétaro has almost as many golf courses as Acapulco (four of them) gives you an idea of the upper-class coloring of this area.

Inevitably, those seeking retirement havens discovered Querétaro, although not to the extent of places like Lake Chapala or the Pacific Riviera locations. Then, a few years ago the Mexican government began encouraging manufacturers and businesses to move to locations like Querétaro to relieve pressure on the already overcrowded metropolis.

Companies needed little encouragement, and their employees were delighted to escape the stress of living in Mexico City.

Today Querétaro Industrial Park hosts more than thirty research centers, Condumex (a Mexican supplier of telecommunications equipment), a manufacturer of auto parts, and a plastics complex. The city is home to several multinational corporations. Their technical and managerial employees have boosted the English-speaking population dramatically over the past few years, making it an expatriate-friendly city. Several foreign clubs and associations help newcomers settle in the community. Some of the most important are the American Society, the International Friendship Club, and Rotary International. The American Society encompasses several smaller clubs and associations based on particular fields of interest.

Querétaro has sprawled outward in recent years to accommodate the manufacturing and business facilities and has grown to at least 600,000 inhabitants. Yet the colonial flavor has been preserved. Today's authentically restored colonial buildings, brick-paved streets, and ornate fountains make Querétaro a textbook example of historic preservation. Mansions and public buildings dating from the seventeenth and eighteenth centuries lend an air of elegant historicism. The area surrounding the main square, the Plaza de Armas, is reminiscent of old Europe, with pedestrian-friendly streets and tasteful shops. Outdoor cafes, enjoyed year-round in the moderate climate, line the spacious plaza and wide walkways leading from the plaza to the main streets of Querétaro's town center.

The expatriates tend to live in Colonia Jurica or Colonia Juriquilla, upscale neighborhoods on the northern edge of the city. An English language school serves expatriate children, and according to residents the classes are more advanced than those in many U.S. schools.

TEQUISQUIAPAN

Almost next door to Querétaro, Tequisquiapan is another traditional escape from the hustle and bustle of Mexico City. Yet the flavor of *Tequis* is much different from its large neighbor. Even though Querétaro is at least 200 years older than Tequis, its rapid development over the past 50 years makes all but the historic center look modern. But much of

Tequisquiapan seems to be caught in a time warp, with many homes and buildings dating from the 1700s. Despite growth in recent years, the town retains a village atmosphere, with winding cobblestone streets lined by colorful and ancient-looking adobe homes.

Tequis has long been famous for its hot baths and swimming pools. Just about anywhere one sunk a well, hot water was available for hot tubs or swimming pools. So it was an easy task to install a spa in the courtyard. Because of this thermal water, the town boasts a dozen or more hotels featuring thermal swimming pools, another reason for weekenders and tourists to visit. An excellent eighteen-hole golf course is open to the public.

Tequisquiapan has changed over the years, as has every other town in Mexico. Some old cobblestone and flagstone streets have been paved over in the interest of speeding traffic flow through the narrow byways. Instead of lounging on the tree-shaded village square, listening to birds and watching wood-laden burros trot past, tourists come here to buy artwork and locally produced handicrafts. What hasn't changed is the feeling of living in an Old Mexican village atmosphere.

Tequisquiapan holds a special place in John Howells's heart because his family bought and restored a 250-year-old home and lived there for almost 20 years. The Howellses' house had 2-foot-thick adobe walls and a large courtyard with arched portals. In those days, the number of full-time expatriates in Tequis was small, but weekends were times of frequent cocktail parties and social get-togethers. Regularly freeloading at cocktail parties was an Argentinean doctor named Ernesto Guevara. He was very popular and had a delightful sense of humor, although he was somewhat intense when it came to politics. He would sometimes mention that he and his friends planned to invade Cuba someday. Most guests would suppress a smile and take a sip of their cocktail. Later on they were astounded when Che Guevara actually did invade Cuba!

MEXICO CITY **AND VICINITY**

In earlier editions of *Choose Mexico* we hesitated to recommend Mexico City as a retirement spot. After many subsequent visits there, we still can't, but we do feel that our readers should know what an exciting and cosmopolitan city it is. We wouldn't want to live there, but we certainly

would want to visit it frequently. Nevertheless, many
North Americans do live in
Mexico City. They love it and
wouldn't consider any other
location.

One caveat we must
emphasize: Mexico City has
suffered an increase in crime

in recent years. Occasionally a wave of robberies by "pirate" taxi drivers
against passengers make headlines. It's difficult to tell just how prevalent
these incidents are. However, it doesn't hurt to repeat the common
advice about taxis in Mexico City. Always travel in legitimate taxis, the
kind you'll find at taxicab stations lined up awaiting passengers. "Pirate"
taxis are those without permits; drivers roam the streets looking for fares.
Most of them are honest, but there are always a few crooks, especially in
a huge megalopolis like Mexico City.

Why do North Americans choose to live in Mexico City rather than
less hectic, less crowded cities? For the same reason some people love
New York, Paris, or London. It's difficult to explain this feeling of urban
euphoria to anyone who has never fallen in love with a large city. For
those who enjoy city life, Mexico City has it all: great restaurants, entertainment, outstanding museums, art exhibits, night clubs, and theaters.
They're all there, in one convenient, easy-to-use package. Every possible
shopping convenience, from native tapestries to WalMart and Costco, is
at your fingertips. Mexico City is so different from Mexican villages, it
could belong to a different world.

Mexico City is steeped in culture; its downtown is famous for its collection of sixteenth-century colonial architectural treasures. The nucleus
of the city is a virtual museum of history and culture. Here you'll find the
Americas' oldest cathedral sharing an enormous open *zócalo* with
ancient, castlelike government buildings and a spectacular museum
that displays artifacts from an Aztec temple, recently unearthed nearby.
One of Mexico's cultural showplaces, Bellas Artes (Palace of Fine Arts),
is also located in the center of town. One of the most beautiful opera
houses in the world, Bellas Artes hosts internationally celebrated opera
companies and symphony orchestras. The famous Ballet Folklórico, a

prime tourist attraction, draws crowds weekly.

Another attraction of living in Mexico City is its cool, temperate climate. Residents here neither freeze nor swelter. This is the place for those who detest hot weather and avoid tropical sunshine; they'll wear sweaters or jackets year-round and sleep under blankets every night. Some folks—especially those with heart conditions—do find Mexico City's mile-high altitude a problem, but most people have no difficulty adjusting. After a day of taking it easy, we jump right back into the swing of things.

Of course many foreigners live in Mexico City because they work for multinational firms, which are well represented in the country. This is nothing new—for decades Mexico City has been the headquarters for foreign business enterprises. In the olden days, when this writer lived in Mexico City, we called ourselves the "British-American colony," and we numbered in the thousands. Because of this large number of expatriates living in the metropolis, you'll find a pool of social contacts among retirees and working residents' families.

Members of the foreign colony tend to congregate in certain elegant neighborhoods, in homes or apartments that look out over tree-lined boulevards or quiet side streets. They live in areas such as Las Lomas, Chapultepec, and El Pedregal. A very popular neighborhood in the center of the city is the Zona Rosa ("pink zone"), a place of upscale apartments, boutiques, and fabulous restaurants. Before making decisions about retiring here, be sure to consult with residents who have lived here for some time. They can guide you to the safe neighborhoods to consider for your new home.

From this writer's viewpoint, an enormous drawback to living in Mexico City is the automobile traffic. Parking is impossible, and the city is so congested that drivers are restricted, with serious fines levied for venturing out on the wrong day of the week. A few experiences with traffic here will turn anyone into a confirmed pedestrian. Many Mexico City residents don't even own cars; they prefer to use taxis, buses, and the excellent subway system, and they rent cars for weekend jaunts around the country.

Of course you needn't live in Mexico City to enjoy its many historic and cultural attractions. Buses and trains are convenient and inexpensive from anywhere in the country. For the average person, Mexico City isn't well suited to retirement living, but if you love the city and its exhilarating atmosphere, be sure to get in contact with the Newcomers Club of Mexico City (www.newcomers.org.mx/). The group comprises almost 700 families who will welcome you to their twice-monthly meetings. The club's cultural and social calendar is extraordinarily full, beginning with welcome and orientation classes and extending to activities such as neighborhood coffees, language classes, tours of interesting places in Mexico, bridge games, and charity affairs.

VALLE DE **BRAVO**

Anyone who enjoys the active life—water sports (including swimming and sailing), tennis, and golf—and has an adequate retirement income should take a look at a retreat favored by those knowledgeable Mexicans who can afford it and by a small group of U.S. and Canadian retirees. Only 90 miles west of México City, perched on a hilltop with a view of a lake and luxuriant, pine-covered slopes, Valle de Bravo is a beautiful contrast to the megalopolis of Mexico City. It comes complete with cobblestone streets and colonial-style homes with lush gardens behind bougainvillea-covered stone walls. It is renowned for its climate, which somehow manages to be significantly warmer than Mexico City in winter and cooler in summer. What's more, there is considerably more sunshine here, and the air is crystal clear. Despite the influx of boutiques and upscale restaurants, it still enjoys much of the serene beauty that must have characterized this country town before the construction of the huge artificial lake that has made it so popular with sports enthusiasts.

Rentals tend to be expensive and hard to come by, but much land is still available and building costs are low. With apologies to those of our readers whose lives, like ours, tend to be sedentary or whose budgets are too limited to consider such a trendy site, we thought we ought to let the more athletic and prosperous retirees know that such a place exists.

There are several excellent hotels in Valle de Bravo. Some of them offer moderately priced weekend packages, so you can see the town for yourself. Even if you don't or can't choose it as a retirement site, it's a wonderful place for vacations.

OAXACA

At slightly higher than 5,000 feet, Oaxaca's climate is a bit warmer than Mexico City's and, without the latter's industrial development, it boasts much cleaner air. Oaxaca's population is passing 300,000, but its large area and the absence of steel and concrete skyscrapers and other visible hallmarks of twenty-first-century life effectively conceal that fact.

Oaxaca is easy to reach from Mexico City by air, bus, or rail. The west coast beaches of Puerto Angel, Puerto Escondido, and Huatulco are close by and are easily accessible by plane.

The great majority of residents, both of the city and of the surrounding state of which it is the capital, are Indians. They are proud of their heritage and their historical resistance to assimilation into the politically, culturally, and economically dominant cultures of the past five centuries: first Aztec, then Spanish, and now Mexican. Oaxaca was the birthplace of both Benito Juarez, "Mexico's Abraham Lincoln," and Porfirio Diaz, an ironfisted president for many years, and was the home of numerous accomplished artists. It is conscious of its colonial and Indian past and has preserved much of its architectural history. Oaxaca is as different in appearance and atmosphere from cities in northern Mexico as Tucson, Arizona, is different from Portland, Maine.

On Saturday handicrafts flood in from neighboring villages and spill out of the huge Juarez market onto the surrounding streets. Black and green glazed pottery, innumerable baskets in a great variety of shapes and sizes, hand-loomed textiles, and many skillful copies of the Monte Albán idols and jewelry beguile even the most apathetic shopper. On other days of the week, there is a market, or *tianguis,* in one or another of the many surrounding towns. A trip to these towns can also provide the opportunity to visit the studios of the many talented artisans whose work is sold in the shops of Oaxaca.

Every Mexican town of any size has its *zócalo* or town square, but few are more sumptuous or lively than Oaxaca's twin plazas. Filled with tall, handsome trees and countless wrought-iron benches where locals and foreigners alike while away many sunny hours, and ringed by sidewalk cafes, it is the heart of Oaxaca.

There is an unusually handsome bandstand on which a variety of instrumental groups play several evenings a week. Almost the entire town

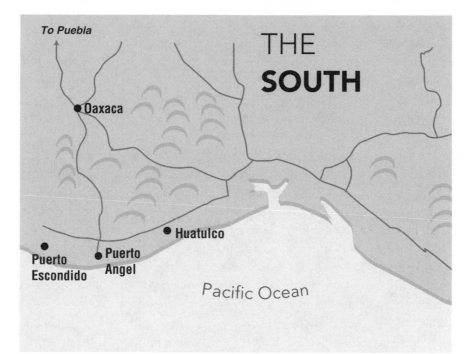

turns out for these concerts, and parents sit around the *zócalo* gossiping while children play on the grassy parts of the park. The stream of peddlers whose wares include carved, painted wooden animals, bird-shaped ceramic whistles, hammocks, baskets, serapes, belts, and even elaborate carpets could become annoying after a while, were it not for the fact that a polite but firm refusal is usually sufficient to send them on their way. Then one can listen to the music, chat with friends, or just enjoy the passing parade.

In the early editions of *Choose Mexico* we reported that the beauty and unspoiled antiquity of Oaxaca were beginning to attract more tourists, particularly those interested in exploring the Zapotec and Mixtec ruins nearby. At that time this mountain city still had only a small colony of North American residents. Most of those who had chosen to live there seemed to indicate that they liked it that way. One reason may be that food and housing prices have remained somewhat lower in Oaxaca than in many other parts of Mexico. We were told apartment rentals were inexpensive, and our experience was that wonderful restaurants were very affordable. Another reason may be what a retired resident described as "freedom from pressures for conformity."

Today the number of full- or part-time foreign residents, mostly from the United States and Canada, has grown in number to what some there estimate to be 2,000 or more. It is hard to be precise, because Oaxaca seems to attract retirees who are more interested in experiencing Mexican life close up than in becoming part of a foreign enclave. Certainly there are opportunities to meet and socialize with fellow *norteamericanos*. One is at the lending library on Calle Alcala just a few blocks from the town center (which has one of Mexico's best collections of English-language books outside San Miguel de Allende). It is the place to go when you want to get together with fellow expatriates to get news from home, to exchange local gossip, and to obtain current information on such practical matters as where there is a particularly attractive house or apartment for rent at a reasonable price. We also found that there tends to be a daily early-morning cluster of English-speaking residents and tourists in one of the outdoor cafes on the *zócalo*. One morning while we were there, more than sixty expatriates gathered for brunch in the sunny patio of a local restaurant to benefit community causes. Several language schools serve the many foreign residents who want to get beneath the surface of this magical city.

A glance at the English-language *Oaxaca Times* reveals a schedule of cultural activities, ranging from concerts to video showings of classical Mexican films to art exhibitions. There are ads for restaurants to suit all tastes and budgets.

Because Oaxaca offers reliably comfortable winter temperatures, it attracts many part-year residents from the United States and Canada. Year after year they desert the cold and damp of their home communities for the warmth and stimulation of Oaxaca for periods ranging from one to three months.

Many foreign residents, whether living in Oaxaca full- or part-time, seem to choose rooms, suites, or cottages on the grounds of the numerous small affordable hotels scattered throughout the city. Some are able to negotiate attractive monthly rental rates in comfortable accommodations that are just a few blocks from the center of town.

Oaxaca is certainly an increasingly viable choice in the Mexico retirement sweepstakes and a wonderful place to visit, even if you have only a few weeks to spend in Mexico.

CUERNAVACA

Cuernavaca is the matriarch of Mexico's "retirement" communities. Long before anyone had heard of Ajijic or San Miguel de Allende, Cuernavaca's superb climate and tranquil ambience held an irresistible appeal for retirees, seasonal visitors, and tourists. From the very early days, famous people were drawn here like a magnet. The Aztec king Montezuma adored Cuernavaca; he maintained a luxurious palace here. Cortez, the conqueror of Mexico, liked the palace so well that he moved in and remodeled it to his taste. Archduke Maximilian and his wife, Carlota, had a mansion here, as did silver baron José Borda. Most of Mexico's presidents either lived in Cuernavaca or spent weekends there. Affluent residents of Mexico City feel obligated to have weekend homes here, and foreigners from all over the world choose Cuernavaca for second homes. Graham Greene loved to winter at his house in "the land of eternal spring," as do several other authors and artists who join less-famous expatriates in making Cuernavaca their home. All of these people can't be wrong. Cuernavaca is a special place.

The location, just an hour's drive via a superhighway to Mexico City, makes it convenient for residents here to visit the capital, enjoy an opera, have dinner, and make a quick return to Cuernavaca's clear air and balmy temperatures. The town sits on a mountain slope at an altitude about 2,500 feet lower than Mexico City; this explains its constant springlike climate. This also explains why so many of the capital's residents flee to Cuernavaca on winter days when temperatures in Mexico City are a dozen degrees cooler than Cuernavaca's semitropical ambience. Magnificent views of the western flank of Popocatépetl volcano can be seen on clear days.

Residents here seldom find it necessary to visit the megalopolis. Everything one could conceivably need can be found right here. Cuernavaca is proud of her own cultural events, theaters, concerts, and university research institutes. Residents can find everything from a Sam's Club to German delicatessens and all other accoutrements of the twenty-first century. As longtime resident Rhonda Tranks (originally from Australia) says, "You feel like you are living in an active and vibrant Mexican city, not just a foreign enclave. We often say, '*we are so close and yet so far from Mexico City*'!"

The wealth that has poured into this lovely valley over the years is readily visible in its stately colonial mansions, palaces, churches, and private homes. Cuernavaca's quiet residential neighborhoods begin close to the city center and feature lovely homes with red-tiled roofs—trimmed in pastel (and sometimes vibrant) pinks, blues, and yellows—and landscaped with brilliant flowers and lush, semitropical vegetation. Houses are often surrounded by high walls to provide privacy for swimming pools and patios with luxuriant landscaping. Flowers are everywhere.

Although Cuernavaca's population has increased tremendously over the years, the town has managed to preserve much of its original charm. The downtown is centered on a colorful and bustling town plaza (it sprawls up the hill to the Palace of Cortez, which today is an outstanding historical and archaeological museum). Adjoining the plaza are narrow streets of the original town, where you'll find artisans' shops, small retail stores, and street merchants selling woven leather huaraches, silver jewelry, antique furniture, embroidered blouses, and handicrafts of all descriptions. Excellent restaurants abound.

Because Cuernavaca lies on a gentle mountain slope, locating above or below the town provides several distinct microclimates. A cool mountain forest lies at the higher altitude above the city, and on the downward side, the climate is drier and warmer. In Cuernavaca itself, temperatures are mild year-round. The rainy season traditionally lasts from May through September, with heavy showers at night and delightfully clear and sunny days. The marvelous weather here makes outdoor recreation a year-round affair. A half-dozen golf courses, at least four of them eighteen-hole layouts, are open around Cuernavaca, and horseback riding and tennis are popular activities enjoyed throughout this area. Several spas with mineral and thermal waters, landscaped grounds, and camping areas are nearby, including Cuauda, Atotonilco, La Fundición, Las Estacas, Oaxtepec, and Temixco.

Living in Cuernavaca offers much more than golf and bridge. The area is incredibly intellectually stimulating, being rich in Mexican archeology and history. The region is saturated with pre-Hispanic, colonial, postcolonial, and revolutionary history. It boasts an extraordinary number of U.N. historical and cultural sites. The romantic revolutionary general Emiliano Zapata was from nearby Morelos.

Cuernavaca has a large number of English-speaking residents.

These are not only North American retirees but also foreigners employed by several international companies located in the region. The town also hosts a large number of Americans who come here to study Spanish at Cuernavaca's highly regarded language schools. Students correctly feel that total immersion classes in Spanish, and staying in a Mexican home, are a great way to begin an investigation of Mexico as a place for retirement.

This large foreign community does something else for Cuernavaca: it makes it a newcomer-friendly place where it's easy to blend into the rich Mexican environment. Several social organizations are in place here, one of the more important being the Newcomers Club of Cuernavaca. The group welcomes all English-speaking residents of the community, regardless of nationality, race, or creed, and provides information, social activities, and friendship to all. More than 150 families belong to the club, with activities ranging from book, film, and dance clubs to lectures, travel, and sports (tennis, golf, walking, hiking), as well as cooking classes, play-reading groups, and holiday festivities. Members contribute to the community through numerous philanthropic activities that take place year-round, including benefit dinners, luncheons, and, this year, a rodeo. Proceeds go to a children's hospital, an organization for the blind, and more. The club's Web site is at www.solucion.com/newcomers/.

To help you settle in, the Newcomers Club has three "must-have" reference materials: (1) *The Newcomers Cuernavaca Survival Guide;* (2) *The Newcomers Directory of Recommended Services;* and (3) *The Newcomers Family Activity Guide.* Other local organizations cooperate in publishing *The Directory of Foreign Residents of the State of Morelos,* which lists hundreds of individuals and families. The book has several pages of associations and clubs, ranging from Alcoholics Anonymous and the American Legion to a home for orphaned children supported largely by U.S. contributions and volunteers. Also in the directory, together with numerous banks, beauty salons, delicatessens, and so on, are a number of veterinarians, a video club, and a washing machine repair service. A listing of physicians and dentists fills several pages.

Another expatriate group is the Guild House, meeting the second Wednesday of each month. The Guild House maintains a rather large library of English-language books, with a wide assortment of paperbacks and hardcovers for sale at very low prices. All Cuernavaca groups unite for a binational July Fourth celebration of both U.S. Independence Day and Mexican-American Friendship Day. Festivities include the trooping of the colors of both countries, the singing of their national anthems, and a feast that includes both hot dogs and *cochinito pibil.*

THE PACIFIC COAST

We often hear people exclaim: "I'd never want to live in someplace like Acapulco or Puerto Vallarta! Much too tourist plagued. I want to live some place more authentic! Someplace more truly *Mexican!*"

Think about this for a moment. Why do so many tourists travel to Mexico's beach towns in the first place? They go there simply because these are wonderful places to visit! They are also wonderful places to live. The scenery is lush and tropical, like a movie set. Balmy breezes caress your skin on palm-fringed beaches. Winter days are typically in the seventies, and summer highs are in the mid- to high eighties; it's shirtsleeve weather year-round. Therefore, it's not surprising that the same folks who look forward to vacations here every year also think about Mexico's west coast when it comes time for retirement. As for being "authentic," will someone define the term? When folks think about retiring in the United States, are they more likely to consider an "authentic" town like Soapy Springs, Nebraska, or some "touristy" place like Palm Springs, California?

When you hear people talking about the great time they had on their Mexican vacation, chances are they visited Mexico's west coast. Termed the "Gold Coast" or the "Mexican Riviera" by tourist agencies and travel writers, this section of Mexico draws by far the most tourists every year. There are many good reasons.

First of all, because of the heavy influx of tourists, accommodations are plentiful, excellent restaurants are everywhere, and prices tend to be competitive. More important is the climate, especially for those who enjoy the warmth of the tropical beaches and the warm ocean waves. The climate here is great because seasonal temperatures and rainfall are moderated by the Pacific Ocean. The Pacific, with its deep, temperate body of water, maintains a steady year-round temperature in the coastal regions. This condition shields you from excessive summer heat, and win-

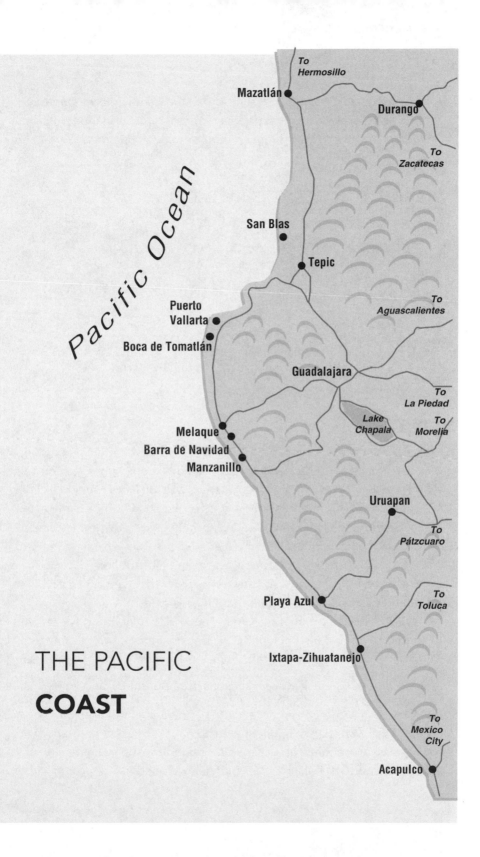

ter "northers" that blow down from Alaska are greatly moderated by the time they reach Mexico's Gold Coast. Temperatures change very little from month to month, with most rainfall coming in summer. Winters are almost totally rain free.

WEATHER ON THE MEXICAN PACIFIC COAST

In degrees Fahrenheit												
	Jan.	Feb.	Mar.	Apr.	May	June	July	Aug.	Sept.	Oct.	Nov.	Dec.
Daily Highs	88	88	88	88	90	91	91	90	90	90	90	88
Daily Lows	72	72	72	73	76	77	77	77	76	76	75	73
Rain (inches)	—	—	—	—	1.5	10.4	9.0	10.5	15.0	6.5	2.0	0.5

MAZATLÁN

Mazatlán is one of Mexico's premier beach resorts. It has long been popular as a place for tourism and escape from northern winters—especially for those snowbirds living in the western half of North America. Even though Mazatlán is the nearest west coast location with a climate that makes year-round retirement practical, until the past few years a surprisingly small number of North Americans have settled in for retirement. This is changing rapidly, although Mazatlán will probably never gain a large enough foreign population to be considered a "gringo enclave." At least retirees who live here hope that never happens.

With a population of approximately 600,000 inhabitants, Mazatlán is located on a long, flat stretch of Pacific beach at a point where warm currents from the Sea of Cortez rendezvous with cool, westerly waves from the open Pacific that brush past the tip of the Baja Peninsula. This bestows on the region comparatively mild temperatures and lower humidity than some of the more southerly resorts along Mexico's "Gold Coast." And Mazatlán's summers are dramatically cooler than anywhere to the north along the shores of the Sea of Cortez, where the desert coast is best described as baking hot in summer, with occasional frost in winter.

Mazatlán is the first place south of the border that can be genuinely called "tropical." In fact the Tropic of Cancer, that imaginary line that defines the tropics, runs just north of the city limits.

Now that the four-lane *Maxipista* (superhighway toll road) zips down from Nogales to Mazatlán, it's entirely possible to make the drive in one long day, although we'd recommend breaking it up into two easy days' drive. It's also practical to take one of the inexpensive deluxe buses from the border, and many daily scheduled air flights serve Mazatlán. This makes it easy for your family and friends to visit from time to time and feel envious of your retirement situation. You really don't need to own an auto here, not with the excellent public transportation. Taxi fares used to be rather expensive, but lately they have become affordable; there's too much competition to justify exorbitant fares. You'll see a fleet of open-air taxis, which are cute but a bit more expensive. They are unique to Mazatlán and are called *pulmonias*. As a resident you would most likely have your own auto or use public transportation, but the taxis are there when you need them. By the way, Mazatlán has greatly improved its bus system, with modern equipment replacing the old, rickety buses that used to lumber along.

CONTINUING DEVELOPMENT Mazatlán continues to develop; each year more condos, apartments, and homes spring up to accommodate the swelling population. Housing choices are plentiful in all price ranges, whether buying, renting, or building. The difference between Mazatlán and other, less popular beach towns is that you'll find few oceanfront homes for sale in the most popular beach areas. The land is too valuable. Mazatlán's precious beach properties have been preempted by large hotels and deluxe resorts. Yet just a few blocks from the beach, many lovely homes are available for rent or purchase. A number of RV parks accommodate winter retirees, with some parks perched right on the beach. Like most Mexican RV parks, they fill up in winter and empty out in summer.

An interesting development here is an assisted-living complex. The Melville was designed for those retirees who would rather stay in Mexico than return home when health problems prevent them from living alone. The complex, consisting of nineteen living units, is located in the Olas Altas area of old Mazatlán.

Real estate here tends to hold its value. According to residents the 1994 downturn in the economy had little effect on prices. At first some homes—particularly properties owned by Mexican families—were placed on the market at reduced prices. However, as in most other retirement communities in Mexico, prices asked by North Americans remained fairly level. Because the demand for upscale homes didn't fall, sellers found little pressure to cut asking prices.

In addition to miles of sunny beaches, Mazatlán also boasts superb sports fishing and a busy commercial port. It deservedly calls itself the shrimp capital of the world. Here shrimpers from the warm waters of the Sea of Cortez routinely unload cargoes of unbelievably enormous prawns. Unfortunately most of these delicious crustaceans—some as large as lobsters—are destined for Japan (where price is no object), and U.S. residents seldom get a chance to sample them. However, you can often buy some if you meet the incoming boats and do some bargaining. Jumbo shrimp taste delicious sautéed with butter, minced garlic, and a pinch of chili powder. ¡Ay, qué rico! (Don't forget to squeeze a lime on them, too!)

At first glance Mazatlán's crowded tourist section of town might seem to be a drawback. As it happens this is also the favorite area for expatriates to live—in enclaves just a few blocks off the main beach drag. Fortunately tourists keep to their beach streets and seem to be oblivious to the peaceful neighborhoods nearby. No one we interviewed in Mazatlán felt that tourists were a particular bother. As one woman put it, "They live in their little beach world, and we live in our world. The only time we meet is when we go to the tourists' restaurants." Incidentally, several excellent restaurants, with surprisingly good food at bargain prices, cater to tourists. Mazatlán's old downtown section is a real surprise, with narrow streets and a real Old Mexico look—a real contrast to the glitzy and modern tourist areas. Elderhostel has chosen Mazatlán as a place to give their cultural courses starting in 2001. This and the fact that the locals are rediscovering their downtown gives a new meaning to Mazatlán!

When we wrote our first edition of Choose Mexico, we reported that traffic wasn't as bad here as in places like Puerto Vallarta or Mexico City. (No place in the world is as bad as Mexico City!) Today we have to rescind that opinion. The population of automobiles has soared along with the population of humans, but the streets remain the same size. Despite the heavy traffic, though, Mazatlán drivers seem to be unusually calm and courteous. The sound of honking horns and the sight of shaking fists are almost nonexistent.

Because tourism is a major industry here, many people around Mazatlán speak English. You'll discover this early on in your first visit— when you're hounded by time-share salesmen, tour guides, and persistent fishing-trip operators. (We get rid of them by saying that our plane leaves in an hour.) Consequently, Mazatlán is a good place to ease into Mexican culture and practice your Spanish; you can feel confident that you can always lapse back into English for a word or two and you'll be understood. In fact, if you speak Spanish well, local people may react with pleased astonishment.

TWO MAZATLÁNS Mazatlán has a split personality. One world is a tourist playground, and the other world is that of foreign residents who have an intimate, close-knit society. Many of the activities revolve around volunteer projects. The American Legion, the Rotary Club, Friends of Mexico, and Hands across the Border coordinate some of these projects, and the Amigos de los Animales is busy saving wildlife. Newcomers will have little problem finding a circle of friends with like interests.

Mazatlán's sea-level altitude is easy on those with heart problems. Residents report that medical care and hospitals are excellent here, and they attest to an abundance of good, English-speaking doctors and dentists. A new medical facility, Sharp Hospital, offers all the latest diagnostic and surgical equipment, with everything state of the art. Although Medicare isn't recognized here, some U.S. medical insurance plans cover expenses that occur outside the country, and permanent residents in Mazatlán carry local health insurance. Retirees here swear by the quality medical care they receive.

Mazatlán's weather is typical of the rest of Mexico's tropical coast. It's exceptionally pleasant from November until May. (These months make up the dry season, a time of little or no rain and balmy temperatures.) The season for rain starts in late May or June and lasts through September. Then the weather turns warm to hot, and the humidity climbs. This is the most beautiful time of the year in Mexico because the hills and fields are green and fresh looking. Yet because of the ocean, summer temperatures are quite pleasant, with highs in the mid-eighties. As in Florida, in summertime you need to get up early and do your tennis, bicycling, or hiking before the weather gets too warm. A leisurely lunch is followed by a long nap and time for reading. Later in the afternoon you can resume outdoor activities, perhaps a swim in the surf, and be ready for a late supper, which is the norm here. Mazatlán boasts three first-rate golf courses. There's El Cid's twenty-seven-hole layout, Estrella del Mar's eighteen-hole beachfront course out by the airport, and a nine-hole public course.

What about crime in Mexican Riviera resort cities? Is it any worse than in other retirement areas in Mexico? Could it possibly be as dangerous as in Florida resort cities? (Hardly.) Below is a quote from Mazatlán residents Henry and Nadine Laxen on the subject of crime in their neighborhood. (Reprinted from their Web page, with permission. Visit their Web site at www.maztravel.com.)

"To give you a feel for the level of crime in Mazatlán, let me tell you about our local newspaper, the *Noroeste*. In their local crime coverage, which is printed every day, they often include pictures of the guys who stole a bicycle, and sometimes of the gun or knife that was confiscated. Finding someone with a gun is a big deal, and gets big coverage, with pictures not only of the villain, but of the firearm as well. Can you imagine the *Los Angeles Times* doing this? They would need to publish a one-hundred-page crime section daily if they were to include pictures of guys stealing bicycles.

"I can honestly say that Nadine and I feel much safer living here in Mazatlán than we have living almost anywhere . . . in the United States. Where we used to live in California, going down the hill to Safeway for some milk was a truly frightening experience. Here, we have walked in the heart of downtown at midnight on several occasions, and have never felt threatened in any way. In fact, even late at night you will still pass young men and girls strolling on the streets or in the parks, holding hands and making out."

Putting all these factors together, Mazatlán might be the ideal place for a three- or six-month experiment in Mexican living. With plentiful rentals, sunny beaches, and a resort atmosphere, what better place to spend a winter?

PUERTO **VALLARTA**

For years Puerto Vallarta was a sleepy village, isolated and cut off from the rest of Mexico—and happy to be so. The only road in was unpaved; visitors had to come by four-wheel-drive, boat, or a DC-3 that bounced to a landing on a dirt airstrip. When the paved road from Tepic finally broke through the tropical forest, Puerto Vallarta suddenly found itself thrust into the modern world of tourism. It also began to accumulate retirees and expatriates from the north, who formed the nucleus of today's foreign community.

Puerto Vallarta never stopped growing; today it is a thriving city of 250,000 inhabitants. Located on a long, narrow strip of land between the mountains and the sea, "PV," as its North American devotees call it, is less than a dozen blocks wide in many places. For this reason the main part of the old town center hasn't developed the usual beach resort facade, with high-rise glass-and-steel buildings. Instead hotel complexes have been forced every year to expand farther north and south, where high-rise condos and luxury hotels sprout like weeds. These are the places where tourists stay—in hotels where they pay top dollar and where it costs several dollars to take a taxi into town. This north-south expansion allows the original town to retain a slight suggestion of its old village atmosphere. Cobblestoned streets and centuries-old buildings add to the charm. The secret to affordable retirement in Puerto Vallarta is to find an apartment in the older section of town where local working people live and where permanently retired couples greatly outnumber the well-heeled tourists. You'll find plenty of apartments available, particularly in late spring, when the flighty snowbirds vacate the premises and begin their annual migration north. This is another town for testing out your tolerance of Mexico; if you find you don't care for living here, the worst that can happen is you will enjoy a long vacation at a seaside resort. The plus side is that living away from the beach is not only inexpensive, it's also relatively uncrowded. The tourist crush isn't concentrated close to your neighborhood; it's spread out over a 20-mile stretch of beach.

Some of the more affordable housing is typically found on the hills behind town—usually 8 blocks or more from the beach. Construction here is older, but in addition to favorable rent, you enjoy the bonus of gorgeous ocean views and vistas of the town below. A nice two-bedroom

TIME-SHARES/**CONDOMINIUMS**

When inspecting any beach city or town along Mexico's west coast, from Mazatlán to Acapulco, you'll surely be deluged by persistent time-share salespeople. They grab you by your shirtsleeve and insist that you accept a complimentary breakfast, lunch, cruise, or car rental. Should you take them up on the "free" offer, you can be sure of several hours of high-pressure sales tactics. These salespeople are experts, so keep your resistance up, or better yet, do as we learned to do when in Mazatlán: Just say, "Sorry, but my plane leaves in an hour."

Time-shares are sprouting on the beaches, and a few blocks back from the water both regular and time-share condos are popping up. Our view of time-sharing is that it should not have a place in anybody's retirement plans. When you pay big money for the right to stay in a condo for a couple of weeks each year, all you're doing is paying rent in advance for a condo you must share with twenty-five other people. It no more belongs to you than does the hotel apartment you rent for a vacation. Vacations are one thing, retirement is another. On the other hand, if you buy a condominium or house and rent it out when you don't plan on using it, that's a different story. You control all fifty-two weeks a year, and should you desire, you can retire full-time to your condo. The key word is *control*.

We investigated one condo development in Puerto Vallarta, and we know of similar ones in Acapulco, Mazatlán, and other west coast locations. Understand that we're neither vouching for these condos nor encouraging anyone to invest, but the management rental plan sounded enticing. Prices of the condos we looked at ranged from $75,000 to $150,000 for two-bedroom units that were located on a desirable stretch of beach in a high-demand tourist area. For a percentage of the rent, a management team operates the participating units as a hotel, renting by the day or week to tourists. According to the sales force, the apartments rent for $75 per day in the low season and $125 a day during the high season. Management withholds the commission and deposits the balance of the rent money to your account.

On paper this sounds like a great idea, but developers have a way of making things sound a lot better than they are. So beware! It all hinges on the ability of management to keep the rentals full and to fulfill all their promises. Should the management have rental units, you can be sure your apartment will be rented only when there is an overflow. The bottom line here is be absolutely sure you know what you're doing when you buy this kind of condo, and *stay away* from time-shares.

apartment with a view can be found for as little as $500 a month through one of the many English-speaking real estate agencies, but you can usually find something on your own for much less. If you don't mind living a bit farther from the ocean, in an all-Mexican neighborhood, you can find an unfurnished apartment for as little as $300 a month. Of course you can pay much, much more for some of the gorgeous homes and villas that perch on oceanside cliffs or cling to the hillsides above the city.

For the ultimate in elegant living, visit the luxury development north of town, Nuevo Vallarta, one of the fanciest places we've encountered in Mexico. Some houses, set back on enormous landscaped plots, would cost several million dollars if they were in a similarly posh U.S. location. But then other homes cost no more than you'd expect to pay for a bungalow in San Marcos, Florida, or Santa Barbara, California. (Those places aren't cheap, either.) Nuevo Vallarta is a breathtaking place, but it's not something for a couple looking for an inexpensive retirement. For an alternative location across the bay from Puerto Vallarta, look at the discussion of Yelapa (see a description in the For the More Adventurous section).

SERVICES FOR FULL-TIMERS Many full-time American residents make their homes in Puerto Vallarta, but as in most tropical resorts, the expatriate population is somewhat impromptu. Many people stay for a few months, then either return home or move on to try some other Mexican location. We've seen estimates ranging from 2,000 to as high as 15,000 expatriates living in Puerto Vallarta. These estimates are difficult to verify. Because people come and go so frequently, it's difficult to distinguish between retirees and visitors who are on extended vacations. Suffice it to say there are many North Americans living here; you'll have no problem finding compatible neighbors.

Because of this large foreign population, two Puerto Vallarta hospitals cater to American and Canadian patients and maintain bilingual staffs. These are the Medassist Hospital and the CMQ Hospital. The Crita Movil Ambulance Service, with well-equipped vehicles, is on call twenty-four hours a day and reportedly has English-speaking drivers.

Several public service organizations are supported by the U.S.-Canadian community. One, which was brought to our attention recently, is the America-Mexico Foundation. To raise funds, this group collects donations and holds benefits and auctions of donated goods. One major goal of the foundation is to provide scholarships for Mexican children who strive for an education but are impeded because of family financial problems. A spokesperson said, "As long as the children maintain B averages or better and sustain good behavior, the foundation will help them obtain their educational goals." The program now has 200 children enrolled. Address: America-Mexico Foundation, APDO 515, Puerto Vallarta, Jalisco, Mexico 48300. They have a Web site at www.pvnet.com .mx/amf.

Another organization is the International Friendship Club (IFC), which was started in 1987 by a small group of U.S. and Canadian expatriates. Their role is organizing the international community to provide services and collect and distribute funds in response to the humanitarian and educational needs of the community. Activities of the IFC include assisting local schools, hospitals, retirement homes, day-care centers, and playgrounds. The IFC also participates in the community-wide toy distribution to children on holidays. Members started the Cleft Palate Project, which is known all over Latin America, and have helped many youngsters get the necessary operation to correct this birth defect.

Following the example of San Miguel de Allende, Ajijic, and Guadalajara, Puerto Vallarta expatriates have started a library. This project will undoubtedly become the social and cultural center of the foreign community as well as further improve public relations by reaching out to the Mexican community. Those of you looking for volunteer work might seriously consider becoming part of a library-project team. This is an excellent way to become a part of the community and meet new friends as well as to contribute to a worthwhile endeavor.

Puerto Vallarta also has an online Internet newspaper (www.pvmiror.com) that reflects the large number of English-speaking residents living there. The local news coverage is very comprehensive and covers local events not only in the city of Puerto Vallarta but also in surrounding communities where expatriates live, including Sayulita and "San Pancho" (described below).

SOUTH OF PUERTO VALLARTA Mismaloya is blossoming into a retirement community. A large hillside development is under way, with some homes tucked in forest settings and others with ocean views. The beach here became famous as the set for Richard Burton's movie *The Night of the Iguana,* but Mismaloya has undergone explosive development—perhaps too fast for its size.

NORTH OF PUERTO VALLARTA For some the attraction of Puerto Vallarta's shopping, social life, and health care is overshadowed by living in the atmosphere of a large resort city, with heavy traffic and throngs of tourists. The solution is found about a forty-five minute drive north to one of Mexico's most charming and desirable coastal landscapes. Small villages are scattered along beaches where forest and mountains meet the blue Pacific. Two preferred locations are the fishing villages of Sayulita (pop. 3,000) and San Francisco (pop. 2,000), known locally as "San Pancho." We looked at these locations years ago, recognizing a potential retiree boom. Already expatriates were "discovering" the area. Today, it's too late to describe these treasures as "undiscovered." Most desirable properties with good views of the bay have been bought, sold, and resold. Still they keep coming.

Lynne Forrette, of Walnut Creek, California, said, "When I first visited Puerto Vallarta in 1968, it looked just like Sayulita today, only a little bigger. After visiting Puerto Vallarta several more times, thinking of a place for early retirement, we decided it was too busy. We would not want to live there. When we first came across Sayulita, it looked like any ordinary Mexican town, and we weren't too impressed. But as the week progressed, quaintness and charm overrode the dust and muddy roads. Soon we fell into the 'Mexican Trance' of lolling around in a hammock, strolling on the beach, hiking the hills. We stopped and talked with expats who were working in their gardens. We actually made some friends that first week in Sayulita—and we returned and bought property!"

Sayulita is still a village, although no longer categorized as "small." There is no police station, post office, government offices, or hospital. (A hospital is located in nearby San Pancho.) You'll still see dogs and roosters wandering along the dirt side streets, yet the pressure of tourism is evident. You'll find thirty restaurants, an Internet cafe, a couple of video rental stores, and several real estate offices with signs in their windows showing that prices of homes in the $250,000 range are not uncommon. Sayulita has an interesting message board for English-speaking residents and visitors: www.sayulitalife.com/wwwboard.

MANZANILLO **REGION**

Manzanillo is one of Mexico's oldest cities. It was settled in 1522, shortly after Cortez overwhelmed the Aztecs at Tenotchtitlán (now Mexico City) during the Spanish conquest. Manzanillo became established as Mexico's major port on the west coast. From the beginning of Spain's occupation of Mexico, treasures from China and the Philippines passed through this calm bay. Located approximately 150 miles south of Puerto Vallarta (in the state of Colima), Manzanillo isn't exactly a tourist destination in the style of Mazatlán or Acapulco. Its main occupation is as a busy marine port and railway shipping terminal. Manzanillo's downtown is strictly commercial. Devoid of elegant restaurants and tourist shops, most of the city seems rather ordinary to us.

It seems unlikely that many foreign residents would choose to live in the city of Manzanillo; instead you'll find them along the coast north of the city. This is where the resorts, condos, and luxury residential communities draw tourists as well as retirees.

The number of foreigners here is small compared with the more successful resort towns along the Mexican Riviera. One reason may be that the beaches aren't as safe for swimming because of the undertow and riptides. It's no problem for experienced swimmers or surfers, but it does keep tourism down. This doesn't displease the expatriate community at all. The places where retirees make their homes are scattered along the beaches and slightly inland. The most impressive landmark hereabouts is a magnificent complex of whitewashed villas and bungalows known as Las Hadas, or "Home of the Fairies." The architecture captures the magic of a tale out of *The Arabian Nights*. One of the attractions here is the eighteen-hole Las Hadas Golf Course.

Manzanillo is clearly a magnet for sports fishermen, billing itself as "the sailfish capital of the world." (Seems like we've heard this claim in other Mexican resorts!) All in all the atmosphere here is more informal and relaxed than in Acapulco or Puerto Vallarta. Like most of the west coast, average monthly temperatures here are in the upper seventies and mid-eighties year-round. The rainy months from July through September bring some hot and steamy days. (Miami, in comparison, is hotter in summer, colder in winter, and far more difficult to escape from when the heat becomes uncomfortable.)

About 70 kilometers north of Manzanillo is one of the prettiest beach areas on the coast: the villages of La Manzanilla, Tenacatita, and Melaque. Strung along a horseshoe-shaped bay with pristine beaches, palms, and quiet residences, this has always been a favorite with the authors. Tenacatita and Melaque are the larger towns, with shopping and tourist facilities. La Manzanilla is a smaller village with about a thousand residents who subsist on fishing from the Pacific Ocean. These places, especially La Manzanilla, have changed very little over the years, seemingly suspended in the Mexican past. The number of expatriates living here has been on the increase lately, with at least a couple of families operating hotels, fishing tours, and other tourist-related businesses.

IXTAPA-**ZIHUATANEJO**

Driving six hours south of Manzanillo, on a fairly good highway, you'll traverse the Costa Grande (the Big Coast). This is where the state of Guerrero angles 200 miles southeast from the Rio Balsas toward Acapulco. You'll travel through some interesting country, places that were unavailable to motorists until a new highway pushed through here about a decade ago. The pavement passes through quaint villages and past rustic coconut plantations, farmhouses, and crops of copra drying along the road shoulders. If you're looking for "authentic" Mexico, this is where you might want to visit.

The most popular retirement location you'll encounter along the Costa Grande is Zihuatanejo, a little more than halfway between Manzanillo and Acapulco. Local residents affectionately refer to the town as "Zihua." The Costa Grande and Zihuatanejo aren't exactly newcomers to the tourist scene. Their gorgeous beaches and steep cliffs circled by forested hills in the background were attracting crowds long before the Spanish arrived. Legend has it that in the 1400s, a Tarascan Indian king built a royal bathing resort on Las Gatas Beach in Zihuatanejo Bay. However, until a paved highway from Acapulco was cut through the mountains in the 1960s, Zihua languished as a sleepy fishing village in isolated splendor. The town woke up abruptly when developers began constructing a luxury resort on the beach at Ixtapa, a few miles north of Zihuatanejo. Before long, Zihua was being "discovered" by tourists and expatriates.

In many ways Zihuatanejo is like the Acapulco of forty years ago. It's evolving from a sleepy little village into a town, but mercifully it hasn't quite turned the corner to become a city. Most residents hope that it never will. Zihuatanejo's town square, the Plaza de Armas, overlooks the main beach, Playa Municipal, just beyond the palm-lined pedestrian walkway, Paseo del Pescador. At least this part hasn't changed since Zihuatanejo was still a village. In the downtown area, shops and restaurants are within a few blocks' walking distance of the Plaza de Armas.

Our favorite beach here is Playa la Ropa, a crescent of white sand about a mile in length. The beach supposedly got its name, Playa la Ropa (the clothes beach), 200 years ago when clothing floated in from an offshore Chinese wreck. The beach is reached via the Paseo Costera, which passes some of the choice residential areas and offers great views of the nearly endless line of beaches around the bay.

Fortunately for those living in Zihuatanejo, the glamorous resort of nearby Ixtapa draws the glitzy tourist trade and crowds, thus keeping Zihuatanejo's prices within reason and its traffic flow relatively calm. Retiring here gives you the best of both worlds—quiet and affordable Zihuatanejo, with the glamour of Ixtapa just a few minutes away.

When bar-hopping in Zihuatanejo, you'll often find yacht captains and crews killing time between sailings. The harbor is popular with yachts cruising between California and Acapulco; the waterside bars never lack new faces. By the way, we always thought that retirement on a sailboat would be the ultimate. Many people do this, of course, and you'll find them in Mexican ports. However, the yachting people we've met report that getting to Mexico is a snap, but getting back north is tough because of currents and prevailing winds. The wealthy sail their boats south, then pay someone to make the slow trek back to California.

At times rentals are reportedly in short supply in Zihua because apartment and home building hasn't kept up with the increasing demand. Most newer construction is taking place away from the town center, especially on hills overlooking the bay. Small mountains ring the town, and the best building sites, with spectacular views of the bay, sit high on the slopes.

IXTAPA AND BEYOND About 15 miles away in Zihua's sister city of Ixtapa, ten beaches invite bathers, surfers, and strollers along a dozen miles of creamy, azure coastline. Ixtapa is a luxurious beach resort with the sophistication of Acapulco but on a smaller scale and with cleaner beaches. Playa de Palmar is the main beach; protective offshore shoals and rocks break some of the surf's energy, keeping the waves safe enough for swimming and body surfing.

Ixtapa's eighteen-hole, Robert Trent Jones–designed Campo de Golf is open to the public. The club has full facilities, including a pro shop, a swimming pool, tennis courts, and a restaurant. A second layout, the new eighteen-hole course at Marina Ixtapa, was rated by *Golf Digest* as one of the best in Mexico. Several Ixtapa hotels also have tennis courts available to the public.

Many condos going up here have time-share arrangements, and you know our opinion on that subject. Regular apartment buildings are available for rent, and an upscale housing development is under way. Therefore, Ixtapa is an alternative for those who prefer the luxury of a busy beach resort to the small-town environment of Zihuatanejo and who don't mind paying the price.

Continuing north along the coast on Highway 200 is the interesting village of Troncones. About 4.5 kilometers past the village of Buena Vista (32 kilometers north of the southern turnoff for Ixtapa), Troncones is to the left on a little-marked turnoff, then about 3 kilometers to the ocean. The area commonly referred to as "Troncones" is actually the 5 or more kilometers of beach from the village of Troncones to the village of La

Majahua to the north. Years ago this lovely beach area was set aside by the government for tourist development, along with Ixtapa. Playa Troncones snoozed for a couple of decades, while Ixtapa became a world-class resort. Now, however, the village area is undergoing rapid growth along with the best beach, Playa Manzanillo, nearer Majahua. Until two years ago many of the more desirable locations were part of an *ejido* and therefore not available for sale. Fortunately this delayed development for so long that there is little danger it will ever become a high-density tourist area like Ixtapa. Its future seems destined as basically residential, a good place for retirement or peaceful vacations. Residential development has blossomed along the beach at Playa Manzanillo, with many tasteful private homes, although there is also a small hotel and a few bed-and-breakfasts. Nearby Ixtapa serves as a place for golf and boutiques.

Recently prices have risen dramatically. One resident said, "When we bought our lot in 1996 (US$14,500), our friends thought we were crazy. There was no electricity, no telephone, no water delivery, no propane delivery—none of the essentials, except home beer delivery. (Honestly!) Eight years later, we now have all the above and more, including the prospect of DSL Internet coming soon. Of course, this has resulted in some changes. Lots are now selling in the US$140,000 to $200,000 range. Home construction is booming. Our little 1,000-square-foot home seems quaint now, alongside homes five times that size—and going up."

Troncones is still too small to have a formal retiree organization. The winter gringo community is probably about fifty, plus vacationers. One resident said, "The community is close-knit in the sense that pretty much everybody knows everybody. But it is an open community in the sense that it welcomes newcomers, since everybody here is a newcomer. The longest resident gringos have been here less than fifteen years."

ACAPULCO

Back in the 1950s Acapulco was one of the world's glamorous "jet-set" destinations. The epitome of tropical luxury, Acapulco became the play-ground of Hollywood and European celebrities. The beaches were incredible, so beautiful they seemed like movie settings of what tropical beaches should look like. Before the town grew into a city and crowded with tourists, it was common to see John Wayne, Hedy Lamar, Susan Hayward, and a gaggle of other famous personalities dining in restaurants, shopping in town, or playing in the surf. Nightlife rocked on into the early dawn, and frosted margaritas were served on the beach by tuxedoed waiters.

Years ago as an experiment in tourism development, the Mexican government launched an intense promotion of Acapulco as Mexico's top tourist destination. At that time it was the *only* upscale resort city in the entire country. Puerto Vallarta and Zihuatanejo were primitive villages isolated by mud roads, and Mazatlán was a grungy fishing port. Cancún and Huatulco hadn't been invented yet—they were still swamps and cane fields.

The experiment was a success. Hotels sprouted from nowhere. Apartments, condos, and luxury homes climbed the hillsides in search of the best views. Elegant multistory hotels and nightclubs lined the beaches like monuments to the gods of tourism. Restaurants and tourist facilities struggled to keep up with the affluent clientele. The winding two-lane road from Mexico City was replaced by a high-speed four-lane highway. Acapulco's population grew from approximately 25,000 to nearly two million inhabitants.

However, too much tourism success has a way of choking itself off. From the very beginning, Acapulco overbuilt. Competition between hotels and rental units became fierce, with price-cutting, bankruptcies, and unfinished buildings dotting the landscape. At that point the Mexican government decided to repeat the experiment elsewhere by promoting other Pacific beach towns: Puerto Vallarta, Mazatlán, and Hualtulco—as well as Caribbean locations such as Cancún and Cozumel. Acapulco stopped sponsoring ads directed at North American markets. The official emphasis shifted toward Mexican tourism, targeting middle- and working-class families from within Mexico. Direct international air service was curtailed; the city became neglected by foreign tourist agencies.

The result has been a bonanza for tourists and retirees who are looking for bargain accommodations. Hotels, apartments, and condos are forced to keep rents in line with the Mexican tourist's ability to pay. What once were luxury accommodations, available only to those who could pay top rates, are now priced within the pocketbook of all. Several of the more luxurious hotels have been converted into affordable condos and apartments. The bottom line is that among all of Mexico's resort locations, Acapulco offers the widest range of lower- to middle-priced housing in the country. You can find a hotel suite 2 blocks from the ocean going for as little as $45 a night. Acceptable rooms near the *zócalo* can be found for $35. Super-luxurious accommodations on Playa Condesa go for as little as $75 a night.

LIVING "UP THE HILL" Competitive rents apply to apartments and houses as well. It turns out that during Acapulco's heyday as a jet-set resort, it was stylish to build on the steep hillsides for terrific views. The higher up, the more expensive the layout. Today Mexican tourists arrive by bus and prefer accommodations near the beach rather than on a steep hill that requires an automobile. Consequently, hillside rents have been forced downward to attract tenants. For less money than in Guadalajara, San Miguel de Allende, or other popular retirement locations, you can rent a spacious two-bedroom apartment with a view of the bay for as little as $300 a month, including utilities. These places are often on the market at affordable prices. Of course you're not on the beach, so you'll need a car or you'll face a long climb uphill to go home. Immediately after the devaluation of 1994, several condo and apartment projects fell into bankruptcy, with units selling at giveaway prices. The market has recovered somewhat, but there still are bargains to be found.

For a time—while the government was concentrating on promoting other vacation destinations—the infrastructure of Acapulco suffered from neglect. Streets were beginning to look dirty, and some public buildings looked shabby. But after a hurricane devastated parts of downtown Acapulco in 1997, a vigorous effort, combined with a substantial amount of resources, was made to refurbish the city. They've done a great job, with everything looking as spiffy as it ever did.

As mentioned earlier in this book, with the appearance of enormous buying complexes like WalMart, K-Mart, and Gigante, shopping patterns have changed in Mexico. In this respect Acapulco was already far ahead. It had large supermarkets and malls long before the rest of the country did. Our favorite was a gourmet supermarket near Hornos Beach—a place where we could find luxury delicatessen treats as well as staples. We always came away burdened with packages. This trend continues, with the full spectrum of U.S.–style shopping.

Restaurants are divided into two classes. You'll find luxurious, exquisitely designed restaurants that cater to affluent tourists, as well as restaurants for ordinary residents. The basic difference, aside from the decor, is that tourist places charge the maximum and don't have to worry about serving top-quality meals (because tourists in a large resort like Acapulco visit only once). Family-owned and -operated establishments must serve excellent food, or they'll go out of business.

Servants are more expensive here than elsewhere and may not be as loyal. This is because of the competition for help among the hotels and tourist businesses. You may find a great cook, only to have him or her discovered by a hotel restaurant and recruited away. Most North Americans aren't used to having servants anyway, so this shouldn't be any barrier to living in Acapulco.

Acapulco's public transportation system is excellent; it's easy to get around on the many city buses plying the streets. Taxis are also plentiful. Although many of those living here insist that an automobile is totally unnecessary, this author believes that Acapulco is one place in Mexico where a car comes in handy. It is, after all, a large city, with beaches and facilities spread all over. And again, with a car you have the ability to go up into the hills and find the best bargains in quality housing.

The exact number of expatriates living in Acapulco has never been determined: suffice it to say there could be as many as 500. Several social and fraternal organizations serve this community, and they are great places to become known and make friends. Acapulco's American Legion Post 4 meets every second Thursday for breakfast at the Club de Yachts de Acapulco. Then there's the Friends of Acapulco club; it doesn't hold regularly scheduled meetings but does sponsor get-togethers and fundraisers throughout the year. This organization focuses on helping poor and needy children in Acapulco.

The bottom line: If you're looking for a place in the tropics, even if only for the winter months, don't overlook Acapulco, even though you may have heard from tourists that the prices are high. Don't be put off by the notion that Acapulco is a tourist town; if it weren't a gorgeous paradise, tourists wouldn't go there in the first place.

PUERTO ESCONDIDO

With the completion of a paved highway south from Acapulco, Mexico's southwestern corner, known as the Costa Chica, is now accessible. The highway passes through some fascinating places, many of which could make outstanding retirement spots for those who don't need English-speaking neighbors. In one area the inhabitants are descendants of black slaves who have lived in isolation here and have preserved some of their old customs from Africa. Another stretch of highway takes you through the only place in Mexico we know of where women still dress every day in pre-Columbian costume: beautifully woven skirts of cochineal-dyed material.

Back in the 1960s Puerto Escondido was "discovered" by the surfing and backpacking student set. Its beaches rank among the finest on Mexico's west coast, and it is known as one of the premier surfing spots in all of Mexico. People come here for the huge waves that come rolling in as high as a house, then curl over to form a tube in which surfers can defy death. The waves here give the term *high-rollers* a new meaning. If you're brave enough, you can bodysurf along the beach with the highest waves, but most people our age tend to go to the southern portion of the beach to catch gentler rollers.

We find Puerto Escondido to be one of the most beautiful and welcoming beach communities on Mexico's west coast. Thankfully the big developers and tourist promoters haven't yet discovered the place. Puerto Escondido has escaped the dramatic changes that over the past decade have altered the faces of less pretty beach areas.

The main street that follows the beach is lined with very pleasant and affordable small hotels and restaurants. While "PE" or "Puerto" (as residents call it) attracts its fair share of tourists, they rarely overcrowd the town. For a few months in winter, many longer-term visitors from the United States and Canada enjoy total relaxation in the sun. But for some reason Puerto keeps few year-round expatriate residents. According to locals, only about fifty North Americans live here more or less permanently—most of them work for or operate businesses. The majority of residents are semipermanent. Some migrate back and forth between Oaxaca and Puerto Escondido, as if they can't quite make up their minds. Because of the marvelous waves here, you'll usually find a contingent of aging surfers trying to recapture those glory days of the 1960s. When you used to say: "Don't trust anyone over thirty," it must be tough to be over sixty!

Surfers of all ages, backpackers, and conservative tourists all combine to lend a special air to PE. One woman I interviewed described Puerto Escondido as having a combination "Haight-Ashbury and Gilligan's Island" ambience.

Most construction in Escondido has been focused on tourism—hotels and time-share condos—so there aren't many apartments and houses for rent. However, just north of town several elegant subdivisions are being laid out near the Posada Real. The Zicatela Beach strip has developed, and a number of houses have been built along the main highway south of town. Again, most of these are for time-share, vacation, and second homes. Residents usually don't think of these areas as part of PE.

To sum up, Puerto Escondido could be a place to investigate for relocation in Mexico, particularly if you are into tropical beaches and monster waves. There are enough fellow North Americans to supply social needs, and developers haven't quite pushed prices out of reach or squelched the quality of life.

BAJA **CALIFORNIA**

Baja California—a place with a reputation for mystery and romance—is a long peninsula that juts south of the state of California for almost a thousand miles. Both sides of the peninsula are lined with almost unexplored beaches. Baja is a world all its own. A wonderland of desert scenery, the peninsula is famous for secluded beaches, lost Jesuit missions, rugged mountains, and deep canyons. Separated from the mainland by the blue, blue waters of the Sea of Cortez (also called the Gulf of California), the peninsula has been isolated so long that it has evolved its own flora and fauna, distinct from anywhere else in the world. Zoologists and botanists pilgrimage here to enjoy themselves.

Baja's economy, similarly isolated from the mainland, has also evolved its own characteristics. With only one highway and one railroad connecting the peninsula with Mexico's mainland, all goods and merchandise must travel over these slow routes or else arrive by ship. This increases prices to the consumer. Much merchandise comes by truck from the United States, which also makes things more expensive. Therefore, it

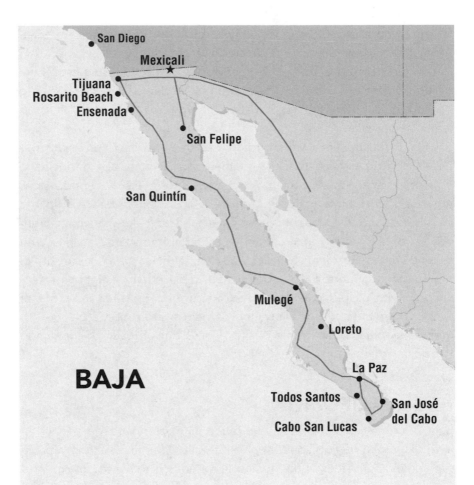

isn't surprising to find that prices and wages are higher here than on the mainland. Despite this, Baja California is still Mexico, and Baja Californians are the same friendly breed you find on the mainland.

For many people living in the western United States, Baja California is the only part of Mexico they know. This is particularly true of Californians. They fondly recall Baja's diverse attractions: long stretches of beach where enormous Pismo clams are there for the taking, moonlit grunion runs, camping, fishing, and soaking up sunshine while drinking Tecate beer flavored with lemon and salt.

Baja is more than simply a place for tourists to let off steam. For uncounted numbers of West Coast residents, Baja has become a retiree's playground. In recognition of this movement, and to encourage retirement, the Mexican government relaxed the rules for property ownership in Baja, which used to be the strictest in the country. Now the land ownership laws are the same as elsewhere in Mexico.

One reason so many Californians retire in Baja California is that it's so conveniently nearby. For people retiring from southern California, having a home in Ensenada means being able to drive north to visit the grandchildren any time they choose. It means neighbors and friends they used to work with are much more likely to drop in for a weekend visit than if they had a similar residence in Puerto Vallarta or Lake Chapala. Some expatriates who own homes in the Rosarito Beach area actually commute to jobs in San Diego and vicinity.

Because most northern Baja California retirement spots are within a few hours of the border, it's no problem to run on up to San Diego or Calexico for shopping. "You'd be surprised how often I find I need a special tool or some nuts and bolts that I can't find here," said one man who is building a home in Ensenada. "In two hours I'm in San Diego. I visit the hardware store while the wife stocks up on hard-to-find grocery items. Then it's back home after a milk shake–and-hamburger fix at some fast-food place."

Because it's convenient and close, Baja offers a way to sample Mexico's graciousness and economical living without investing excessive time or money in the adventure. Baja is an excellent place for preretirement planning—an opportunity to see whether you actually like Mexico and its people. Baja is a place from which to move into the Mexican culture gradually, yet be close to Hollywood and Disneyland, if that somehow makes you feel more secure. If you like what you see, you might decide to investigate a different type of Mexican retirement on the mainland.

As we pointed out earlier, because Baja is isolated from Mexico proper, you'll find prices and wages higher and Yankee influence more apparent. Yet for the novice these differences aren't so obvious, because prices and wages are so much less than back home that they seem downright ridiculous. In Ensenada, for example, a maid will come in to clean your house and do your laundry for $10.00 to $13.00 a day. On the mainland the wage might be $6.00 a day. (This would be a generous wage, because $4.00 a day is normally the minimum wage.) Maybe your Mexican neighbors can hire help a little cheaper, but anyone who would complain about paying these wages or even more (after all, you are comparatively wealthy) shouldn't even consider living in Mexico.

DRIVING **IN BAJA**

Baja roads are average for Mexico—which says a lot for Baja. Until a few years ago, most roads were dirt trails liberally spotted with 2-foot-deep potholes filled with powder dust. Some of us maintain that it was better that way, but then, others probably didn't have four-wheel-drive vehicles or enjoy riding around with red bandanas over their face to cut the dust.

Shirley Miller, in her travel article "Baja Alone" (from *Mexico West Newsletter*), describes her trip driving alone from California to the tip of Baja and back. She reports, "Well, all I can say is that a woman alone driving the Baja highway from Tijuana to Cabo San Lucas is safer than she would be driving into downtown Los Angeles. Nary a problem with gasoline, my trusty 1980 Chevy pickup, the roads, or anything else, for that matter." Her only caution is that one should bring plenty of cassette tapes or CDs, because reception on the car radio fades rapidly farther away from civilization.

FREE **ZONE**

The northern part of Baja is known as the *zona libre* (free zone). The government deliberately keeps this area quite relaxed as far as immigration and customs are concerned. You don't need tourist papers or an automobile permit to enter, but don't forget your automobile insurance. You can usually cross the border without even saying "hello" to Mexican customs and immigration officials. Don't misunderstand: This doesn't give you any rights of residency or any legal status at all. By law your stay is limited to seventy-two hours, although the law is seldom enforced—unless you're a troublemaker. Because there is no way to prove when a tourist actually crossed the border, many Californians spend days, weeks, even months at their weekend getaways.

By no means are we encouraging you to break Mexican immigration laws by staying longer than the seventy-two-hour limit—we're merely reporting on the present practices. If you plan on staying for a while, we recommend that you follow the entirely reasonable rules of the Mexican government. There are several ways to do this, all covered in the Your Legal Status section. It used to be that getting a tourist visa was simple; you just asked for your card and it was yours. The rules on tourist visas have been undergoing a series of changes lately. They are explained in detail in the Living with Mexican Laws chapter, but briefly the present rule is: after receiving your tourist card at the border, you must validate it at a local bank by paying a fee of approximately $20, good for up to 180 days. The fee can vary, depending on the rules in force at the time.

Gringo investment in real estate in the *zona libre* is impressive. Everywhere you turn, particularly along the beaches, you'll find single homes, condos, and luxury gated developments. But we encourage you to check with a locally recommended lawyer before laying out money for that oceanfront Baja property. Several scandals and horror stories have muddied the water here, with people buying homes from sellers who didn't own the properties.

THE MEDITERRANEAN **COAST**

The long string of beach communities stretching some 70 miles between Rosarito Beach, Ensenada, and Punta Banda is probably the fastest-growing retirement region in Mexico. Since residency restrictions have been loosened with multiple-entry FM-3 residency and property owner-ship liberalized, a flood of gringos have taken advantage of the close-to–San Diego locations. Not all are retired, either. Some regularly commute to jobs or businesses in the San Diego area; others work for U.S. compa-nies' facilities in Baja California. The recent addition of a "commuter lane" across the border makes a commuting trip even easier. New home construction is at an all-time high. At least 25,000 North Americans (pos-sibly a lot more) have homes here, either weekend places or permanent residences.

When asked why they chose this region for residence, all those inter-viewed listed weather as a major consideration. "It has a balmy Mediterranean kind of climate," points out one retiree. "It rarely gets over eighty degrees and almost never below fifty degrees at night. We have a San Diego climate with a Mexican environment." Another resident said, "I live in the most expensive neighborhood in Ensenada, yet I don't have air-conditioning, nor do I know anyone who does." Few houses have heating systems, either, because the ocean keeps winter weather from dropping to extremes. For all but the most luxurious homes, an electric heater or a fireplace suffices for most of the year, although the coldest January days can be frosty. Continual breezes from the cool Pacific Ocean moderate temperatures along the coast, but a few miles inland, temperatures are anything but "Mediterranean." (See for yourself on the temperature chart.)

WEATHER IN THE BAJA CALIFORNIA/ROSARITO BEACH/ ENSENADA AREA

| | In degrees Fahrenheit | | | | | | | |
	Jan.	Mar.	Apr.	May	July	Aug.	Oct.	Dec.
Daily Highs	66	68	70	72	75	77	75	66
Daily Lows	48	50	55	57	63	66	57	50

ROSARITO BEACH Here in the *zona libre*, just a few miles from the California border, Rosarito Beach is a very popular place for retirement, second homes, and vacation retreats. A four-lane highway takes you back to convenient shopping on the U.S. side of the border in short order. Rosarito Beach has a population of more than 80,000, with estimates of 5,000 or more North Americans, mostly Californians, living here.

The town abounds with small ranch-style homes, crowded together and landscaped like suburban neighborhoods across the border—but with a taco flavor. Although many sections of town are typical Baja-grungy, you'll also find several upscale, gated communities reminiscent of southern California developments. Folks who live here claim that the beach is one of the finest in Baja.

The retirees here have formed a club called the United Society of Baja California, complete with a monthly newspaper filled with local news and listings of rentals and property available in the Rosarito Beach area. This place is for those who need to be within easy driving distance of San Diego. It's Mexico, of course, but less Mexico-like than the rest of Baja.

As you travel farther south, you'll encounter numerous attractive gringo communities perched along the ocean cliffs, San Antonio Shores being one of the largest. These are mostly gated or restricted access developments and almost exclusively inhabited by gringos. Most homes are used as weekend getaways, but many are lived in full time. The architecture tends toward tasteful Old Spanish homes, with red tile roofs and adobe-like walls. Along with the upscale communities between Rosarito and Ensenada, you'll find a few areas distinguished by cheap, slapjack construction, more on the order of fishing camps. In fact, that's exactly what some places are: fishing camps. The better developments have security guards and limited access to outsiders.

ENSENADA Ensenada is located a little more than one hour south of Tijuana by four-lane divided toll highway. Duty-free shopping, very low prescription drug prices, nice beaches nearby, and friendly people make Ensenada and surrounding communities very popular for retirement and weekend homes. In Spanish the word *ensenada* means bay, or cove. The cove was discovered in 1542 by Sebastián Vizcaíno, who was so impressed with its beauty that he named it Ensenada de Todos los Santos (All Saints' Bay). Over the years it has grown from a sleepy fishing village to a bustling city of more than 300,000 inhabitants, and it likes to call itself Cenicienta del Pacifico (Cinderella of the Pacific). Fishing and tourism are still big industries, but the momentum of industry and shipping business has grown impressively. Ensenada's ship harbor is the third largest seaport in Baja. Education is another big source of jobs in Ensenada; the city has campuses of the University of Baja California, the National University of Mexico's Institute of Astronomy and Physics, a private medical school, and several private research centers.

Although Ensenada gets plenty of tourists, it's basically a genuine Mexican city. You'll find all the services you would expect from a city, from shopping malls to excellent hospitals and fine restaurants. A few gringos live in the city proper, but the majority live in one of the communities on the northern and southern beaches. Ensenada is their commercial center, with residences in a wide variety of locations, from elegant gated communities to ramshackle fishing camps. Many elegant homes are perched on hills overlooking the ocean, some on cliffs overlooking the surf below.

The actual number of gringos living here is difficult to ascertain—so many are continually coming and going. But there's no question that several thousand *norteamericanos* permanently make their homes near Ensenada, and that thousands more are part-time residents. Ensenada, by the way, has three language schools where you can immerse yourself in Spanish. This may be the nearest place to the border where you can get total immersion in Spanish learning, small classes, a native Spanish teacher, and living quarters with a non–English-speaking family.

Ensenada has several motels with small apartment units that rent by the month. Staying in one of these is an excellent way to try out the area and see whether this might be your dream retirement place. The town itself is full of house rentals at rock-bottom prices (provided you don't insist on having English-speaking neighbors). One man we interviewed, a widower from Tacoma, told of his living in a working-class neighborhood, paying an embarrassingly low rent, saying that his neighbors are very friendly and keep an eye on his house while he is away. (We didn't check the neighborhood, so we can't guarantee that his flowery descriptions are accurate.)

Living expenses in Ensenada are somewhat higher than on the mainland, but this is to be expected anywhere in Baja California. The region is isolated from the rest of Mexico, and much of the economy is connected to California. Local residents complain that utilities are constantly on the increase and that telephone service is substandard. Of course, these complaints can be heard all over Mexico.

PUNTA BANDA AND LA BUFADORA About 13 miles south of Ensenada, along the shore and at the end of Bahía Todos Santos, are several small retirement communities. The main ones are Punta Banda and La Bufadora, although the entire area past Ejido Cantu is usually referred to as Punta Banda. The name La Bufadora refers to an interesting "blowhole" in an oceanside cliff, where impressive spouts of water are created by the pounding waves.

Punta Banda started out as a collection of the most rustic and innovative homes you can imagine. Early residents began living in travel trailers or motor homes, which evolved into permanent structures in an interesting way. Typically a residence began with something like a 20-foot travel trailer. The first year the owners would lay out a patio and put up a picket fence to spiffy things up. Because a 20-footer is somewhat cramped for living space, the next year they built on a living room so that they could spread out a little, and perhaps added a storage room. Then, as the grandkids started coming to visit, they added on a bedroom or two. By this time the old travel trailer was beginning to fall apart, so they pulled it out and replaced it with a kitchen. In its final stage the compound rambles all over the place and has no relationship to the original conception of an RV lot. Today many conventional—and sometimes elaborate—homes have been added to the housing selections.

Punta Banda and La Bufadora began rather modestly a couple of decades ago, but today you'll find plenty of services, including restaurants, a large building supply store, small grocery stores, a fresh fruit/vegetable stand, and even an insurance agent and a post office! Recently an arts and crafts store opened, displaying the work of local craftsmen and offering supplies for "do-it-yourselfers."

The total number of residents in Punta Banda and La Bufadora is approximately 1,000 permanent gringo residents, 1,000 Mexican residents, and another 2,000 or more temporary gringo residents. They've developed an unusually active social structure. Among the most important clubs is one called Sociedad de Amigos de Punta Banda, which has several hundred members. They've also organized a volunteer fire department. Among the several civic and social clubs, there's an active local theater group that gives performances at the Gertrude Perlman Theater, an ad hoc theater in nearby La Jolla Camp (on the road to La Bufadora).

Of course we caution everyone to be very careful about purchasing leases in the restricted maritime zone, but extra prudence is due here. The problem began with certain leases granted to several gringos on *ejido* land. At the time this was illegal, but the government took action to make it okay. Then thirty years later—after some really nice homes had been built—the Mexican Supreme Court ruled that it was illegal after all and that the land belonged to the original owners who had it before the land was made into *ejidos*. To date the government has been quite reluctant to enforce this ruling, and negotiations with the U.S. government are under way. Our understanding is that the problem is confined to a place called Punta Estero, about 3 miles from Punta Banda. But we've cautioned over and over: Beware of *ejido* lands!

This problem has produced much negative publicity, leaves many land owners feeling nervous, and has had an effect on tourism in the region. Everyone hopes that it will be resolved soon.

A few miles south of Punta Banda the *zona libre* ends. From here onward you need tourist papers. (Be sure you get your papers stamped here, because the next place to do it is in La Paz.) This is where the real Baja starts, according to four-wheel-drive enthusiasts and true desert lovers. Here rolling hills and rugged clifflike mountains are sparsely covered with strange plants, like the majestic cardon cactus (similar to the saguaro cactus on the mainland), squat barrel cactus, and spiked plants of all types. This is the only place on earth where you'll see the weird-looking cirio trees—commonly called bojuum trees—which grow like upside-down carrots, or thick-trunked elephant trees, which bleed a blood-colored sap when punctured with a knife. Smoke trees, salt pines, and cacti of all descriptions add to the inventory of desert wonders. Several small communities, with occasional North Americans in residence, string along the paved highway. Some interesting places, like the wine-growing valleys around Santo Tomas and San Vincente, might be suitable for gringos who can get by without speaking English every day.

SAN **FELIPE**

On the Sea of Cortez side of the peninsula (but still in the *zona libre* part of Baja), the town of San Felipe has mushroomed in just a few years from a small fishing village into a major center for vacationers and retirees. The attraction here is miles of sandy beaches washed with warm gulf waters—a scenic desert setting with a mysterious panorama of the towering peaks of the Sierra San Pedro Martir in the distance.

San Felipe has always been a favorite with RV retirees and snowbirds, those who customarily winter in Tucson or Yuma. They discovered that by driving 120 miles south of the border on a good paved road, they can enjoy a pleasant winter retirement on Mexico's Sea of Cortez. RVers found it a great place to wake up in the morning and look out over the sea, shimmering and blue-green, with fishing and shrimp boats criss-crossing in the early haze.

Fishing, by the way, is why many journey to San Felipe in the first place. It's fabulous, with huge sea bass and enormous red snappers elbowing each other aside to gobble up your bait. And San Felipe is conveniently located close to the California border. Family and friends can visit for the weekend without a major transportation problem. The present two-lane road is currently being widened into four lanes.

The town has changed tremendously over the past thirty years, when we first started spending winter months in the beachside RV parks. The sand and dirt streets are now paved, and the long main street is a bustling commercial artery that parallels the beach, loaded with good restaurants and thriving businesses. San Felipe boasts several banks and supermarkets that are expanding rapidly to meet the demands of the growing retirement population. This is no longer the exclusive domain of the home-on-wheels crowd and weekend fishermen. Conventional housing and year-round retirement living are taking over.

San Felipe is undergoing a construction boom. Retirement residences are popping up everywhere, with housing styles ranging from fish-camp rustic to Mediterranean deluxe. Although many North Americans own property in town, most lease or build homes away from San Felipe's center, on individual beach- or ocean-view lots or in one of the many tasteful developments. Rentals are not plentiful, but real estate people in town can often find something for you.

Between 20,000 and 22,000 Mexican citizens live here today, joined by an additional 7,000 Americans and Canadians who have either part- or full-time living arrangements during the cooler months. Some of the more heat-proof northerners (about 700 of them) stick it out all year, but most flee north for the summer months. Summers here, unlike those on the Baja peninsula's Pacific side, are fierce. Temperatures often top 110 degrees Fahrenheit. At that level you needn't mention low humidity; it's just plain hot!

To be fair we must admit that summer in San Felipe is only a little warmer than that in Phoenix or Las Vegas. The pleasant fall, winter, and spring make up for cruel summers by providing gloriously sunny days, perfect for enjoying the desert-sea environment. You can be pretty sure it won't rain on your picnic here; sometimes a year or two can go by without a drop. But when it does rain, as anywhere in Baja, the desert suddenly bursts into a symphony of lush green and brilliant flowers. This spectacle is an emotional experience that makes waiting worthwhile.

The ambience here is Mexico–Baja California, but because of the high numbers of North Americans in residence or visiting, most folks aren't exposed to Mexican culture to any extent unless they choose to get involved with natives. Almost all your neighbors will be from the United States or Canada. Many prefer it this way. One retired lady said, "I didn't come here to learn a new language or study a new culture. I simply want to kick back and enjoy my winter retirement." However, those who care to will find every opportunity to practice Spanish and make Mexican friends.

Kay and Bill Gabbard live year-round in a San Felipe development called Club de Pesca (a combination of houses and RVs fronting on the beach). Bill says, "One of the things I like about living here is that it is family oriented. It's great fun to watch kids playing as they explore the beach and tide pools. Personally, I would not want to live in a place where kids are excluded, nor would I want to be in a self-contained American community."

Labor costs are higher here than in Ensenada because of the booming economy. Still, by stateside measures, wages are very low. Kay Gabbard says: "We do not have a lot of property around our house, so we just have a man come in twice a week to sweep, rake, clean up, and water the plants. I pay him $20 per month. Of course, he works at our development, so some of this is part of his job, and he does it during work hours. We have a lady come in one morning a week. She cleans the patio, carport, and house and charges $15 for a little over two hours of work. This seems a little high, but she does a good job and can be trusted when we are not at home. Local women who do housework like that can actually make much more than their husbands." For folks who don't want to hire their own housekeepers, a housecleaning service has recently opened.

As in most expatriate communities, volunteer organizations are the centerpiece of social activity. Cocktail parties, luncheons, and breakfasts are all excuses to get together and plan cooperative action and make new friends in the process. This is a great way to become acquainted with the community while undertaking worthwhile projects.

One of the most active groups is Las Amigas, an organization of Mexican, American, and Canadian women who help local schools improve the quality of education. They also provide needy families with clothing and food. Fund-raising events turn out to be fun events for the entire community; Las Amigas sponsors entertainment such as casino nights, dances, chili cook-offs, dinner theater melodrama, and parties celebrating everything from St. Patrick's Day to Halloween. Several Las Amigas–sponsored students are currently attending universities, pursuing degrees in architecture, education, medicine, and nuclear physics.

Another social group is the San Felipe Players, a group of actors, writers, set builders, and lovers of live theater. They enjoy bringing the magic of the stage to San Felipe. And there's the San Felipe Association of Retired Persons, an informal, apolitical, nonprofit organization open to all San Felipe residents and visitors. Volunteer projects aren't limited to social organizations. Kay Gabbard's pet project is the San Felipe Book Buddies, an outreach project dedicated to getting quality picture books and reading materials to the town's schoolkids. Classrooms have government-supplied textbooks but no children's literature in Spanish. The Book Buddies Web site is www.inet-toolbox.com/bookbuddies.

To sum it up, living in San Felipe makes for a different kind of Mexican retirement, one that is basically part-time and an alternative to the usual Padre Island, Brownsville-McAllen, or Lake Havasu kind of winter escape.

BAJA **CALIFORNIA SUR**

The peninsula is broken into two political entities, north and south, with the territory of Baja California Sur only recently elevated to statehood. The first time John Howells visited Baja California Sur was in 1963, on a four-wheel-drive camping adventure. In those days driving the unpaved trails of Baja was a true safari, with many hard days of bouncing through clouds of dust and climbing rocky ledges from the top to bottom of the peninsula. Baja fans formed a sort of cult in those days, with adventurers who actually made it all the way to La Paz or Cabo San Lucas being awarded the highest honors. During the journey John reports asking himself many times, "Why am I doing this?" His wife asked the same question, although in a much more intense manner. An overnight ferry from La Paz to the mainland avoided a return trip and probably saved a marriage.

Today a fairly good asphalt highway links the northern and southern parts of Baja; driving is a snap. A long expanse of almost uninhabited country separates the population centers of the north from the south. The drive is long, but worth it; it's liberally endowed with spectacular and unforgettable scenery. Scattered along the way are some tiny settlements, an occasional town, and always-friendly, helpful people. Sometimes residents seem quite shy, but if you practice your Spanish with them, you'll find they warm up very quickly.

The people in the lower parts of Baja interact with Americans differently than do Mexicans who live nearer the border, and for good reason. Here they see a different type of American tourist. Those "ugly Americans" in search of boisterous weekends, gaudy souvenirs, cheap thrills, and hell-raising usually don't stray very far from Tijuana or Mexicali. Tourists who bother to travel this far are different; they obviously appreciate Mexico and the fascinating Baja scenery, or they wouldn't be here. The local people sense this, and they treat you accordingly. They haven't met the other kind of gringos.

As in other parts of Mexico, you'll see the Green Angels (Angeles Verdes) as they patrol for motorists in trouble. At last report, the Green Angels' funding has been reduced somewhat, but the workers try to cover their routes at least once every day. They carry a truckload of spare parts and gasoline. The drivers are excellent mechanics and speak some English, and the services are free (except for parts and gasoline, all available at cost). The trucks are all equipped with two-way radios, so they can be reached either by CB or by calling the hotline number: 01–800–903–9200.

Incidentally, along this stretch of highway are some of the most innovative automobile mechanics in the world. Just because there are few or no parts for repairs doesn't stop them. They perform miracles by recycling parts from old hulks, reworking them, and fitting them into automobiles that aren't even closely related. Still, don't let this lull you into venturing into the open country of Baja without a vehicle in good repair, and don't forget to keep an eye on the gasoline gauge.

The highway is paved and, although pockmarked in places, is in fairly good shape. Signs posted along the way proclaim that the highway was not intended to be a "high-speed" highway and caution you to drive carefully. Good advice. Many stretches have no shoulders, so wide vehicles, such as RVs and travel trailers, should use special caution. At times every other vehicle seems to be an RV. Fortunately traffic along the highway is usually light and relatively tension free.

It isn't until you get as far south as La Paz that you begin to encounter North Americans in any considerable number. From here to the tip of the Baja Peninsula, the weather undergoes a subtle change. The cool water of the Pacific Ocean pushes its way into the Sea of Cortez, moderating the temperature a bit. Summers are tolerable from La Paz south to Los

Cabos, at land's end, and expatriates aren't forced to evacuate every May. When it rains here, it rains in summer rather than in winter, as is the case up north. Therefore year-round living is feasible.

Make no mistake—this is still desert country. Rainfall is scanty, with as long as two years between storms. Then it comes in torrential downpours that turn the arroyos into raging rivers. By the way, be very careful when driving in one of the infrequent rain storms—*anywhere* in Baja. Slight dips in the road can quickly become deep, swirling currents of water. It's best to wait for someone else to splash through before trying to ford what looks like a shallow rush of water crossing the highway. Okay, so it only comes halfway up on the ducks—wait anyway.

LA PAZ: THE PEARL OF BAJA When early Spanish explorers discovered the sheltered bay of La Paz off the Sea of Cortez in the mid-1500s, they also discovered an astonishing wealth of pearl oysters in the warm sea waters. This led to the founding of the town of La Paz. Centuries of harvesting the valuable crop have eliminated pearls as an industry, although today an occasional oyster will yield a small treasure.

Over the years La Paz has grown to be the largest city in Baja California Sur, with close to 200,000 inhabitants. An unusually clean city with all services and enjoyable winter temperatures, it's not surprising that La Paz attracts a large number of North American residents. Approximately 1,500 of them choose to live here year-round, and at least double that number come here on a seasonal basis. Because the bay is so well protected, hundreds of yachts are always in attendance, with an estimated 400 yacht owners living full-time on their vessels. Several well-kept trailer parks draw seasonal visitors. Some RV enthusiasts claim this is absolutely the best place in Baja for winter retirement.

Although tourism and retirement are important to the economy, they have a relatively small impact on the overall scheme of things. La Paz gives you the feeling of a substantial, prosperous Mexican city—without the helter-skelter of some Baja locations. It's prosperous and bustling, with tourism and retirement incidental to everyday commerce. La Paz has an attractive downtown, nice shopping centers, and excellent non-tourist restaurants scattered throughout the city. The inviting *Malecón,* or walkway, runs alongside the broad street that curves about the picturesque bay. It's popular with early-morning joggers as well as strollers throughout the day and evening. Most tourist shops, restaurants, and tour agencies are found along a 6-block stretch of the *Malecón*.

The harbor and marina form the focal point of the city for retirees. A good place to meet fellow expatriates is by the marina at the Dock Cafe, where gringos convene for informal breakfasts every morning and for dinner and music in the evening. Throughout the winter a seagoing-oriented group, the Club Cruceros, meets on the third Tuesday of each month at Los Arcos Hotel. Meetings are open to everyone (whether you own a yacht or not), and the club maintains a trading library at its clubhouse at Marina La Paz. The clubhouse hosts informal social gatherings, where friends meet and discuss current events, lie about the fish they almost caught, and debate the best places to find lobsters.

La Paz lives up to its name (the word paz means "peace") in that it is quiet and safe. During the authors' last visit, we looked at the local newspaper's "police page" to see what kinds of crimes were being reported. Two stories made large headlines. One reported that two youths had been arrested for drinking and driving at excessive speeds. The other major story told of another youth who ran through a red light and crashed into another automobile. One driver was slightly injured. Would these crimes be reported in your local newspaper? That's not to say that La Paz doesn't suffer the petty theft normal in other Mexican retirement locations, but local residents insist that violent offenses are rare and they feel personal safety is exceptionally high.

Several agreeable neighborhoods in the town of La Paz are quite suitable for retirement. Most are in mixed Mexican–North American areas rather than gringo enclaves. Housing costs can range from very affordable to exorbitant, all in the same neighborhood. The bulk of the expatriates seem to gravitate toward neighborhoods on the southern edge of La Paz, where well-to-do Mexican families and gringos cluster. There don't seem to be many, if any, exclusive enclaves of foreign residents who keep to themselves. Most residents prefer to be integrated throughout the city, enjoying the cultural experience of having Spanish-speaking neighbors.

The local expatriate community is well regarded by its neighbors because of its participation in local affairs. With the Club Cruceros leading the way, the community holds fund-raising events to collect money for children in need of medical and other help. Every December they host a bazaar, with an auction, food stands, and entertainment. The proceeds are used for Christmas gifts and school supplies for the kids.

LOS CABOS One of the biggest explosions of development and population increase is under way on the lower end of the peninsula, an area known as Los Cabos. Consisting of the area between Cabo San Lucas and San José del Cabo—once widely separated, now almost twin cities—the Los Cabos area is sprouting hotels, condos, and housing developments. Some folks come because of Los Cabos's classic desert scenery and balmy climate, but most have designs on the game fish, so abundant just off the coast. Others love the area's four excellent golf courses. Sometimes dubbed the Pebble Beach of Baja, Cabo San Lucas boasts two championship courses, and San José del Cabo claims two famous courses.

An international airport sits halfway between the towns, making it convenient for friends and family to visit those ensconced in their retirement homes. Frequent flights from Los Angeles, San Francisco, Portland, Vancouver, and other West Coast cities make getting here a snap (only three hours from San Francisco), so residents here can expect frequent visitors. Every flight seems to carry a full load of enthusiastic tourists looking forward to fishing, surfing, and just plain loafing in the sunshine. Because of the dry desert climate, there is abundant sunshine. The total rainfall is less than 5 inches a year. Most of it falls in August and September, making the landscape unexpectedly green at that time of year.

Because of its popularity, housing prices in the Cabos area can be shocking. We've seen condos that would barely fetch $100,000 in Mazatlán, selling for more than $200,000. Most houses on the beach, or with good ocean views, command prices that would be expensive even in California or Florida. Prices go up daily, and North Americans seem to be buying condos and houses as fast as the Mexicans can build them. So much construction is going on that skilled workers have to be imported from the mainland to keep up with the demand. To give you an idea of how big the market is, the Mexican immigration offices here released the figure of 4,500 foreigners living full-time or most of the time in the Los Cabos area.

Why the boom? We really don't understand it at all. Although Baja is wonderful, after a while you may get homesick for some green plants, forests, and wildflowers, instead of sand and cactus. (And the parts of Baja that we like best are the rustic, undeveloped places where gringos are still novelties.) Yet when interviewed, most North American residents insist this is the best place in all of Mexico to retire. "I wouldn't even consider living on the mainland," is the typical reply. "We love Baja, and we wouldn't care if it costs *more* to live here than it does back home!" They point to the astonishingly blue ocean, the rugged cliffs with surf frothing against the rocky shore, and the crystal-clear skies. "Where else in the world could I have a view like this from my living room?" To quote a cliché, it's all in the eye of the beholder.

This economic boom has had an effect upon the cultural atmosphere of Baja. With higher prices and practically a dollar economy, wages have naturally risen for the natives, and employment is at an all-time high. Construction workers earn from $150 to $300 a month, as opposed to $90 or less on the mainland. However, even though workers earn big money for Mexico, prices are so high in tourist facilities that Mexicans seldom patronize them. Nice restaurants and bars are exclusively gringo. After all, a worker making $12.00 a day can't really afford to hoist many $2.00 beers with the gringos. Here, there are *three* economic realities—one for tourists, one for gringo residents, and one for Mexicans.

SAN JOSÉ DEL CABO In our first edition we hinted that San José del Cabo was Baja's "well-kept secret." Today it's undergoing an even more vigorous boom than Cabo San Lucas. Some secret! About 30 miles north of Cabo San Lucas, San José del Cabo was our favorite town in all of the peninsula; at that time, it was totally unspoiled, like something out of a Hollywood movie set. In an early edition we described San José del Cabo as "an old town with sparkling white houses, dressed in flowers, neat as an old maid's bedroom."

Not surprisingly San José del Cabo was "discovered" (we hope not because of our book), and retirees began moving in. They bought empty buildings, some centuries old, converted them into plush homes, then waited breathlessly for new condo developments to become available. Restaurants opened on side streets, competing with one another to bring in gringo customers.

Although the town has tripled in size since we reported on it in the original version of *Choose Mexico,* this growth was mostly outward. The center of town has fortunately escaped "renewal" and modernization. It looks pretty much as it must have a century and a half ago, with the landscaped squares and grassy parks intact and the old-fashioned flavor of Mexico.

The town's main street is a landscaped boulevard with restored nineteenth-century buildings housing boutiques, restaurants, and shops. The boulevard provides a promenade for tourists and residents as they enjoy the peace and quiet of San José del Cabo. The central square is a place where folks gather in the evening to chat and make new friends—as is traditional in old-fashioned Mexican towns—instead of seeking out discos as they might in Cabo San Lucas. Plans are afoot to close the main thoroughfare to motor traffic, thus turning it into a pedestrian mall and an even more user-friendly place. Yet for those who crave nightlife, loud music, and overpriced drinks, Cabo San Lucas is only half an hour's drive away.

The expatriate population is substantial, probably close to 2,000, and retirees have considerable economic influence over the town. Restaurants compete for their business and turn out some surprisingly good menus. Local stores stock everything a foreigner might desire.

The southern edge of town is where the most development has taken place, although a nice section known as Chamizal sits above the town and is still expanding. If the boom continues, numerous condominium complexes and individual homes threaten to spread all the way to Cabo San Lucas. The builders deserve credit for the tasteful designs, with Spanish colonial styles prevalent.

Time-share developments are fewer here than in the Cabo San Lucas area, with most new construction either condos or private homes. We have friends here who own both condos and private homes, and they seem to have no problem renting them out when they are back in the States. Of course in the summer months, when it really becomes hot here, renters are scarce, but not totally absent.

The cost of living here is, like most of Baja California, higher than average. On the other hand, most of San José del Cabo's residents and visitors are affluent enough that higher costs are not relevant. The upscale housing in the area attests to this. This is not to say that there aren't some economically priced neighborhoods—and in fact some gringos prefer to live in some of the small villages not far from the town center, where rents are almost gifts.

CABO SAN LUCAS The name *Cabo San Lucas* seems to have a magical quality for many people, and they're convinced that "Cabo" is the ultimate place in all of Baja California. We have never understood its fascination for many North Americans. To us Cabo San Lucas is a large, sprawling place, without a real "downtown" section—unless you count a concentration of souvenir shops and incredibly loud gringo bars. (For some reason gringo tourists feel an obligation, when patronizing Cabo bars, to pour tequila down their gullets, shout at the top of their voices, and do all the other things that they can't do back home without going to jail.)

This is a new town, with few buildings more than thirty years old, so it isn't surprising that Cabo doesn't maintain the traditional Spanish-Mexican architecture found in San José del Cabo. Most construction doesn't bother pretending to be anything other than new, utilitarian, and no-nonsense.

Nevertheless, countless North Americans have fallen in love with Cabo and seem to be standing in line to buy the next new house or condo. Tourists fly down from everywhere in the United States and Canada for the incredible sailfish and marlin sportfishing and are happy to pay $900 a week for a one-bedroom apartment that would cost $900 for *two months* on the mainland. Several developments offer luxury homes and condos starting at $250,000. That's for a small one—who knows how much for a "big" one? We've heard rumors that a million bucks isn't out of range. Of course there are affordable homes and condos with great views of the ocean. But *affordable* is a relative term here. What you'd pay for a modest little home would buy something breathtaking on Mexico's mainland.

Despite our puzzlement as to why people are fighting to buy property here, the fact is that many of those who love Baja wouldn't consider living anywhere else. There's something special about the desert that attracts some people but repels others. Of course the fishing there is marvelous, and for many Baja residents, that is reason enough to love Baja.

You needn't live in Cabo San Lucas or San José del Cabo to enjoy the best of this southernmost part of Baja. Take a look at our section on retirement sites for the more adventurous to learn about small towns, villages, and beach hangouts in the Los Cabos area.

At the risk of making enemies of some Baja lovers, we have to question the inflated prices in the lower tip of the peninsula. Is it worth the extra investment to live in Baja Sur? Obviously the answer to the question by many who live in Cabo San Lucas and its environs is a resounding "yes." Indeed there's a sense of romance, beauty, and mystery about the Baja desert that isn't to be found elsewhere. There's a certain crispness in the dry air and the breezes off the sea that makes it a special place. The way nature balances life and environment with delicate perfection reveals some deeply miraculous secrets of the universe. Again, the only answer seems to be found within yourself. You have to go and "try it before you buy it."

About 40 miles north of Cabo San Lucas, the small town of Todos Santos is in the process of becoming a much bigger town. The boom is being fueled largely by foreigners buying up old homes and constructing new ones. Until the paved highway reached Todos Santos back in 1986, the town was isolated from the rest of Baja. A highly prosperous sugar cane center back in the nineteenth century, Todos Santos was abandoned when the market suddenly collapsed, making it a virtual ghost town. The small town center contains many fascinating old buildings that have been renovated for use as stores, galleries, and restaurants. This provides a quiet atmosphere of historic old Mexico, contrasting sharply with Cabo San Lucas's modern glitter and hustle. The nearby tall smokestack of an old sugar mill stands as a reminder of Todos Santos's historic past.

With an abundant water supply flowing underground from a nearby mountain range, Todos Santos is in an unusual position for Baja California. There's enough surplus water to irrigate orchards of avocados, mangoes, and papayas, as well to supply an anticipated tourist and retirement boom. Within reason, of course. Persistent and credible rumors circulate to the effect that a large luxury development is on the way. Besides a four-figure number of condos and luxury homes, plans include an eighteen-hole golf course. According to those "in the know," the developers have promised to install a water and sewage system for the entire town, promising to use reclaimed water for the golf course (to lessen fears that water shortages will ensue if the planned golf course becomes a reality).

The first time we visited here, about ten years ago, only a handful of North Americans had homes here. Most of them returned to the United

States or Canada for the summer. But during our last visit, we were astounded at the growth, with many new homes popping up alongside restored old adobes. Local people estimate that 300 people live here year-round and perhaps a thousand spend a good part of the year in Todos Santos. Despite the increased population, this is a quiet, laid-back place. During the siesta hour the streets are all but deserted.

Because of its proximity to the Pacific Ocean, Santo Tomas is considerably cooler than locations on the Sea of Cortez side of the peninsula; thus, it's more livable year-round. Curiously, the town is not on the beach but several kilometers inland. Miles of beautiful, yet deserted, beaches stretch south to Cabo San Lucas and north for hundreds of miles, with just a few homes and small hotels scattered sparsely along the way. One reason for residents ignoring beachfront properties could be the frequent warnings against swimming or even wading in the surf; riptides and undertow are common.

BAJA CALIFORNIA **OFF THE BEATEN PATH**

Driving the highway south of Ensenada, below the *zona libre,* treats you to some spectacular desert landscapes. Occasionally, but not often, you'll encounter a North American or two living in one of the small villages along the highway. Two of the most striking towns, San Ignacio and Mulegé (two of the prettiest places in Baja), have a few North Americans living there, and we suspect these places will become more popular with gringos in the near future.

San Ignacio was founded in the seventeenth century by Jesuit missionaries who discovered that the high water table around San Ignacio naturally irrigated the soil. Even before the church and mission were completed, groves of oranges and lemons, grapevines, and date palms were thrusting roots into the damp soil. The Jesuits were expelled from Baja more than two centuries ago, but dates, citrus, and grapes survived fabulously. Today they grow like weeds, sometimes like a jungle. Here and farther south in Mulegé, the trees and vines grow lushly. You will understand the meaning of oasis if you ever visit these two towns.

Before the paved highway, Mulegé was a favorite destination for off-road adventurers. They looked forward to the shade of tall date palms, tropical flowers in profusion, and the cool waters of one of Baja's few real rivers. An old town—dating from the 1600s, with buildings that have defied centuries of weathering—Mulegé was in itself fascinating. But even more interesting was the fact that before the new highway, it was a penal colony. On a hill overlooking the town sits a large pastel-colored building: the territorial prison. Convicts who were judged to be nonviolent and who could be trusted to be part of society (yet legally couldn't) were exiled to places like Mulegé to serve out their sentences. This was not only a very humane practice but also wonderfully practical. Instead of placing a prisoner into a cage with the taxpayers spending $40,000 a year to keep him there (U.S. style), Mexico sent nondangerous prisoners into "exile." (They may still do this—I'm not sure.) The convict's family then joined him, and together they somehow managed to earn a living. (Remember Mexican taxpayers are very much against pampering convicts by paying room and board for them.) The family either found jobs or started a business, much the same as if they were still on the mainland. The children went to school, the parents worked, and the family lived normal lives as responsible members of the community. The prison on the hill was reserved for someone who occasionally misbehaved, perhaps appearing intoxicated in public or quarreling with neighbors. If a convict misbehaved too often, he was shipped back to the mainland and tossed into a regular prison. As you can imagine, few people ever misbehaved. If you were looking for a crime-free environment, you couldn't have found any safer place than Mulegé!

However, in the interests of tourism, the government closed the "prison" (which rarely held prisoners in the first place). Today the children and grandchildren of convicts might be the owners of the stores or restaurants in town. These days serious crime is almost nonexistent; Mulegé is no different from almost any small town in Mexico.

A river—slow-moving and tropical, fringed with bamboo, tall trees, and massive date palms—runs through town and down to the gulf. A half dozen trailer parks face the river. These parks are very popular with winter retirees. Although we're getting farther south, where cooler currents from the Pacific Ocean temper the warm gulf water, the summers here are still not particularly livable. Even so, some people talk of plans for a 300-unit condo and a marina on the river.

Just south of town is a development called Villas de Mulegé. Houses there can be built to your specifications. Without electricity, this development features solar energy. Because approximately 98 percent of Mulegé days are sunny, this doesn't seem to be such a bad idea. Our guess is that before long, the town is in line for development.

LORETO

The desert-by-the-sea town of Loreto is the oldest permanent Spanish settlement in Baja. It was founded in 1697 when missionary Juan Maria Salvatierra and his band of loyal followers established a mission and a fishing village. The location on a bay of the Sea of Cortez was selected because it was protected by the Isla del Carmen that sits offshore. About seventy years later, in 1769, Father Junípero Serra set forth from Loreto on his famous undertaking to establish a chain of seventeen Jesuit missions— stretching as far north as present-day San Francisco, California.

For years Loreto languished as a sleepy village, hosting infrequent gringo tourists who flew there in private or chartered planes for a few days of fishing adventures. Then when the paved highway made its way south from the border, making automobile travel practical, Loreto's future began to look better. It looks even better today, with direct air service from Los Angeles to the new airport at nearby Nopolo Cove making it relatively easy to get here. Other ambitious facilities are under way here, particularly at Puerto Escondido (not to be confused with the mainland's west coast town of the same name), 16 kilometers to the south. The big attraction here, of course, is still fishing, but lately more and more people are considering full- or part-time retirement in Loreto. With more and more North Americans coming every day, this area is growing from a sleepy fishing resort into a bustling complex. An eighteen-hole golf course and eight professional tennis courts are some recent additions to the recreation scene. Some local boosters believe that when all the projected facilities in the area are completed—including a European-style village somewhat like Manzanillo's Las Hadas, with red-tiled roofs and sparkling white walls—Loreto will be as popular as anywhere on the mainland. A new Cancún, they say.

A new Cancún? Maybe; maybe not. Again, the problem with all the Sea of Cortez side of Baja California Sur is the fierce summer heat. As soon as the temperatures begin climbing in May, the gringos begin packing, not to return until October or November. Another problem is the water supply; some say it isn't adequate to support a large population. So Loreto will not likely become a new Cancún but will remain Loreto. There's nothing wrong with that.

BAHÍA DE PALMAS

On your way south, about halfway between La Paz and Cabo San Lucas, is an interesting, fast-growing North American colony, spread along the Bahía de Palmas. This colony is on the Sea of Cortez side of the peninsula (although it's just about open ocean at this point), so the weather is more civilized. Some fancy homes, as well as some ordinary places and RV lots, have been built next to the beaches. Homes aren't cheap around here, with a few selling for prices as high as $200,000. Nothing is crowded, and if you're looking for isolated beaches, beautiful ocean water, and quiet, then you've found it.

Los Barriles and Buena Vista are the larger communities along the bay. But neither is really large enough to be called even a village. From here on southward runs a dirt and gravel road that follows the coast (and some really spectacular scenery) all the way to San José del Cabo. Very, very few people live here, but you'll find RVs and gringo houses scattered along the way, taking advantage of the view.

Because of the way the wind blows across the bay, this area is reputed to have the best windsurfing anywhere. It seems that high-velocity thermal winds swoop down from the high inland mountains, sending winds of 20 to 25 knots to really speed the windsurfers along! (Better know what you're doing, though.) Several really nice hotels in the area cater to the windsurfers as well as to tourists who want someplace different to visit.

Just south of here is a place called Santiago, one of the most interesting towns in Baja Sur. It sits in a broad canyon that is continuously watered by volcanic springs and not affected by drought and low rainfall. The result is a lush oasis of trees, tropical plants, and flowers. Some of the streets are lined with flowering trees with brilliant red blossoms that look almost surrealistic. The Palomar Hotel there has one of the best chefs in Baja, and it's worth a detour just to taste one of his soups. But according to local people, not one North American resident has ever chosen to live here. We don't understand this.

CHAPTER TEN

FOR THE MORE
ADVENTUROUS

The vast majority of North Americans who choose retirement or long-term living in Mexico would be well advised to join one of the well-established English-speaking colonies in popular places such as Lake Chapala, San Miguel de Allende, and Cuernavaca. This makes good sense because you know you'll find a welcoming community of expatriates and friendly neighbors to help you get settled in your new surroundings. You'll be able to choose your friends on the basis of mutual interests: golf, bridge, politics, or whatever. You'll find excellent medical facilities with English-speaking doctors and nurses. Transition into a new culture is infinitely easier when you're surrounded by people who speak your language and who, themselves, have had to adapt to living in a foreign country.

However, not everyone needs to be immersed in the ambience of a large gringo society. Some might prefer to blend totally into the landscape of an ancient Mexican village or a small fishing community where the dawn begins with a rooster crowing or the clip-clop of burro hooves on cobblestone streets—a town where English is a foreign language. These people are more interested in adventures than comforts. This is particularly true of some of those newly entering the age of retirement:

the advance guard of the "baby boomer" generation who are already in their early sixties and rapidly moving on.

With early retirement incentives, job outsourcing, and downsizing in today's business world, many younger folks are being cut loose into the world of leisure time and retirement, whether they like it or not. This new wave of retirees (voluntary and otherwise) were just becoming adults during the Vietnam War era, and they tend to view the world differently from those who matured in Korean War times or earlier. The new retirees were the "younger generation" of the 1970s. Before they settled down to becoming successful yuppies, these baby boomers (now graying at the temples) preferred roughing it when they traveled. They enjoyed backpacking and international travel on a shoestring. Rustic accommodations were just fine—part of the adventure. For many of them the luxury of Puerto Vallarta or the picture-book glamour of San Miguel de Allende could be a bit bourgeois and "older generation" for their taste.

For these adventurous souls—as well as any others too free spirited to march to the conventional drumbeat—we'll now take a look at some alternative living situations in Mexico. But before you start packing, you ought to think about how you will fit into some of these lifestyles.

Some places described here are small towns or villages with just a few expatriates in residence. In some towns and cities mentioned, only a handful of gringos make their homes. If you don't need a wide circle of friends and acquaintances, that's not a bad situation. It's fascinating how a tremendous level of camaraderie develops among gringos who reside in places where the English-speaking population is small. It doesn't take long before you know every expatriate in town, even those who live in the boondocks and only visit the village to shop occasionally. On the other hand, since the non-Mexican population will be small, there's always the chance that some of the English-speakers might be people you wouldn't want to associate with in the first place. For this reason, before you buy property and settle in for the long haul, be sure you will be compatible with the potential neighbors in your new retirement location.

An important item that younger retirees seldom consider is medical care. Typically one doesn't begin to worry about hospital quality and doctors until one's health begins to falter. Therefore, along with descriptions of these alternative retirement possibilities comes a recommendation to check out the health care situation. (If you're in good health and consider

yourself made of iron, you'll probably ignore this advice.) Small-town clin-ics can be *very* rustic, and village doctors are often newly graduated med-ical students fulfilling their required assignment of one year of public service. (They're stationed in the village because no regular doctor is will-ing to work there.)

SEA OF CORTEZ COAST—ROCKY POINT Californians have Baja California as their convenient destination for Mexico adventure or full- or part-time retirement. Residents of Arizona have their Mexico getaway in the Sonoran Desert's Rocky Point (in Spanish, known as *Puerto Punta Peñasco*). A relatively new development, uninhabited until the 1920s, Rocky Point is the closest Sea of Cortez beach for Arizona and New Mexico residents. About ninety minutes from the U.S. border, at the Sonoita crossing, Rocky Point is in the midst of an expatriate boom. Condos, second homes, RVs, and mobile homes are popping up every-where. Local developers claim that more than $50 million of real estate changed hands in 2004 and predict that this could double in the near future. Prices are anticipated to increase as Rocky Point continues its metamorphosis from a weekend resort to a retirement and winter-home community.

Four megaresorts are under way, along with several gated communities. There is talk among enthusiastic developers of an international airport to bring easy access to more sportfishing enthusiasts and vacationers. The area will continue to grow because of its affordability and its being only four to eight hours' driving time for individuals in West Texas, New Mexico, Arizona, and Southeastern California. Obviously, Rocky Point is no longer one of those "authentic" Mexican villages where you need to know some Spanish. On the contrary, some RV developments are self-contained, with built-in shopping and conveniences, so one never has to mingle with the natives. But it is off the beaten path.

Like several other Baja California locations, the limit on development here as a full-time retirement destination will be the hot and muggy summer weather. Another drawback, for the time being at any rate, is the lack of satisfactory medical services. This will probably change as the number of expatriates grows.

GUANAJUATO

Many people consider Guanajuato to be Mexico's most beautiful and romantic of the colonial cities. Certainly its architectural splendor, physical setting, and pervasively European look and feel place it in the running for that title. Its location, on the slopes of a canyon, makes for narrow streets and numerous stairways. Rather than having a single central plaza, or *zócalo*, like most Mexican towns, it has a number of small parks, each with its own special character. The main plaza is the scene of Sunday band concerts and is a place to socialize and meet other expatriates.

The University of Guanajuato, with a 250-year history and a modern campus, is considered one of Mexico's best. Inside and out, the Juarez Theater displays nineteenth-century opulence but annually plays host to the Cervantes Festival, which showcases the international cultural treasures of the twenty-first century.

During the festival's duration, two or three weeks in October, performances overflow into theaters, parks, and plazas throughout the city. Students take part, along with nationally and even internationally known actors. Guanajuato is a year-round venue for the worlds of music, art, and theater.

There are several theories as to why this beautiful and lively town has attracted so few North Americans. David Gardner—who recently moved there from Berkeley, California, with his wife and young son—suggests that older people may be intimidated by the topography, which is even steeper than San Miguel's. He observes that Guanajuato is not automobile-friendly, with many streets that can be negotiated only on foot. Finally, he notes, you really must speak Spanish to participate in what the town has to offer.

That may be changing, however, with a growing expat population. Estimates run as high as 400, including students in Guanajuato's numerous, excellent, and affordable Spanish language programs. Some expats meet in informal groups around interests as diverse as arts and crafts, politics, and animals. A Sunday brunch brings together foreigners and Mexicans to exchange information and ideas. In the absence of an English-language newspaper of its own, the expat community has to rely on occasional coverage in San Miguel de Allende's *Atencíon*.

YELAPA: **A TROPICAL PARADISE**

Some people dream of living in a tropical village, where there are no automobiles or electricity and where pigs and chickens run loose in the streets. Those of you who've vacationed in Puerto Vallarta have probably taken the cruise boat to Yelapa, about an hour's sail from PV. The beach is a delightful medley of tropical sand, sun, and music, with a few tequila sunrises thrown in. Typically the visitor has lunch in one of the palm-thatched *palapa* restaurants, strolls the narrow streets of Yelapa's small village, and returns to Puerto Vallarta on the boat, with the band playing and margaritas flowing.

These visitors miss the "real" Yelapa, much to the delight of the "real" Yelapa residents. Yelapa is as different from modern, urban Puerto Vallarta as different can be. The village features dirt streets and tropically rustic homes. It's a place where electricity is a new innovation and communication with the mainland is mostly via cell phones. Yelapa's semi-isolation is the delight of residents, who know that "civilization" is a short boat ride away should they wish to go out for a night on the town or buy a new microwave.

Thea and Roger, who've lived there off and on since 1981, said, "There are probably a hundred of us gringos living here at any given time. Not so many that we don't recognize almost everyone as we do our shopping in the one grocery store." They also pointed out that the kinds of retirees living here permanently are truly unusual people: "Writers, artists, musicians, philosophers, we have 'em all."

However, it isn't all sweet music and tropical breezes. Several drawbacks prevent more people from moving to Yelapa. For one thing, you can't own the land your house is built on. This land is officially part of the Indian reservation, so title belongs to the tribe, to the municipality, or to somebody other than the residents. Nobody is completely sure. So when gringos "buy" a house or build one, they're always aware of their tentative position.

Another drawback is the difficulty in getting back and forth to the mainland; the only way is by water. Until recently the only public transportation was by the tourist steamers, but today there are five "water taxis" that carry passengers for about $7.00 each way. Some residents resent this innovation, for that may mean even more visitors.

SAN BLAS

For a tropical village (small town, actually) that's "unspoiled" and truly Mexican—yet not as unspoiled as Yelapa—you might consider San Blas. Reputedly a pirate hangout during the days of the Manila galleons, the town tries to maintain a "buccaneer" motif. Actually the town was founded as a naval base to *chase* pirates and as a place to outfit expeditions for the colonization of the west coast. Ships sailing out of San Blas established colonies as far north as Alaska. Yes, Alaska. The city of Valdez, Alaska, was named for the Spanish captain Valdez, who sailed out of San Blas to plant a royal colony there. Enough history.

As a tropical village San Blas is a jewel. It's a subdued place of a few thousand inhabitants, where often you'll see a mama pig herding her litter of piglets along the sandy streets. (Most streets are unpaved.) Many local people live in thatched-roof houses. Some buildings along the square date back to the time when the king's sailors used San Blas's main street for shore leave.

For some reason or other, this part of the coast always seems to be green and lush while the rest of the west suffers from lack of rainfall during the winter season. Even during the severe drought of 1988, this stretch of beach looked marvelously tropical and verdant.

Housing and food are as inexpensive in San Blas as anywhere else in Mexico, according to the year-round, English-speaking residents we interviewed. One person, who was in the process of finding a place for the summer, told us that he had his choice of half a dozen houses for very low rents. (Costs vary widely depending upon the season.) Summers here are hot and exceptionally humid—the kind of weather that makes you understand the custom of an afternoon siesta. One serious drawback to year-round living in San Blas is the seasonal appearance of no-see-ums— tiny, almost invisible gnats that delight on feeding on any victim not lib- erally doused with insect repellent. The town has never been able to bat- tle the little critters successfully. For this reason you can have San Blas almost to yourself during the summer.

Matachén and Playa los Cocos are about a ten-minute drive from San Blas and are very rustic but picturesque villages. The view of the moun- tains and Matachén Bay are marvelous. Then, if you follow the road that skirts the ocean, you come to a village called Santa Cruz, which is also worth investigating. We've met several people who regularly haul fishing boats there and spend several months with the surf lapping at their beachfront site.

North of San Blas are a string of picturesque beach villages. The peo- ple here are friendly, and the villages are small. Most have a few American residents. A particularly inviting village is San Francisco, about an hour north of Puerto Vallarta. It is growing quickly, but prices of homes are still at bargain levels.

PUERTO ANGEL **AND HUATULCO**

Puerto Angel is another place we predicted would become a hot spot for tourism and retirement. The area beaches are so beautiful and varied and the panorama is so gorgeous, we were convinced it couldn't miss. We envisioned cruise ships docking here and spiffy condos and view homes going up on the steep hillsides that overlook one of the most gorgeous bays we've ever seen. Well, we were wrong again. Puerto Angel remains the charming, unsophisticated village it was seventeen years ago. There are still only a couple of main streets and remarkably few tourist busi- nesses. Until recently the town didn't have a single curio shop—not even a place that sold postcards. There are some moderately priced hotels and some excellent restaurants specializing in the fresh fish and lobster that are brought in daily by local fishermen. But Puerto Angel is still a very quiet and restful place, with most beach activity taking place away from the village.

If you follow a dirt road a few miles west of Puerto Angel, you'll find the small village of Zipolite, with its mile-long beach of warm, white sand. A strip of tiny restaurants and bars compete for the tourist business, which isn't terribly crushing because of the beach's isolation. This is a ruler-straight beach that faces the open ocean, so riptides and currents make it rather dangerous for all but experienced swimmers. But the biggest attraction here, particularly for the younger set, is that Zipolite Beach is "clothing optional." Technically nude bathing is against the law, but local cops seldom enforce this law. Several beaches in this area enjoy the same laxness—something unusual in Mexico.

Huatulco, about 35 kilometers from Puerto Angel, is where we should have predicted a tourist boom. But at the time Huatulco was little more than a shabby village situated on a nice, sandy bay. When the Mexican government decided to construct a spiffy resort here, they went to work with a vengeance. Before long there was an airport, a Club Med, and four large hotels, including a Sheraton. All of this expansion happened rather rapidly. Then suddenly things slowed to a crawl. Apparently tourism wasn't keeping pace with the expansion of facilities.

The original idea was to make the resort into an "authentic Mexican village," but the large luxury hotels destroyed this possibility. Those who've visited Huatulco as tourists rave about how wonderful their stays were, but who knows how it will be for those actually wishing to live there. There are several condos in place, presumably time-shares, but regular housing may be in short supply.

TAXCO: **THE FORGOTTEN SILVER QUEEN**

This colonial gem, nestled in the mountains just three and a half hours southwest of Mexico City, has been the favorite of John Howells since he was a teenager. In those days, when the family lived in Mexico City, they spent one or two weekends a month in Taxco. Although it's grown from a small town to a city, the main part of town hasn't changed a bit;

it still looks like 1948.

Taxco is another must-visit place—a scenic delight of genuine colonial architecture (few modern reproductions here), with narrow, cobblestoned streets rising sharply toward the main plaza. If Walt Disney had wanted to design a sixteenth-century mining town, it probably would have looked just like Taxco.

Like San Miguel de Allende, Taxco owes much of its current fame and popularity with foreigners to an American. In this case it was William Spratling, an Alabama-born architect and college professor. He came for a visit in 1929, fell in love with the place, and decided to stay. In 1931 he started the process of resurrecting Taxco's long-dormant silver industry. Today his efforts can be seen in the town's highly successful silver commerce.

Back in the eighteenth century, Taxco's wealth was based on the silver mines that had been worked since the time of Cortez. Today the economy is based on silver far more than on tourism; the town has about 200 shops, mostly family operated, where silver is handcrafted into jewelry and flatware. Many of today's best silversmiths are the grandchildren of Spratling's apprentices.

Why hasn't Taxco become a popular retirement center? Perhaps it is a consequence of progress. At one time the only practical way to get from Mexico City to Acapulco was by highway, and you had to pass through Taxco. The drive used to take twelve hours, so Taxco was the logical stopover between Mexico City and Acapulco. Many visitors were so fascinated by the town that they couldn't resist joining the artists already in residence and making Taxco their home. Before long several hundred expatriates owned or rented homes here, and a thousand or more stayed for lesser periods of time.

Taxco was on its way to becoming as popular with retirees as San Miguel de Allende. Then progress came in the form of a high-speed toll road, which bypassed the town and drastically cut the number of tourists who are exposed to Taxco. Now most people drive or fly directly between Acapulco and Mexico City. Consequently those who might have considered retirement in Taxco no longer get the chance to look it over. Most tourists today are Mexican, European, and Japanese. Just one factor that could account for Taxco's comparatively scanty retired population: Its steep streets might intimidate older, less vigorous retirees and send them toward more level colonial towns. But with people taking retirement at much earlier ages today, we might expect to see additions to the numbers of retirees, both in town and on small ranches that sit in tropical splendor toward the base of the mountains.

XALAPA

As a place for gringos to congregate, Xalapa may be Mexico's best-kept secret. This would appear to be true if you count the small number of expatriates who have "discovered" the town and who have decided to live here. Some estimate that about 200 English-speaking foreigners live here, augmented by 150 or so Americans who study at the University of Veracruz. The university and its student population have a strong cultural influence on Xalapa, with art galleries, the Ballet Folklórico, outstanding anthropology and science museums, and the first-rate Xalapa Symphony Orchestra. The town proudly bills itself as the "Athens of Veracruz."

Xalapa is a beautiful city nestled on the side of a steep hillside and surrounded by lush coffee plantations, banana groves, flower gardens, and tall pine trees. The town is encircled by the black volcanic peaks of the Sierra Madre Oriental in the distance and enhanced by breathtaking views of Mexico's tallest mountain, the snow-covered Pico de Orizaba. The surrounding region is sprinkled with a number of interesting small towns, many of them great places to retire if you like to be near a larger city but enjoy the intimacy of a village. Tourists haven't discovered Xalapa either; they naively bypass the region by speeding along the superhighway directly to Veracruz or on their way to the Yucatán. Tourists don't know what they are missing, although the English-speaking residents here don't seem to miss the tourists.

When considering Xalapa as a place to live, expect higher-than-average rainfall and a greener-than-average landscape. In winter a light but persistent winter rain known as the *chipichipi* nurtures the plant life; in summer, frequent evening mists create a natural greenhouse environment. Plush with bougainvillea, gardenias, roses, and other flowers of all descriptions, Xalapa deserves its reputation as the "Flower Garden of Mexico."

Although a bustling city of more than 300,000, as well as the capital of the state of Veracruz, Xalapa doesn't seem that large at all. It artfully manages to combine its role as a modern commercial center for coffee and fruit growers with the charm of its antique colonial heritage. The old downtown section preserves its cobblestone streets, neoclassic architecture—with antique doorways and wrought-iron balconies—and buildings painted in bright pastels and primary colors. In addition to good downtown shopping, there's a Costco store just outside downtown, in the Las Animas area. You'll even find gyms and fitness/aerobic centers, good Internet services, and just about anything else you might need to ease into retirement here.

The name *Xalapa* comes from the Aztec (Nahuatl) language and means "water springs in the sand." Don't be puzzled if you see Xalapa (pronounced *ha-LA-pa*) spelled "Jalapa" on your road map or travel guide. In archaic Spanish the x and the j sounds were practically identical and used interchangeably. *Mexico* was often spelled *Mejico*, and *Xalapa* was spelled *Jalapa*. (*Xalapa* was the original form, and locals want to return to that spelling.) By the way, those hot chile peppers we know as jalapeños are so named because they originated here.

Those hot peppers contrast with Xalapa's pleasant, cool climate. Perched at an altitude of approximately 4,500 feet, Xalapa enjoys year-round spring weather. The town has been a traditional weekend haven for residents of the hot and steamy port city of Veracruz, only a couple hours' drive from this cool mountain setting. Had Xalapa been closer to Mexico City, it would surely have rivaled Cuernavaca as a place for weekend homes and tourism. The climate and ambience are similar, except that Cuernavaca gets much less rain. This writer recalls several pleasant visits to the region when he was a youngster and his sister's fiancé lived in Jalapa (would that make him a jalapeño?). We loved it then, and during our last visit a few years ago we were relieved to find that population growth hadn't diminished the city's charm.

Alan Cogan, who lives in the Lake Chapala region, agrees with my assessment. He had this comment about a recent trip to Xalapa: "Of the six cities my wife and I visited—Morelia, Cholula, Puebla, Xalapa, Veracruz, and Queretaro—Xalapa is, for us, the hands-down winner. If we were ever to leave our lakeside home for another destination in Mexico, that's where it would be."

An investigation of Xalapa isn't complete without a visit with Roy Dudley, a resident of the "city of flowers" for more than thirty years. Roy, a professional photographer, is also Xalapa's biggest booster. He came to Xalapa three decades ago to finish his bachelor's degree in Spanish at the Universidad Veracruzana and has lived here ever since. Roy loves to point out the advantages of living here and offers tours and retirement seminars in addition to operating his photography studio. He lives in the center of downtown with his wife and children and says, "We rarely use our car, since taxis only cost around a dollar! Why hassle finding a parking place when a taxi will drop you off right where you want to go? And for 'walkaholics' like me, who love to explore new sights and sounds on foot, Xalapa is wonderful, with narrow and often steep streets. Xalapa is the place to make lasting friends where you can meet for a delicious cup of *capuchino* or *Americano* at the myriad cafes and restaurants this city has to offer." If you are considering moving to Xalapa, be sure to contact Roy about his retirement seminar, which includes a tour of the region's cultural and scenic marvels. E-mail him at roydudley@xalapa.net or visit his Web site: www.xalaparoy.com.

SAN **CARLOS BAY**

On Mexico's west coast, the first place south of Arizona that attracts a considerable number of retirees is San Carlos Bay, located near the fairly uninteresting agricultural center of Guaymas. Originally San Carlos was a "discovery" of winter retirees—those RV addicts who wintered in nearby Kino Bay or Puerto Peñasco. But it quickly became exceedingly popular with conventional retirees as well. With a backdrop of rugged mountains, balmy winters, and gentle, protected beaches, San Carlos Bay is a place retirees come back to year after year to hold reunions with friends.

Visitors from Arizona, New Mexico, and Texas began staying longer and longer; then they started building homes, both modest and elaborate. The steadily increasing numbers of North Americans sparked an astounding expansion in construction. Today the area has the appearance of a true resort town. Locals estimate that more than a thousand homes in and around San Carlos belong to gringos. The RV parks are still evident, but they're dwarfed by conventional home developments and condominiums.

Several gated communities of rather elaborate homes occupy strategic positions on the shore of San Carlos Bay. These developments are popular with those who want to tie up their yachts and fishing boats at a dock in their backyard. Beachfront lots are plentiful for those who wish to build, even though prices aren't always exactly cheap, particularly in the town itself. During our last visit, we were fortunate to find four open houses being held the same afternoon in the main part of San Carlos. All four homes backed up against the beach. The views were spectacular, the interiors were luxurious, and the prices were exorbitant, ranging from $175,000 to $400,000. Farther north of town, beach and view homes were considerably less expensive, ranging from $50,000 upward.

Boating is part of the scene here. During summer, while you do your retirement thing in cooler climes, a marina at San Carlos's largest RV park will store your boat. Several retiree organizations are quite active here, sponsoring Spanish classes, dancing, and art lessons for their members. North American residents also support an orphanage and buy school supplies for local children.

San Carlos Bay now has a dozen restaurants, several grocery stores, a drugstore, some small shopping malls, two marinas, and everything you might need for a winter's retirement. At least one Mexican bank has established a branch here. The downside here, as anywhere along the Sea of Cortez, is the scorching summer sunshine that sends most folks scurrying north for a couple of months of cooler weather. Some may protest that because most residents do not live here year-round, they shouldn't be considered "retired" in Mexico. However, those who retire in Montana and travel to Arizona for the winter are still considered Montana retirees, aren't they? Predictably, more and more are sticking it out, enjoying having San Carlos to themselves during the hot months.

ALAMOS: **A GHOST TOWN REVIVED**

South of Guaymas you'll pass through two more agricultural cities: Ciudad Obregon and Navajoa. Neither has much to propose for retirement living. However, we can highly recommend Alamos, a fascinating colonial town about a seven-hour drive from the Arizona border and about 35 miles east of Navajoa. There's even premier-class bus service direct from Nogales.

Spanish conquistador Francisco Coronado explored the area in 1531 on his expedition north. The Jesuits began constructing a mission here in 1613. One of Mexico's oldest silver-mining cities, Alamos started its boom more than four centuries ago, in early 1683, with the discovery of rich ore bodies. By the late 1700s it had grown into a prosperous city with a population of more than 30,000—for a while the richest silver producer in all of Mexico. Its many substantial buildings attest to its former grandeur.

But like many mining towns, Alamos's fortunes rose and fell with changes in the world economy. By the early twentieth century, the mines were pretty much worked out. The Mexican Revolution exploded about that time, and wealthy landowners fled as the revolutionaries confiscated their land. Pancho Villa's troops entered Alamos in 1915, but refrained from sacking it because of Villa's high regard for the colonial jewel. Alamos became a ghost town after the revolution, unpopulated for decades. Alamos is a living museum where little has changed over the centuries. Today nobody seems to remember where the original mine workings were located.

Somewhere back in the 1950s the town was "discovered" by a small group of North Americans: artists, sculptors, and writers. Recognizing the ghost town's inherent beauty, they bought—for less than a song—old homes and silver baron mansions and set to work restoring them. The project was so successful that the Mexican government declared the town to be a national monument, just as they did with San Miguel de Allende and Taxco. Modern buildings are forbidden, and remodeling must faithfully preserve the structure's original appearance. Today artists' studios and apartments are hidden away in these old colonial mansions, which once housed silver barons and wealthy merchants. Typical decor of these mansions includes Moorish arches, covered walkways decorated with intricately fashioned wrought-iron work, and graceful fountains in landscaped gardens.

The population is said to be approximately 6,000, but that must include everyone living in the area. The number of North Americans is difficult to pin down because they are constantly coming and going, but the average is about 250. You never get the feeling that the place is crowded. The number of expatriates in Alamos is small compared with some other gringo colonies discussed in this book, but the residents are just as loyal to their adopted home as those living in San Miguel or Ajijic.

Residents here are totally convinced they've found Mexico's ultimate retirement mecca. Because summers are livable in this high-altitude desert, many live here year-round, others retire here just for the winter, and many others visit on a regular basis. The English-speaking community is very active and engages in several worthwhile community projects that boost the retirees' image with the local people. One fund-raising project is a regularly conducted house tour that permits tourists and residents to enjoy the restoration miracles performed on these centuries-old mansions. One holiday tradition is the Christmas Posadas; another is the Children's Carnival. Both are celebrated through the month of December, when part-time residents are often in town.

The Casa de los Tesoros, a remarkable hotel—claimed by some to be one of Mexico's finest—is located here. Several less expensive hotels are found on or near the main plaza. Three RV parks accommodate motorized retirees. Almost all of the RV folks are snowbirds who fly home for the summer. A few who own private airplanes literally do fly home, using the town's excellent paved 3,900-foot landing strip (1,346-foot elevation). For those with a desire to fish, the beaches of Huatabampito, on the Sea of Cortez, are about ninety minutes away by car. World-class bass fishing can be enjoyed at nearby Lake Mocuzari.

THE YUCATÁN **PENINSULA**

The Yucatán is historically, geographically, and culturally separate from the rest of Mexico. In fact the Yucatecans do not think of themselves as Mexican. The region enjoys a distinct Caribbean flavor tempered by an ancient Maya culture. People here speak Spanish with a distinct accent, and many natives speak a Mayan dialect exclusively. Their homeland, closer to Miami than to Mexico City (only an hour and forty minutes by air), has become familiar to great numbers of North Americans who are drawn by the peninsula's resorts and ruins. Because the Yucatán is easily accessible from the east coast of the United States and Canada, it is one of the most popular travel destinations in Mexico. Some visitors, particularly those who get to know the inhabitants, decide to make the Yucatán their retirement home.

The huge peninsula juts far to the north, bounded by the Gulf of Mexico on the west and by the Caribbean on the east coast. The interior features tropical jungles and colonial cities, mysterious archaeological sites, rustic villages, and modern cities. Nowhere else will you find such an exotic blend of elements. Parts of the Yucatán catch extremely heavy rainfall; other areas are exceptionally dry. It's a land of perpetual summer, with temperatures in the high eighties and low nineties year-round.

WEATHER IN THE YUCATÁN PENINSULA

	In degrees Fahrenheit			
	Jan.	April	July	Oct.
Daily Highs	82	92	91	86
Daily Lows	64	70	73	67

Although the Gulf of Mexico coast of the Yucatán is somewhat boring, the Caribbean coast from Cancún south has some of the most delightful beaches in the world. Long stretches of sand and coral are fringed by low jungles and an occasional coconut plantation or vegetable farm. Numerous peaceful bays are perfect for snorkeling, diving, and boating, with an abundance of coral reefs easily enjoyed, even by novices. Overuse and development have threatened some coral reefs, but many towns, like Puerto Morelos and Akumal, are taking vigorous steps to correct the problem of water consumption and sewage treatment.

Much of the beachfront land is tantalizing as a site for that dream home, but be warned against potential legal pitfalls. Often people who "own" this land don't realize that they are living on their property only because "possession" is that well-known percentage of the law. When they try to sell, they discover that their family land belongs to someone else. When they move, the legal owners will swoop in and take possession. Don't let this discourage you, however: property is always available, but do find a reliable lawyer. Away from the beaches land ownership is more available and more reliable but, alas, less desirable.

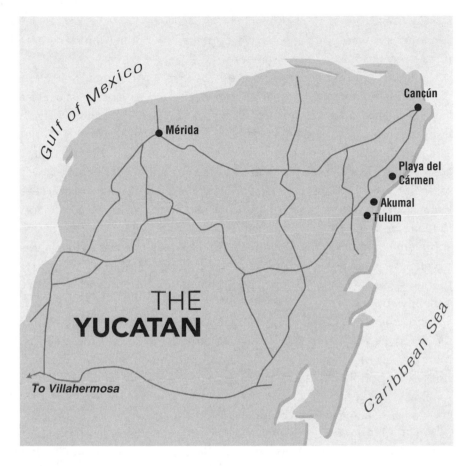

Gulf of Mexico

● Cancún

● Mérida

Playa del
● Cármen

● Akumal
● Tulum

THE
YUCATAN

Caribbean Sea

← To Villahermosa

MÉRIDA

Mérida is a most unusual Mexican city. Residents call Mérida the "Paris of the West" because of its charming, tree-lined boulevards, lovely colonial mansions, and spectacular estates of the henequen barons of the 1800s. Mérida is widely known as the "White City," partly because its buildings are mostly of limestone construction but also because of its cleanliness. Streets, plazas, and parks are cleaned twice daily. Residents also claim that Mérida has the lowest crime rate per capita in Mexico.

Over the years the city has managed to maintain much of its colonial charm, and if it weren't for unmuffled motorcycles and trucks, it could be described as a sleepy paradise. One problem here is the summer weather. Located 33 kilometers from the Gulf of Mexico, without tempering Caribbean breezes to help cool things off, Mérida can get hot during summer. Fortunately it doesn't have oppressive humidity, and temperatures rarely rise above the low nineties.

Yet the North Americans who live here love it. After the publication of an earlier edition of Choose Mexico, we received an enthusiastic letter from a college administrator from Texas who had just bought a new, three-bedroom, two-and-a-half-bath, two-floor town house in Mérida. The purchase price (complete with full-time security) was $23,000, but it cost another $6,400 to add a carport, balcony, patio, water heater, stove, refrigerator, ceiling fans, cabinets, and shelving. Furnishing the house—kitchen, bedrooms, living room, and dining room—with custom-made furniture and original art brought the total close to $34,000. Our correspondent couldn't say enough about how delighted he was to live in the Yucatán, with all its human and ecological riches. He did say, however, that there were few North Americans in his neighborhood and he wasn't unhappy about it.

Previous editions of Choose Mexico suggested that only retirees who didn't require the company of fellow expatriates would be likely to enjoy Mérida. That has certainly changed, with informed estimates of the resident expat population ranging as high as 1,000.

The thriving Mérida English Library, with events ranging from chili cook-offs to garage sales to programs for ESL teachers, is one of the centers of North American residents' life. The International Women's Club of Mérida is another. The Friends of Oasis de San Juan, an HIV–AIDS hospice, brings together expats and locals in fund-raising activity.

Residents give good marks to the community's physicians and health care facilities. Shopping offers choices between several WalMarts and the typical Mexican mercado. Beaches are a short trip away at Progreso. Many of the small towns and villages around Merida are now attracting foreign residents as well.

CANCÚN

While Acapulco was enjoying the title of "Jet-set Capital of the Americas," Cancún could barely claim the title of a backwater village. Dirt trails connected Cancún to the rest of the world, and airplanes larger than a two-motor DC–3 were unknown hereabouts. Then when the Mexico Ministry of

Tourism decided to shift the tourist emphasis away from Acapulco to places like Puerto Vallarta and Mazatlán, developers began looking at Cancún. By an astounding coincidence, some high-ranking politicians, including the president of Mexico, just happened to own many acres of land along the beach, so the decision to turn the location into Mexico's most popular tourist destination wasn't a difficult one to make. Of course the year-round summer weather, amazingly blue waters, and soft-sand beaches fringed with coconut palms helped the decision, too.

Today Cancún is one of the hemisphere's most popular beach resorts. Some three million tourists visit annually. Luxury hotels and condo developments line the beach. Prices in the tourist areas bear a much closer resemblance to those elsewhere in the Caribbean than to those in most of Mexico. Condos are being marketed aggressively, but before you sign up for one—in Cancún, Acapulco, Lake Tahoe, or any resort town—figure out what your weekly and daily costs will be. A popular ploy is to sell condos on a two- or three-week time-share basis. This is for tourists, not for anyone who seriously wants to live in Mexico.

If you choose to live in Cancún, look at one of the many small houses being built in or near the downtown area. They are far less expensive than the beachfront hotel area and look very comfortable. Other nice residential areas are found in the small towns surrounding Cancún.

Puerto Morelos is one example of a place near enough to Cancún to enjoy all the tourist benefits, yet far enough away to feel like you are living in Mexico and not Miami. Located just twenty minutes south of Cancún on the Maya Riviera, Puerto Morelos is a haven of peace and solitude, an authentic fishing village on the Caribbean coast. An American retired couple owns Cabanas Puerto Morelos—the village's only room accommodations, which consist of three one-bedroom, one-bath units with kitchenettes. They describe the village this way: "The road into town leads directly to the *zócalo*, a gathering place at day's end. Children's games, gossip, and music are daily events in this tree-shaded town park, and impromptu guitar music frequently fills the air. Brightly painted cement benches and lovers' chairs that face one another are spread throughout the square. Several intimate restaurants, markets, a pharmacy, and gift shops surround the *zócalo.*"

Local people are convinced that Puerto Morelos will retain its small village atmosphere and avoid the overdevelopment taking place along the coast. They point out that the government has declared the reef area and the mangroves behind the village to be ecological preserves. This means that development will be very limited.

THE YUCATÁN'S **EAST COAST**

A booming area for retirement is the east coast of the peninsula, from Cancún down to Tulúm. A great four-lane highway leads south, passing through or near a dozen beach towns, each with a small population of North American expatriates happily living there. Some call this region the "Mayan Riviera," but local residents object to this description, partly because the region clearly lacks the sophistication of a true riviera, and partly because they hope it will always stay that way. Pristine beaches, quiet jungles, and clean air are why they live here, and they shudder every time a multinational company buys another beach to erect a megaresort.

Along the length of the highway, numerous side roads—often 2 or 3 kilometers long—lead to beach communities too small to be called villages. The largest town here is Playa del Carmen, where condominium and home building is booming. It sits about 75 kilometers south of Cancún. From there the island of Cozumel is just a short trip by auto ferry.

Both places are attracting Americans and Canadians for retirement living. Playa del Carmen is *the* place for heavy-duty shopping, with a supermarket the size of a large Safeway and a wide selection of goods. Three banks serve the town, each with a *cajero automatico* (automatic teller machine).

Akumal, about 110 kilometers south of Cancún, is undergoing an extraordinary wave of development, partly as a result of incoming gringos. Building is said to be "going wild." New developments are spawning from the Akumal boom, with Akumal Sur and Aventuras Akumal under way. Nearby Puerto Aventuras is a planned community with a marina, great shopping, and a bilingual school. The bay is particularly lovely for swimming.

Besides the great weather, one of the attractions of the Akumal area is exotic snorkeling lagoons with underwater caves and spectacular varieties of small and large fish. Local retirees become involved with volunteer efforts to preserve these miraculous *lagunas*. They work with the Centro Ecologico Akumal to help preserve the pristine water quality and to educate tourists to help them have an ecologically aware vacation in the Yucatán.

CHAPTER ELEVEN

DOING BUSINESS
IN MEXICO

Ten years ago the United States, Canada, and Mexico negotiated the North American Free Trade Agreement (NAFTA). The purpose of the treaty was to lower or eliminate trade barriers, allowing a free flow of goods that would stimulate the economies of all three countries. It was predicted that NAFTA would boost Mexico's economy into first-world prosperity. So far, this hasn't happened. NAFTA clearly has been a boon to foreign companies and manufacturers, yet many economists question whether Mexico is receiving many of the heralded economic benefits NAFTA promised.

NAFTA's major beneficiaries are foreign manufacturers, which take advantage of Mexico's low wage structure to produce goods for export to the United States or Europe. Unfortunately the profits from these inexpensively produced goods do not return to Mexico. The money is deposited in banks in the United States or Europe, distributed to stockholders, and spent elsewhere. Numerous Mexican-owned factories dropped by the wayside, unable to compete with more efficient and better financed foreign corporations. The Mexican economy remains fairly stagnant despite the establishment of foreign manufacturing facilities all over the country. However, this has helped control the inflation-

ary spirals that traditionally plague Mexico. Ten years without significant inflation is probably a record.

Instead of the predicted higher wages for Mexican workers, those who haven't already fled the country have seen their wage levels remain static—around $4.00 per day—over this ten-year period, while prices have risen slowly but surely. For most workers in Mexico, the minimum and maximum wages are the same. Mexican President Vicente Fox recently admitted that Mexico's primary source of U.S. dollars comes from wages sent home by millions of small farmers who emigrated to the United States and who send money to help family and relatives survive. In 2004 Mexicans working in the United States sent more than $13 billion dollars to Mexico, making these dollars exceed, for the first time, income from foreign investments and tourism combined.

Although the NAFTA treaty has fallen short of the promised benefits for the Mexican people, there have been some positive impacts on expatriate retirees as well as those wanting to work or do business in Mexico. Until NAFTA, going into business in Mexico was almost out of the question for most expatriates. The government erected so many barriers that the authors of *Choose Mexico* used to suggest that the easiest way to go into business was to marry a Mexican citizen. Under most conditions, foreigners could not own the majority interest in their business; a Mexican citizen had to control at least 51 percent of the enterprise. Just about the only way to control 100 percent of the business was to have a spouse who had Mexican citizenship and put the business in his or her name. Otherwise you could be in a precarious position as a minority partner or stockholder in your own business, with someone else controlling your investment.

Expatriates and retirees have benefited also. Several U.S.–based corporations, such as Kellogg, General Mills, Wonder Bread, and more, have installed local production facilities in Mexico. These goods are competitively priced. However, goods imported from the States, for example, cranberry sauce, Campbell's soups, and Cool Whip, are still expensive. With tariffs lifted, the cost of many other imported goods dropped dramatically. The establishment of giant U.S. retail outlets such as Sears, Costco and WalMart changed retirees' shopping habits by making higher quality imports available at affordable prices. When shopping, we seldom need to weigh the choice between lower quality, Mexican-produced items or higher priced imports.

FEWER **RESTRICTIONS**

Several restrictions against hiring foreign employees have been lifted, allowing foreign corporations doing business in Mexico more free-dom to hire North American workers for executive, supervisory, and tech-nical positions. This dramatically increased the expatriate population in industrial and commercial centers throughout the country. Although it has become somewhat easier to get working papers when employed by international companies, restrictions are still in effect for those who work for other employers. You still must prove you have skills that Mexican workers cannot supply—that you are not keeping a qualified Mexican from working

A big change for foreigners doing business in Mexico is that it is no longer required that Mexican citizens own 51 percent of your business. A welcome change indeed! Today a North American expatriate can have complete control over the enterprise. Note that while some restrictions have been lifted on doing business in Mexico, the situation is still not totally wide open. You still run the obstacle course you might expect when dealing with any government bureaucracy—and Mexico's bureau-cracy is tangled. Also, do not confuse ownership in your business and working in your business. You still need at least an FM-3 status, plus a work permit, to obviously be working in the business. Work permits are not automatically granted. Just as with a foreigner working at a job, the business owner must prove that he is not taking work from Mexicans and that there is a logical reason why the owner can perform the work better than a local Mexican. Alternatively, the businessperson can show that a certain number of Mexican employees will be hired or that his employees will be engaged in learning a valuable new trade or skill.

The general rule is that all foreigners are prohibited from doing work that Mexicans are capable of doing and who are available for hire. This means the owner is expected to keep a low profile—not working "out front" dealing with customers, waiting tables, working the cash register, or performing visible work of any nature. It's okay to do bookkeeping, ordering, and general overseeing (behind the scenes), but leave the cooking and waiting tables to your employees. Of course this does not apply to business owners who are engaged in technical work that involves special training and knowledge. Those who run language schools or edu-cational institutes usually receive permits without problems.

Those who try to ignore these rules can be fined heavily, ordered out of the country, and forbidden reentry for up to a year. So if you are obviously performing work in public view, you better have working papers. You never know when some local official might be watching you, hoping to catch you in a violation so that he can extract a *mordida* (bribe) from you. Anyway, with the low cost of labor in Mexico, why not hire someone else to do the work, while you kick back and supervise?

FORMING **A CORPORATION**

When considering going into business in Mexico, you will be well advised to seek out the help and advice of a specialized attorney known as a *notario publico.* As explained earlier in the book, this is a specialized attorney who can not only advise you on what you can and cannot do in your business, but also is specially authorized to do the paperwork necessary to set up a corporation, or *Sociadad Anónima.* The *notario* will guide you through the legalities, making sure you have control over the corporation. He will explain what your role in the operation of the business can and cannot be. If you are buying an existent corporation, have a *notario publico* look things over to make sure you are in control.

PROFESSIONAL **LICENSES**

Mexico no longer requires citizenship or permanent residency for such professionals as dentists, doctors, and engineers. The catch is that Mexico is not required to recognize foreign professional licenses. Our understanding is that medical doctors, for example, are rarely granted permission to work here. To open a practice, they'll need a license, and the Mexican government is reluctant to grant licenses. Under NAFTA, the government is committed to providing a procedure by which foreigners may obtain validation of their credentials. We understand that it is easier for engineers to gain approval of work permits. Check with your professional colleagues to ascertain the current state of bureaucracy.

Even if you are licensed in your professional field, such as engineering or refrigeration, remember that when working for other than an international company, you will be competing with Mexican professionals. In some fields $300 a week is considered excellent money.

BUSINESS **PROTOCOL**

We interviewed a number of expatriates who are doing business in Mexico, asking for their insights and advice about entering the Mexican world of business. The one theme everyone mentioned was the importance of developing a personal relationship with associates, clients, and customers. As one businessman in Ajijic pointed out, "If you're not willing to take time to engage in some pleasantries before starting your business meetings, you can be sure it will cost you." Mexicans believe in pleasure before business. Exchanging pleasantries, talking about their families, and maybe commenting on the weather are considered polite before jumping into the reason for the meeting. Keep your meetings easygoing and relaxed, and if the meeting is at your office or home, be a gracious host.

Like most other Latin Americans, Mexicans are uncomfortable with direct confrontation and heated arguments. Politeness, dignity, and the appearance of integrity are most important. When dealing with Mexican associates or employees, it's important not to "pull rank," raise your voice, or use sarcastic comments. Your associates, partners, customers, and suppliers will often avoid giving you a direct and impolite "no," which could risk your displeasure or appear to be rude. Instead you might get a vague "maybe" or "we'll see" when they really mean "no." This is called *dar largas*, "beating around the bush," and is why getting your final agreement in writing is crucial. You need to recognize the difference between a "polite yes" and a "genuine yes." Remember, "*mañana*" can be a polite way of saying "never"!

THE **"LITTLE BITE"**

A prevalent practice in Mexico when dealing with officials is the *mordida*—literally, "little bite," or in plain English, a "bribe." If you need something done in a hurry, an under-the-table handout often does the trick. However, one businessman we interviewed gave this advice: "Do it right the first time, or it may come back to haunt you. We made sure that our contractor had all the permits and paperwork done for construction. We paid the insurance and social security fees for the workers. Some others build without doing these things, but five years from now, some inspector could demand to see the paperwork. If you don't have it, you could end up paying not only the fees but fines and interest as well. I'd rather pay a bit more at the beginning and know that I'm legal."

To function successfully in a different culture requires patience and insight into the system. You cannot assume that everything works the same way in Mexico as it does in Canada or the United States. For one thing, you must be prepared for a great deal more government interference in your business. One bit of advice given by expatriate entrepreneurs: "Before you get too deep into the business, be sure you have a good lawyer and accountant." One woman told us that she was informed that her workers needed to belong to a union. When she explained that there was no union available for the type of work her employees were doing, she was urged to "start one for them."

BUSINESS **PROFILES**

During our research to revise *Choose Mexico* we like to profile a few expatriates who are successfully making a living by doing business in Mexico. You'll find them in every good-size city where North Americans congregate. From our observation, one key to success is finding a location where they can cater to foreign tourists and the expatriate community: customers with money. Obviously, any type of business that deals principally with the native population will be handicapped by the fact that ordinary Mexicans can rarely afford the services or products that attract tourists and affluent expats. A fancy boutique or fashion clothing store will surely fail in a village where *rebozos* are the latest fad. A spiffy restaurant serving tastefully prepared meals for only $10 will attract few Mexican working-class families when $10 equals at least two days' pay.

An exception to this rule is any type of business conducted by Internet. Your business is located wherever your computer is plugged into a telephone line. You'll see several examples of this type of enterprise listed below.

DO WHAT YOU KNOW BEST! The time-proven key to success for those entering business in Mexico is: Do something you already know! Judy King, who came to Mexico almost fifteen years ago, reiterated the advice about knowing what you are doing before considering going into business. She says, "So often I meet newcomers who act as if they're in one of those old Mickey Rooney movies. They exclaim, 'Hey, I know! We can start a business! We'll export pots to the United States! It will be really fun! Just like shopping, and we will make a lot of money!'

"These poor folks have no idea what they are getting into!"

Judy continues, "When I first came to Mexico, moving here permanently was the farthest thing from my mind. I was on a vacation, pure and simple. But on the third day, even in the center of Guadalajara and not speaking Spanish, I suddenly felt like I had come home. From that moment on, it was like I was watching my life go by, as opportunities fell from the sky into my lap."

Because Judy knew real estate, she took a position in a small real estate office (there were no franchise companies in those days). Eventually she switched to larger offices and finally, with several associates, received a franchise.

About four years ago, Judy began rolling a new opportunity around in her mind. She'd enjoyed selling real estate, but she realized that her special expertise was beyond merely selling property to newcomers. She was adept at helping them get comfortable in their new home, teaching them the ins and outs of living in the Lake Chapala area, and providing the essential inside information needed to make a successful move to Mexico. Logically, her idea for a new business opportunity was an information service for newcomers and those considering the Lake Chapala–Guadalajara region for relocation. Judy says, "I really want visitors and newcomers to avoid the mistakes I've seen others make so often."

Most of Judy's earlier working experience had been with Midwest newspapers. It was a natural evolution when her brainstorming sessions with local author Karen Blue resulted in the creation of two vehicles for showcasing information about real estate, immigration requirements, health care and insurance, foods, markets, cost of living, cars and driving, communication, and, most of all, the unique culture and customs of their Mexican neighbors. One tool is the online monthly magazine *Living at Lake Chapala,* launched in January 2002. They also planned sessions and handout packages for the presentation of weekly seminars on "Living at Lake Chapala" (every Thursday morning in Ajijic at La Nueva Posada). Adopting the slogan "We tell it like it is . . .," they're so confident of the value of the seminars, they offer a money-back guarantee.

"Our seminar participants tell us we answered questions they never would have thought to ask," Judy reports. "We hope newcomers won't have to make the same mistakes we did in our first year."

"Living at Lake Chapala" has steadily grown and gained well-deserved recognition for its clearly presented, accurate, and in-depth information. The American Association of Retired Persons' monthly magazine quoted Judy and Karen, recommending "Living at Lake Chapala" as an excellent source of relocation information. The magazine can be found at www.mexico-insights.com. By 2004 Christine Potters, with years of Mexico experience and perfect Spanish language skills, had stepped into the coeditor's position, working with Judy to produce a new issue to their Web site each month. (The authors of *Choose Mexico* would be remiss if we did not point out that Judy's online publication was a valuable source of information for this latest revision.)

ONLINE INTERNET BUSINESS When David and Dona McLaughlin of Saskatchewan, Canada, were researching their move to Mexico, they found scanty resources on the Internet to answer questions about living, working, or starting a business in Mexico. Few travel books provided the answers either. David says, "Using the Internet for research made us realize its potential to assist others who were seeking the same answers. So when we moved to Mexico in 1995, our idea came along on a 3.5-inch floppy disk." Their popular *Mexico Connect* became Mexico's first online magazine.

The endeavor was a success from its inception. Today it is much more than a forum for retirees and travelers; *Mexico Connect* is a virtual treasure trove of information about Mexico, an encyclopedic resource of more than 10,000 articles, documents, and photographs. You'll find everything from history and current events to Mexican cooking and travel hints. Art and culture, political commentary, and up-to-date legal advice are offered in addition to the invaluable bulletin boards where topics about living and travel in Mexico are discussed in great detail. (You can check it out at www.mexconnect.com.)

WRITING, NEWSLETTERS, AND SEMINARS More than thirty years ago, as a college student backpacking around Mexico, Stan Gotlieb fell in love with Oaxaca. When he decided he'd had enough of the rat race and the freezing weather in Minnesota, it seemed only natural to settle in

Oaxaca. After getting an unexpected payment for letters he had sent a friend who publishes a monthly newspaper, Stan began writing in a serious way as a method of supporting himself. Another friend suggested he start publishing his monthly *Letters from Mexico* on the World Wide Web, thus launching him on a career as a "man on the scene" in Oaxaca. Later he introduced a Web-based subscription newsletter about Oaxaca and Mexico, incorporating photos by his mate, Diana Ricci, also an expat, whom he met at a Day of the Dead party in Oaxaca. Her professional photos have become popular with writers and illustrators. Providing twenty issues a year for $30, they send e-mails to subscribers to announce new issues.

To supplement his writing income, Stan conducts newcomer seminars to orient folks on the ins and outs of living in—or visiting—Oaxaca. The seminars (www.realoaxaca.com/orient.html) are by appointment only. Stan says, "I don't live in Mexico to work; I work in Mexico in order to live here." With two newsletters a month, plus a newspaper article, plus the orientation sessions, he estimates that he spends about fifteen hours a week in preparation: reading, writing, and talking to folks.

His popular *Letters from Mexico,* sample newsletters, and some of Diana's photo albums can be viewed at www.realoaxaca.com, along with a list of their recommended books and CDs, links to other useful sites, and answers to frequently asked questions.

COMPUTER REPAIR Another success story is Dennis Setera, a computer repairman who found a niche that needed filling and employed his special skills to start a business. During a trade mission visit to Guadalajara, Dennis realized that computer technology in Mexico lagged far behind the latest developments in the United States. Businesses here use a lot of outdated but perfectly usable equipment that is constantly in need of maintenance and repair to keep it functioning.

Dennis imported some inexpensive, last-generation equipment for repairing hard drives and other computer hardware and went into business. With virtually no competition, Dennis soon found his business booming. He reports his biggest difficulty is negotiating with Mexican businesspeople. "They act as though they hate to make a decision," he says. "And just when you think the deal is off, they suddenly stop stalling and want to close the deal immediately."

BED-AND-BREAKFAST Many people dream about a small hotel or a bed-and-breakfast as their retirement business project. This is a business for which experience isn't absolutely necessary; the important ingredients are capital and elbow grease. Ernie Gorrie and his wife, Glenna Jones, found their opportunity in Troncones, a small beach village near Ixtapa. Starting very small, the building was designed to be expanded to fit future demand. It is now a flourishing bed-and-breakfast.

How do they find guests from all over the United States and Canada to vacation at their House of Tropical Dreams? At first it was tough. They once distributed 4,000 brochures at a travel show, with no results. Then they hit on the idea of Internet. Ernie says, "About 90 percent of our guests learned about us from our Web page (www.mexonline.com/dreams.htm), about one hundred inquiries a week. Of course they don't all make reservations, but at least our presence is known. Once we get another couple of years behind us and expand our base of happy vacationers, we'll be OK."

Recently we checked in with Ernie and Glenna to see how things are going. Ernie reports that "rentals have gone surprisingly well. We anticipated the house being empty from June through October, the slow season, but as it turns out we have 80 percent occupancy during those months, at 50 percent of our high-season rate." He continues, "It is a shame so many people are convinced they cannot have their dream in Mexico. I used to believe that, but I have proved myself wrong. When we started this project, I posted a reminder to myself saying, 'I used to have a dream; now I have a plan.' I recently changed that to 'I used to have a plan; now I have my dream!'"

HOME MAINTENANCE SERVICES Pam Pastore, a Yankee from Connecticut, fell in love with the Baja California community of San Felipe. Too young to "retire," she decided to look for some kind of business opportunity and took a survey of what local residents felt was lacking. Pam reports, "One of the many answers I got over and over was the need for a good housecleaning service. I thought, *I can surely do that.*" She had started Maid Marion, a housecleaning service, in Connecticut some twenty years ago, and she understood the concept of working in teams for maximum efficiency.

Most foreign residents live in San Felipe part-time, and many do not want full-time help they have to lay off at the end of the season. Also many people do not want to have a housemaid hanging around all day. They would prefer to have a team come in once or twice a week, spend an hour or two blitzing the place, and be done with it.

"I immediately went to work getting my corporation started, my accountant set up, and my working FM-3. I trained a team of girls, and we began to work. After only six months, Maid Marion employees were working three days a week for weekly maintenance clients and two days for big cleans such as new construction. We're very busy with closing or opening cleans for private residences. By the way, I do not speak Spanish very well, but we manage fine."

The business has expanded into a company called RedWagon Enterprises, which provides property management and computer services as well as house maintenance. Their Web site is www.blueroad runner.com/Redwagon/aboutus.htm.

SPECIALIZED BOUTIQUE Debbie Mounts, originally from California, first settled in San Miguel de Allende, where she founded and operated a Spanish language school. After eleven years, she felt ready for a change. Oaxaca attracted her attention because it was a bigger city and had an indigeneous population and an evolving tourist base. She continued operating a language school there for a while, then decided to open a boutique. Calling the business *Milagros Para Ti,* Debbie assembled an eclectic selection of fine crafts and other handmade objects, as well as a collection of books. She found a great location for the shop, in an enticing colonial building located in Oaxaca's *Centro Historico.*

The theme is a tranquil oasis opening onto a secluded patio filled with plants, where folks are welcome to come browse, chat, or stay and read a book for as long as they like. The shop is filled with antiques from Debbie's home. Most of what she originally opened with (copper, brass, Talavera, pewter, textiles, and shoes) came from Michoacan and Guanajuato. When she opened, however, local artists and craftspeople started bringing their work to Milagros Para Ti on a consignment basis. Debbie specializes in featuring promising new artists and proven *artesanos* who have made the "who's who" list in Mexico by either winning national competitions or having been included in the *Grand Masters of Mexico* book.

She insists that the quality of the "miracles" folks encounter in her shop is of the highest quality. She now offers Oaxaca rugs, miniature ceramic figures, woven baskets, art, *alebrijes*, stained glass, and antique jewelry. The mix has proved successful. Debbie says, "I really try to focus on service. I am happy to send folks to other stores where they can find what they are looking for. I provide info on classes, tours, living arrangements, and 'best buys' to be found here."

Asked what advice she would offer to someone thinking about doing business in Mexico, Debbie responds, "One needs to accept the fact that Mexico, and perhaps Oaxaca in particular, is very traditional and continues to value that over having cutting-edge products. One should also be fluent in Spanish and have lots of patience!" (A Web site featuring Debbie's shop is found at www.MiligrosParaTi.com.)

CHAPTER TWELVE

MEXICO ON
THE INTERNET

The experience of living in Mexico has been radically changed by a revolution that started about a decade ago and is continuing today—we are referring, of course, to the digital revolution. As profoundly as the computer, e-mail, and the World Wide Web have affected the lives of Americans living in the United States, its impact is even greater on those living in Mexico.

The Mexican postal system is notoriously slow and inefficient. A letter to or from the United States typically takes a week or two in transit. This means an average wait of about twenty days to get an answer to a letter mailed home. Long-distance calls from Mexico to back home can be expensive. Today, however, it is possible to keep in touch with friends and loved ones on a daily, or even hourly, basis by sending e-mail messages over Internet.

You don't even need to own a computer; Internet cafes are everywhere! Hourly fees can be as low as 50 cents, making it inexcusable not to keep in touch with friends and family. Even more convenient would be an Internet connection in your home. For a small monthly fee, you can connect to the Web just as you did back home. A laptop is just fine for this purpose and can be brought into Mexico without problem.

Computers are custom-free nowadays. One to a customer, however—additional used computers are charged at their depreciated values.

But E-mail is far from the only use of the Internet. You can keep in touch with Wall Street, buy and sell stocks and bonds, and read the latest *New York Times* articles. (In all likelihood, you can read your hometown newspaper on the Web as well.) Up-to-the-minute weather reports are also available, and you can pay bills, transfer money between bank accounts, and buy or sell just about everything imaginable—all without leaving your Mexican retirement home.

And now you can make your PC the hub of your voice communications, as well. Inexpensive computer-to-computer telephone programs abound. Some are even free, making expensive international telephone calls a thing of the past.

The Internet is also useful for learning more about the country before you go there. *Mexico Connect* (www.mexconnect.com) has numerous features, links to other useful sites, and bulletin boards where current and prospective residents trade questions and answers, tips, and observations. Many popular communities are represented by Web sites with color photographs, real estate listings, detailed information about facilities, and other useful facts too numerous to describe. We have found it invaluable in our research for this edition of *Choose Mexico*.

If you aren't computer literate, it's time to learn. Adult education courses on using the Internet, some of them specifically for seniors, are available almost everywhere, but chances are your kids and grandchildren can teach you everything you need to know to get started.

CHAPTER THIRTEEN

QUESTIONS
AND ANSWERS

Retirement in Mexico is an ever-changing process. Each time we revise *Choose Mexico*, we update the book to reflect changes in laws and contemporary conditions. We've received many letters and e-mails from readers asking for more information about living in Mexico. It's impossible to answer every query, and we cannot always provide a detailed reply. While reading e-mail from readers, we often discover areas of information that we overlooked or didn't stress enough in the previous editions. We've covered most of those topics in the main text of this edition, but we feel it may be helpful to reiterate them and to provide answers to some of the more frequently asked questions.

QUESTION: What does it cost to live in Mexico?

Answer: Although this is one of the most frequently asked questions, it can only be answered with another question: What does it cost you to live in the United States (or Canada)?

If you ask me that question, I will give one answer. If you ask my doctor, she will give another; and if you ask the person who bags my groceries in the supermarket, he will give still another. Obviously different people have different lifestyles, different expectations, and differ-

ent ideas about what is a necessity and what is a luxury.

We have spoken to people in Mexico living on incomes ranging from several hundred to several thousand dollars a month. They all seem to be content with the way they are living.

What we can tell you from our examination of rents, food prices, health care costs, and other expenses all over Mexico is that—at the time of this writing—most of the basic cost-of-living items are about two-thirds of what they would cost in the United States. This is not true of every location in the country. In the Los Cabos area of Baja, for instance, many prices are almost the same as north of the border. In some of Mexico's more isolated spots, both in Baja and on the mainland, costs are much lower.

Do not go to Mexico expecting to live royally on an income insufficient to maintain a decent standard of living in the United States or Canada. Remember, there is no safety net in Mexico such as welfare, food stamps, or other public assistance. If you get into trouble financially, your fellow expatriates are unlikely to help. Above all, do not go to Mexico just because you hear living there is cheap. Nothing is a bargain, unless it is what you want. Go to Mexico because you want to share in the richness of life there and be happy that if you can afford to live well in the United States or Canada, you can afford to live better there.

QUESTION: What is involved in driving my automobile into Mexico?

Answer: If you are on a tourist visa (FM-T), you are entitled to bring a vehicle into Mexico for 180 days. You will need:

- The original certificate of title
- An affidavit from the lien holder authorizing the temporary importation of the car (if the vehicle is financed)
- A valid state registration and current license plates
- A valid state driver's license
- A VISA, MasterCard, or American Express card in the driver's name (This card will be used to post a bond to ensure that the car is returned to the United States.)

QUESTION: How long will my imported automobile be legal in Mexico?

Answer: The Mexican government no longer allows unlimited time for your automobile to remain legal in Mexico. Today's limit is 180 days in a one-year period. However, any vehicle with foreign plates remains legal as long as its owner maintains legal immigration status. That is, you could enter on a 180-day tourist permit, then convert your visa to a one-year permit and automatically change the validity of the auto permit to match the owner's visa. Bottom line: Your New Hampshire–licensed vehicle will be legal as long as your visa is legal. That could be for years!

QUESTION: What is happening in Mexico concerning inflation? I am concerned that if prices rise, retirement might become unaffordable.

Answer: Like United States and Canada, Mexico is undergoing gradual inflation. The government seems to have much better control over the disastrous hyperinflationary spirals that plagued Mexico a decade ago. Mexico's everyday inflation is keeping pace with that of her NAFTA partners to the north. At the time of publication of this edition of *Choose Mexico,* the authors believe that the Mexican economy is on a steady course. Since we are not fortune-tellers, we hesitate to guarantee that economic conditions will not change in Mexico. We do believe that inflation will continue to be in tandem with what happens in the United States, and whatever changes occur in the United States or Canada will not particularly affect expatriates living south of the border.

QUESTION: What are the age limits and income requirements for retirement in Mexico?

Answer: Nowadays it's relatively easy to qualify, because there is no longer a "fifty-five-and-older" requirement. Currently the FM-3 *rentista* status is available to anyone who can show a monthly income of about $1,000, plus $500 for each dependent. If you own property in Mexico, the amount of income required is reduced by one-half. All you need to do is present bank statements for the past three months showing that you have deposited at least this amount each month. The requisites for residency are listed in this book in the Your Legal Status section.

QUESTION: Can I bring a firearm into Mexico?

Answer: Don't even *think* about bringing guns into Mexico without permission! Mexican jails always contain persons who crossed the border, forgetting they had a handgun in the glove compartment or the trunk! In

Mexico this is an extremely serious offense.

The best advice we can give concerning guns is this: If you feel you can't travel without a weapon, then do not travel in Mexico! Shotguns are just about the only firearms permitted across the border, and the red tape involved is incredible. Besides proof of citizenship, you need a character reference in duplicate from your local police department; the serial numbers, calibers, and makes of your guns; up to fourteen passport-size photos; and several days of running around to various Mexican government offices. Fees, stamps, and papers will cost about $120, plus *mordidas* and a doozy of a headache.

QUESTION: I'm looking at a beach property in Mexico. Is buying property safe? Can the government suddenly decide to take it away?

Answer: Land that changes hands legally is perfectly safe. The key word here is "legally." We have never heard of a single case where non-*ejido* property held by a non-Mexican in a legal bank trust (*fideicomiso*) has been taken from the non-Mexican. (See Can Foreigners Own Property for an explanation of *ejido*.) Problems arise when someone buys ejido land without going through the process of obtaining the *fideicomiso*. It's important to have a competent *notario publico* (a special kind of lawyer) handle the transaction. He will make sure the property is free and clear by checking with the Land Registry Office and will obtain a no-lien certificate and tax statement from *Hacienda* (treasury department). Your *notario* will also check for outstanding water bills, municipal taxes, or other encumbrances.

QUESTION: Can I get a job in Mexico?

Answer: Working in Mexico has become somewhat easier, because foreign corporations have more freedom to bring employees in from outside the country. However, those seeking work for other employers are still restricted to work that Mexican citizens cannot do. Restrictions are somewhat relaxed in such fields as real estate sales, teaching English, and other specialty endeavors.

QUESTION: Can I bring my pets with me?

Answer: Dogs and cats can be brought into Mexico if they are healthy, have received the required immunizations, and you have a veterinarian's certificate to prove it. Ask your vet for a U.S. Interstate and International Certificate of Health and have it dated within seventy-two hours of crossing the border. To bring a pet back into the United States, you'll need another health certificate and a rabies certificate not more than thirty days old from a Mexican veterinarian.

QUESTION: How about moving my furniture to Mexico?

Answer: You can legally move your furniture and other household goods to Mexico once you have resident status. This is done by a process called *Menaje de Casa.* (Details can be found in the Living with Mexican Laws chapter.) Whether it pays to transport your property to Mexico, rather than selling and replacing it with new purchases in Mexico, is something you will have to decide after comparing prices in Mexico with what it will cost to import your belongings.

QUESTION: Do American appliances work on Mexican electrical current?

Answer: Yes; the current is the same as in the United States. No adapters are needed, and anything that works at home will work in Mexico (although we have heard that electric clocks do not keep good time). However, you'll find that occasional intermittent voltage fluctuations can eat your electrical appliances, so it pays to buy surge or spike protectors for your plug-ins—especially for your computer equipment! Telephone lines aren't grounded, so remember to unplug phones during thunderstorms or use a high-quality surge protector.

QUESTION: Can I have my Social Security check automatically deposited in my Mexican bank account as I do at home?

Answer: At the present time, Social Security checks cannot be automatically deposited into a foreign bank account. Most expatriates maintain an account with U.S. banks that have connections with their Mexican bank. Then they simply transfer the money as they need it by calling a toll-free Mexican number.

QUESTION: What income taxes do retirees in Mexico have to pay?

Answer: If you receive income from the United States or Canada, you will continue filing returns as you did when living there, as well as with your state or provincial agencies. You do not have to report this income to the Mexican government. Since most expatriates do not work in Mexico, the only taxable income they are likely to have is interest on their deposits in Mexican banks. This tax on bank account income is withheld before the interest is paid. Those who have businesses will pay Mexican income taxes on their business income.

QUESTION: Is my Medicare health insurance good in Mexico?

Answer: Although there's substantial discussion and lobbying to allow Medicare coverage to citizens living in foreign countries, at the moment its coverage doesn't extend to Mexico. The good news is that you can join the Mexican Social Security medical plan for around $300 a year. (You must pass a physical by a certified IMSS doctor.) Private health coverage is available for those who prefer private physicians, at a cost as low as $150 a month.

QUESTION: Is obtaining legal residency in Mexico very difficult?

Answer: Not at all. You can either apply for the FM-3 at the Mexican consulate nearest to your home in the United States or Canada, or you can apply for residency when you arrive in Mexico. Details about applying for immigration papers are found in the Living with Mexican Laws chapter.

QUESTION: Isn't Mexican automobile insurance very expensive?

Answer: It can be if you buy it at the border and pay a daily rate rather than by the year. Daily insurance can cost $10 to $20; therefore, for a two-week jaunt you could pay $140 to $280 for protection. Purchasing a six-month policy in advance (by mail or Internet) can cost no more than two-week coverage. In any event, do not drive in Mexico without insurance!

QUESTION: Are there schools for English-speaking children and adolescents?

Answer: Every large city in Mexico (and some smaller ones, too) has at least one bilingual school to which many American (as well as some

Mexican) families send their children. Because this book is primarily for retirees, or those "empty-nest" people who have already raised their children, we do not list these schools.

QUESTION: What happens if I die while I am in Mexico?

Answer: Your spouse or friends can get a certificate from the local authorities that allows your remains to be flown back to your home country, if that is what you wish.

QUESTION: Are U.S. television programs shown in Mexico?

Answer: Of course. Just about anywhere you choose to live, you'll have good cable or satellite reception.

QUESTION: Can you recommend a real estate broker we can contact who can help me buy a home or rent a house or apartment in Mexico?

Answer: We don't feel that dealing with a real estate broker by long distance is a wise way to shop for housing in Mexico. As for recommending a real estate agency, be aware that the ownership and personnel of real estate firms can change during the life of a an edition. As we discussed at greater length in The Real Estate Game, we strongly urge you to visit a community before you make any commitments. Searching the Internet real estate listings for the communities you are considering will give you an idea of what the upper-end properties might cost you. However, be aware that only a tiny fraction of properties for sale will make the Internet. Many are overpriced and hard-to-sell properties. Ordinary homes and bargains seldom make the Internet; they are snapped up immediately.

CHAPTER FOURTEEN

WILL YOU
LOVE IT?

Most foreigners either love Mexico or hate it. This phenomenon is so well known that just about every guidebook to the country, after listing the numerous reasons for the author's deep affection for the land and its people, finds it necessary to warn that "Mexico is not everybody's cup of tea." (Someone should offer a prize for an alternative to that cliche—"cup of tequila" would not qualify.) No doubt the principal reason for these strong feelings is that Mexico, like many of its favorite foods, is highly spiced. Nothing is muted—neither the colors nor the sounds. Mexico does not sneak up on you. It confronts you immediately and totally.

The shock is particularly intense for the North American who has gone right next door to find himself in a country vastly different from his or her own. Mexico quickly shatters the illusion that foreignness is a function of distance.

Are Mexico's differences from the United States and Canada good or bad? We know our answer to that question, but we don't know yours. Even if we knew you very well, we are not at all sure that we could predict which it would be. Yes, there are some people whose reaction to the country we could confidently guess. Most of them are so rigid,

impatient, or demanding that we cannot imagine them tolerating the inefficiencies and delays of Mexican life. We're proud that after a number of months in Mexico, we have learned to sit in a restaurant for twenty minutes before the waiter takes our orders and for another twenty until the food arrives, without any knotting of our insides. (We're doubly proud that we can even do it back in the United States.) We are not, however, sufficiently unreasonable to expect or demand that everyone master this trick. Would you be outraged or amused by the fact that each time postage for an airmail letter to the United States goes up, it is many months before stamps are available for the new amount or that often envelopes and packages have to be mailed with wall-to-wall small denomination stamps because no larger ones are available? Trivial? Of course. But if your answer is "outraged" or even if you would merely find that situation annoying, it's quite possible that Mexico is not for you. There are just too many little things that, if you let them, could add up to constant annoyance.

Somewhat more serious are the seemingly arbitrary and unpredictable shortages that plague Mexico for months at a time. Unlike the United States, where many brands of almost every product are available, Mexico usually has only one brand, and anything that interrupts its manufacturer's operations cuts off the supply altogether. Mexicans and longtime foreign residents there learn to deal with these shortages in a variety of ways. Approached in the right spirit, obtaining the seemingly unobtainable becomes a game. Of course it may not be the kind you enjoy playing.

Most North Americans are deeply offended by the sight of people spitting in the street. In the days when spittoons were a ubiquitous feature of the American domestic landscape, the aesthetic aversion to that practice was probably much weaker. However, a very effective antispitting campaign by the Tuberculosis Association succeeded in sensitizing our grandparents, and we continue to view it with an intense distaste that Mexicans do not seem to share. To be comfortable in Mexico, you do not have to enjoy the sight, but it does help to be able to ignore it.

Drinking only bottled or boiled water is a nuisance. How much more convenient it is to place your glass under any tap and enjoy, without any trace of concern, the clear liquid that pours out. It is also pleasant to pick up a piece of fruit in the market and eat it as you find it or, if you're fastidious, after running some cold water over it. After you have returned from Mexico, it usually takes some time before you are able to resume those practices without a moment of hesitation. Water in Mexico is not safe, and while there you must learn to avoid everything uncooked with which it may have come in contact. Are these inconveniences serious enough to spoil your enjoyment of the country, or are they somewhat like the necessity to retrain your reflexes before you can drive or even cross streets safely in England? You may not know what your reaction will be until you have been in Mexico for a while. Part of the initial strain is fear that you will forget and inadvertently expose yourself to danger. That worry soon fades as the required new behaviors become second nature.

Many North Americans are appalled by what they see as the pervasive corruption of Mexican political life. Indeed it's true that few Mexican presidents have left office without arranging for themselves and their friends to live in luxury for the rest of their lives. However, to see this as contrasting sharply with universal probity north of the border requires that one forget the sleaze factor that has figured so prominently in our own political history. Of course every scandal on the federal level has many counterparts in our statehouses. Less visible but far more widespread are the abuses of power routinely encountered in the world of commerce. It is all too easy to jump from the unquestionable fact that U.S. or Canadian customs inspectors are much less likely to take bribes than their Mexican counterparts to the dubious conclusion that North Americans are honest and Mexicans are crooked. It's not even a question of degree but rather of different culturally approved manifestations of what, sadly, appears to be a universal weakness. However, most North Americans do need some time to become comfortable with the idea of "tipping" minor public officials.

One certainly does not have to approve of the Mexican government to be happy living there. North Americans have fallen in love with the country under regimes that have covered the full spectrum from right to left, and often their affection has been very much in spite of the ideology and behavior of the party in power. Even today Mexico is full of Americans who deplore everything about the government's foreign and domestic policies, would love to see them become carbon copies of ours, but would not think of moving back to the United States where they could enjoy the originals. Very few are too poor to afford the higher prices in their homeland, so there must be something else about Mexico that holds them.

This brief recitation of some things North Americans find to dislike about Mexico is far from exhaustive. It does, however, include many of the most frequently heard complaints. For those who allow them to, they constitute ample reason for choosing other places in which to spend time. For many others—the authors included—they are part of the price one must pay for sharing in the riches of Mexican life.

Uppermost among those riches are the people of Mexico. If we have repeated this observation too frequently throughout this book, it's because we know that although anyone who has spent much time in Mexico will agree, those who have never been there may not be easily convinced.

Of course there are other attractions. One is the climate. At any given time the weather may not be perfect everywhere in Mexico, but chances are that it is someplace, and usually not too far from where you are. The residents of Mexico City discovered at least five centuries ago that when, as occasionally happens, the winters there are a bit too nippy, it's easy to find temperatures a dozen degrees warmer in nearby Cuernavaca. In Guadalajara they know that in January, descending to the Pacific Coast (only a few hours away) takes you from the fifties to the balmy eighties. In San Miguel, Morelia, and dozens of other cities and towns of the Central Plateau, spring is "eternal." If you live in a climate that is bearable year-round, it may be hard to understand the thirst for warmth and sunshine that historically—for Northern Europeans from England to Russia—has made Italy an earthly paradise and that draws flocks of sun-starved Scandinavians to Spain every winter. Unless you have gasped for air in a New York, Washington, or Houston summer, the annual exodus to the mountains and the beaches may seem inexplicable. If, on the other hand, you suffer either extreme heat or cold in the course of a year, it may not be necessary for us to tell you much more about why the Mexican climate draws so many refugees from the extremes of U.S. winters and summers. Yes, parts of Mexico can be hot, but the bulk of the population lives in, and visitors flock to, places where altitude or sea breezes provide year-round moderation.

It's difficult to avoid sounding crass when discussing how reasonable living in Mexico can be. Compulsive bargain hunting is an illness and, many would say, one of the least attractive characteristics of North Americans abroad. Perhaps, though, retirees who are trying to make limited incomes provide the comfort they have been encouraged to expect as the reward for a lifetime of work can be viewed a little differently than tourists seeking cheap vacations. In Mexico we observed North Americans who would be barely making it at home living comfortably. This gave us renewed optimism about our own futures and colors our perceptions of Mexico as a place to retire. Certainly we would not advise anyone to move there for the low prices alone. Nothing is a bargain if you don't enjoy it. Nevertheless, the stretch that the low prices give to a modest income must be counted as one of the major advantages of Mexico as a place to visit or live.

In the end, although we hope that these observations may help you make some guesses about whether you will love or hate the Mexican experience, you will not know for sure until you've tried it. If you go there expecting to find a replica of life in the United States or Canada, but with palm trees and *mariachis* in the background, you'll be disappointed. Some things that you value highly are not considered important there. On the other hand, you may learn to appreciate some qualities—such as patience, courtesy, and simplicity—that our culture often slights. Even if you decide, after you have seen it for yourself, that you can't love Mexico as we do, we doubt that you will regret having tried.

APPENDIX

ENGLISH-LANGUAGE MEDIA **AND ONLINE RESOURCES**

Atención San Miguel (San Miguel de Allende weekly)
Apdo 119
San Miguel de Allende
GTO, Mexico

El Ojo del Lago (Lake Chapala area monthly)
P.O. Box 279
Chapala, Jalisco
45900 Mexico

Guadalajara Reporter (news of the Guadalajara area)
9051-C Siempre Viva Road, Suite 5–452
San Diego, CA 92173-3628
www.guadalajarareporter.com

Oaxaca Times (free weekly)
307 Macedonio Alcalá
Oaxaca
Oax 68000, Mexico

Miami Herald International (Mexico Edition)

Lake Chapala Review
E-mail: review@laguna.com.mx

Cuernavaca Calling
Apdo 4–587, Cuernavaca
C.P. 62431, Mexico

Vallarta Today
Puerto Vallarta online newspaper
www.vallartatoday.com

Mexico Connect (subscription)
Popular online magazine, message board, and information about living and retiring in Mexico.
www.mexconnect.com

Living at Lake Chapala (subscription)
Comprehensive online magazine with twelve accurate new articles each month focused on relocating and adjusting to life at "Lakeside"
www.mexico-insights.com

Atención San Miguel
English-language weekly in San Miguel de Allende lists events of interest to expatriates, as well as local news; free at most hotels

MexOnline
Web site with news stories and lots of information about Mexico

Cuernavaca Calling
Apdo 4–587
Cuernavaca
C.P. 62431, Mexico

Citizens Emergency Center—U.S. State Department—Situation reports on any destination around the world; locates travelers abroad to deliver emergency messages. Phone (202) 647–5225. Available: 8:15 A.M. to 5:00 P.M. weekdays, 9:00 A.M. to 3:00 P.M. Saturday (Eastern Standard Time).

MEXICAN CONSULATES IN THE **UNITED STATES AND CANADA**

U.S. CONSULATES
ARIZONA
Douglas: 1201 F Avenue, Douglas, AZ 85607
(520) 364–3142; fax: (520) 364–1379

Nogales: 571 North Grand Avenue, Nogales, AZ 85621
(520) 287–2521; fax: (520) 287–3175

Phoenix: 1990 West Camelback, Suite 110, Phoenix, AZ 85015
(602) 242–7398; fax: 242–2957

Tucson: 553 South Stone Avenue, Tucson, AZ 85701
(520) 882–5595; fax: (520) 882–8959, e-mail: contucmx@mindspring.com

CALIFORNIA
Calexico: 331 West Second Street, Calexico, CA 92231
(760) 357–3863; fax: (760) 357–6284

Fresno: 2409 Merced Street, Fresno, CA 93721
(559) 233–3065; fax: (559) 233–4219; e-mail: consulado@consul
mexfresno.net

Los Angeles: 2401 West Sixth Street, Los Angeles, CA 90057
(213) 351–6800; fax: (213) 389–9249

Oxnard: 201 East Fourth Street, Suite 206-A, Oxnard, CA 93030
(805) 483–4684; fax: (805) 385–3527

Sacramento: 1010 Eighth Street, Sacramento, CA 95814
(916) 441–3287; fax: (916) 441–3176; e-mail: consulsac1@quiknet.com

San Bernadino: 532 North D Street, San Bernadino, CA 92401
(909) 889–9837; fax: (909) 889–8285

San Diego: 1549 India Street, San Diego, CA 92101
(619) 231–8414; fax: (619) 231–4802; e-mail: info@consulmexsd.org

San Francisco: 532 Folsom Street, San Francisco, CA 94105
(415) 354–1700; fax: (415) 495–3971

San Jose: 540 North First Street, San Jose, CA 95112
(408) 294–3414; fax: (408) 294–4506

Santa Ana: 828 North Broadway Street, Santa Ana, CA 92701–3424
(714) 835–3069; fax: (714) 835–3472

COLORADO
Denver: 48 Steele Street, Denver, CO 80206
(303) 331–1110; fax: (303) 331–1872

DISTRICT OF COLUMBIA
Washington (Embassy of Mexico)
1911 Pennsylvania Avenue NW, Washington, DC, 20006
(202) 736–1000; fax: (202) 234–4498; e-mail: consulwas@aol.com

FLORIDA
Miami: 5975 Sunset Drive, South Miami, FL 33143
(786) 268–4900; fax: (786) 268–4895; e-mail: conmxmia@bellsouth.net

Orlando: 100 West Washington Street, Orlando, FL 32801
(407) 422–0514; fax: (407) 422–9633

GEORGIA
Atlanta: 2600 Apple Valley Road, Atlanta, GA 30319
(404) 266–2233; fax: (404) 266–2302

ILLINOIS
Chicago: 300 North Michigan Avenue, Second Floor, Chicago, IL 60651
(312) 855–1380; fax: (312) 855–9257

LOUISIANA
New Orleans: World Trade Center Building
2 Canal Street, Suite 840, New Orleans, LA 70115
(504) 522–3596; fax: (504) 525–2332

MASSACHUSETTS
Boston: 20 Park Plaza, Suite 506, Boston, MA 02116
(617) 426–4181; fax: (617) 695–1957

MICHIGAN
Detroit: 645 Griswold Avenue Suite 1700, Detroit, MI 48226
(313) 964–4515; fax: (313) 964–4522

MISSOURI
Kansas City: 1600 Baltimore, Suite 100, Kansas City, MO 64108
(816) 556–0800; fax: (816) 556–0900

NEBRASKA
Omaha: 3552 Dodge Street, Omaha, NE 68131
(402) 595–1841 or (402) 595–1844; fax: (402) 595–1845

NEW MEXICO
Albuquerque: 1610 Fourth Street NW, Albuquerque, NM 87102
(505) 247–4177; fax: (505) 842–9490

NEW YORK
New York City: 27 East Thirty-ninth Street, New York, NY 10016
(212) 217–6400; fax: (212) 217–6493

NORTH CAROLINA
Charlotte: P.O. Box 19627, Charlotte, NC 28219
(704) 394–2190

Raleigh: 336 East Six Forks Road, Raleigh, NC 27609
(919) 754–0046; fax: (919) 754–1729

OREGON
Portland: 1234 Southwest Morrison, Portland, OR 97205
(503) 274–1450; fax: (503) 274–1540

PENNSYLVANIA
Philadelphia: 111 South Independence Mall E, Suite 310,
Bourse Building, Philadelphia, PA 19106
(215) 922–3834; fax: (215) 923–7281

TEXAS

Austin: 200 East Sixth Street, Suite 200, Austin, TX 78701
(512) 478–2866; fax: (512) 478–8008
Brownsville: 724 East Elizabeth Street, Brownsville, TX 78520
(956) 542–4431; fax: (956) 542–7267

Corpus Christi: 800 North Shoreline Boulevard, Suite 410, North Tower,
Corpus Christi, TX 78401
(512) 882–3375; fax: (512) 882–9324

Dallas: 8855 North Stemmons Freeway, Dallas, TX 75247
(214) 252–9250, ext. 123; fax: (214) 630–3511

Del Rio: 300 East Losoya, Del Rio, TX 78841
(830) 775–2352; fax: (830) 774–6497

Eagle Pass: 140 Adams Street, Eagle Pass, TX 78852
(830) 773–9255; fax: (830) 773–9397

El Paso: 910 East San Antonio Street, El Paso, TX 79901
(915) 533–3644; fax: (915) 532–7163

Houston: 4507 San Jacinto Street, Houston, TX 77004
(713) 271–6800; fax: (713) 271–3201

Laredo: 1612 Farragut Street, Laredo, TX 78040
(956) 723–6369; fax: (956) 723–1741

McAllen: 600 South Broadway Avenue, McAllen, TX 78501
(956) 686–0243; fax: (956) 686–4901

Midland: 511 West Ohio, Suite 121, Midland, TX 79701
(915) 687–2334; fax: (915) 687–3952

San Antonio: 127 Navarro Street, San Antonio, TX 78205
(210) 271–9728; fax: (210) 227–7518

UTAH

Salt Lake City: 230 West 400 South, Second Floor,
Salt Lake City, UT 84047
(801) 521–8502; fax: (801) 521–0534

WASHINGTON
Seattle: 2132 Third Avenue, Seattle, WA 98121
(206) 448–3526; fax: (206) 448–4771

CANADA

BRITISH COLUMBIA
Vancouver: 710–1177 West Hastings Street, Vancouver, BC V6E 2K3
(604) 684–1859; fax: (604) 684–2485

ONTARIO
Ottawa (Embassy of Mexico): 45 O'Connor, Suite 1500,
Ottawa, ON K1P 1A4
(613) 233–8988; fax: (613) 235–9123

Toronto: 199 Bay Street, Suite 4440, Commerce Court West,
Toronto, ON M5L 1E9
(416) 368–1847; fax: (416) 368–8141

QUEBEC
Montreal: 2000 Mansfield Street, Suite 1015, Montreal, QC H3A 2Z7
(514) 288–2502; fax: (514) 288–8287

INDEX

ABOUT THE **AUTHORS**

John Howells was born in New Orleans and grew up in suburban St. Louis. His teen years, however, were spent in Mexico City, and he has been returning to Mexico as often as possible ever since. Now a resident of California, he has worked on newspapers from coast to coast—forty in all. He has been a Linotype operator, English teacher, silver miner, and a travel and feature writer. John earned a B.A. in Anthropology and a M.A. in Mexican-American graduate studies from San Jose State University. He is the author of nine travel-retirement boosk.

Don Merwin is a native New Yorker who now lives in the San Francisco Bay area. He began his career in communications as a writer for Edward R. Murrow in the early 1950s and spent the next three decades as publicist, administrator, and planner in the health and human services organizations. From 1984 until 1997 Don and his wife, Judith, were the publishers of Gateway Books. They are enjoying a retirement that gives them the opportunity to spend part of the year south of the border.